*Information
and Coding Theory*

Information and Coding Theory

FRANKLIN M. INGELS

Department of Electrical Engineering
Mississippi State University

Visiting Staff Member
Los Alamos Scientific Laboratory

 INTEXT EDUCATIONAL PUBLISHERS
College Division of Intext
Scranton ● San Francisco ● Toronto ● London

The **Intext** *Series in*
ELECTRICAL ENGINEERING

ISBN 0-7002-2378-9

Preface

This text is intended for the first-year graduate student and for the capable senior student. The main objectives in writing this text have been twofold:

1. To give the reader an introduction to the subject of coding theory using the basic results of information theory as a set of tools for analyzing various coding schemes.
2. To establish a base from which the reader may expect to read the current literature in this area.

Chapter 1 is a short introduction including a discussion of the subject's meaning, a brief history, and a description of a basic communication system. Chapter 2 develops the information measure in an axiomatic manner and describes some of the properties of the information measure, which we see is termed *entropy*. Chapters 3 and 4 discuss communication systems with and without memory. In Chapters 5 and 6 we take up coding theory as a natural outcome of our studies in Chapters 3 and 4. In developing the basic tools of information theory a somewhat formal style of presentation has been used. While this style is appropriate for that subject matter the rest of the text has been written in a more relaxed manner which lends itself well to the subject of coding.

Throughout the text the principles and quantities discussed are illustrated with examples and diagrams so that the student will have both a theoretical knowledge and a physical "feeling" or insight into the material. For this reason the text should be valuable to the practicing engineer as well as the student. In particular, Chapters 6 and 7 should be very helpful to the practicing engineer.

For those readers who do not wish to pursue the axiomatic derivation of the information measure, a reading of Secs. 2-1, 2-2, and 2-5 will provide a sufficient background for reading the rest of the text, if the reader is willing to accept a few statements at face value. In an effort to prompt the student to utilize the digital computer for the often tedious process of solving problems, a series of problems to be solved on the computer have been provided. Several computer programs for the more interesting problems such as Muroga's technique for the general binary channel have been included as an appendix to various chapters. These programs are in Fortran and are included to illustrate the general method. The student should develop his own program library as suggested by the problems at the end of the chapters. The problems at the end of each chapter are meant to deal with each topic and all should be solved by each student. A solution manual for teachers will be available shortly after the text is published and answers to selected problems are included in the appendix.

A short section dealing with some elementary probability theory is included in the appendix for those readers who either have not had a course in that area or who feel the need to renew their acquaintance with it. The appendix also contains some tables useful in working the problems.

I wish to express my appreciation to the publisher for the helpful suggestions and to my wife who has willingly spared time from her favorite endeavors to type the manuscript—a formidable task.

FRANKLIN M. INGELS

State College, Mississippi
August 1971

Contents

List of Symbols

CHAPTER 1

Introduction

1-1. WHAT IS INFORMATION AND ITS THEORY?

The word *information* has many connotations. What meaning it may have to the reader depends largely upon his background. If one were to consult the IEEE *Standards on Definitions of Terms on Information Theory*[1] one would find definitions for many related terms such as *information content* and *information rate*, but no definition of the word *information* itself: while from Webster's *Seventh New Collegiate Dictionary* we find several definitions of varying meaning. One begins to form the opinion that perhaps there exists no single "correct" definition of the word. This is indeed the case. The word has many meanings. About the best we can do is to point out that any given statement carries different information to different people. "To have a great deal of potential" does not mean the same thing to an electrical engineer as to a businessman.

We shall have to look further into what we mean when we say one statement carries more information than another. To learn that John hit a tree with a rock would not seem very informative until we also learn that he did this by hand from a distance of 1,000 feet. The rarity of the event would startle us. In fact, if one stops to consider what properties of communication convey information we must come to the conclusion that the more "unlikely" a message is the more informative it is.

Thus information of a message, while an elusive concept in some ways, may be measured in a relative manner by considering the uncertainty associated with the message. The subject of information theory is thus the study of the uncertainty of messages and the efficiency with which we transmit these messages.

1-2. BRIEF HISTORICAL SKETCH

Information theory as modern science thinks of it today had its beginning in the early twentieth century stemming from the work of H. Nyquist and

R. V. L. Hartley. In 1917, Nyquist had started working on the problems of telegraphy for AT&T. His work was made public in a paper published in 1924.[2] In 1928 Hartley, possibly known better as the inventor of the Hartley oscillator, published a paper entitled *Transmission of Information*.[3]

Shortly after World War II two other researchers, Claude E. Shannon[4] and Norbert Wiener[5] generated some written works that started a chain reaction in the newly defined area of information theory. From this point on Shannon and Wiener established themselves in the area of communications but with slightly different objectives.

Wiener concentrated on the very troublesome but highly important problem of extracting signals of a known ensemble from noise of a predictable nature. This problem is common to the receiving end of any communication system.

On the other hand, Shannon associated himself with the problem of encoding messages chosen from a known ensemble so that they can be transmitted accurately and rapidly, even in the presence of noise.

The study of efficient encoding and its consequences, in the form of speed of transmission and probability of error, is the main objective of information theory. For this reason Shannon is often regarded as the father of information theory.

From these initial works a surging interest and a wealth of publications have literally exploded in and around the central theme.[†] (As a matter of interest, things started moving far afield in the middle 1950's, and this prompted Wiener to write a note in an issue of IT-1[6] pleading with the profession to turn itself back to the original objectives and main stream of the area of information theory as he saw it.)

Thus it is with a newly generated area of interest. Elegant mathematical proofs of many of the early ideas and relations soon followed. Perhaps the most concise of these are presented in a short but very powerful presentation of the mathematical formulation of the basic relations of information theory.[7]

Currently the results of almost twenty years of intense labor by many investigators has resulted in various techniques for coding messages for achieving accuracy while approaching the maximum allowable sending rate, but despite all this progress we still have a long way to go to approach the promise of error rates and transmission speeds envisioned in Shannon's original work.

1-3. BASIC COMMUNICATIONS SYSTEMS AND DEFINITIONS

Communication is a process by which we transfer messages from one point to another by use of symbols or signals. Determination of the capacity of com-

---

[†]This is always the case when someone makes a statement of fundamental importance. The reason is that many others have also been beating the bushes but missing the key points. When these keys are presented, many hitherto unexplainable items suddenly become quite obvious, leading to many new journal articles.

munications systems and what factors affect this capacity is our main objective. A basic communications system is outlined in Fig. 1-1.

The first element of this system is an information source, or message source, from which we draw a message to be transmitted. A message may be thought of as a sequence of symbols intended to convey an idea, or some fact.

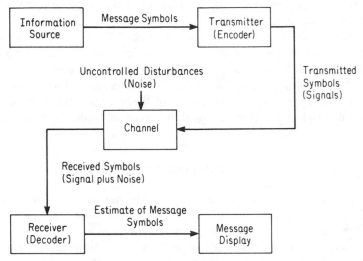

Fig. 1-1. Basic communication system.

DEFINITION. A *message* is an ordered selection from a known set of symbols, intended for communication of information. A message may be speech from a person talking, or a blinking light, or a series of electrical pulses.

The message symbols are then passed through a transmitter which transforms the message symbols into a suitable form for passage over the *system channel* (which may be current through a wire or radiation through the atmosphere, etc.). The form that the symbol takes on is termed a *signal*. Thus the input to the transmitter is the message symbol, and the output of the transmitter is the electrical signal which is the physical realization of the message.

The system channel is the medium through which the signal passes from the transmitter to the receiver.

DEFINITION. A *channel* is a combination of transmission media and equipment capable of receiving signals at one point, the *input*, and delivering related signals at another point, the *output*.

This channel may be a system of wires or the atmosphere or space between the locations of the transmitter and the receiver. It is while the signal is passing through this channel that it becomes altered by noise or distortion. *Distortion* is usually thought of as a deterministic (fixed operation) alteration of the signal, while *noise* is considered to be a statistical and unpredictable (nondeterministic) alteration of the signal. Since distortion is a deterministic operation on the signal, such as loss of high frequencies by 3 db per octave, we may correct most of these effects at the receiver. The effects of noise are not so easily handled, and it is these alterations that have given the communications engineer an interesting if frustrating area in which to work.

Later on we will see that a given channel has a capacity to transmit information in much the same manner as a bucket carrying cubes. In both cases we may or may not be clever enough to "pack the bucket" to the theoretical capacity. In a later chapter we will want to formalize our definition of channel capacity.

After passing through the channel the corrupted signals enter the receiver. The receiver is constructed to do the best job of reconstructing the original signal from the received signal. The output of the receiver is the received message and may be displayed in printed, visual, or acoustical forms, or combinations of these.

1-4. OUTLINE OF TEXT

In planning the layout of the text each chapter has been prefaced with a short history of the development to follow, plus a description of what will be done in the chapter—with some reasons why we want to do it.

In Chapter 2 a short heuristic exposition of the information measure has been included before presenting the axiomatic approach to development of the information measure as presented by Feinstein. One might question the inclusion of Feinstein's lemmas and theorems with all their details. However, the insight gained by working through these formalized mathematics on the subject is well worth the effort. For one thing, the articles in the current literature are written in this fashion and with good reason—one must substantiate one's results in a logical fashion. Secondly, some sort of maturity factor seems to be gained by students who have tackled this sort of thing and won out. Another benefit is the fact that once we have mastered only a few of the lemmas and theorems, many short statements are obvious, needing only a line or two to prove as opposed to many lines of argument otherwise required.

Our first step will be the development of the information measure and its properties. Using these results, we will investigate the properties of a message source, communications channel, and received signals for both memoryless and memory type systems.

In the process it will become obvious that we may help ourselves communicate more efficiently by working on the structure of the message to be sent. This introduces us to the discipline of *coding*. It will be to our benefit to study the purposes and techniques involved in coding and some of the basic relations and bounds. Finally, we shall learn some of the coding schemes available.

It would be worthwhile for the reader to review the section on basic probability theory in the appendix.

CHAPTER 2

The Information Measure

2-1. INTRODUCTION

In 1948 when Shannon published his basic work outlining the fundamentals of the mathematical theory of information, it was essentially from the engineer-scientist point of view. In 1958 there was still no single reference to which an interested researcher could turn for a concise but rigorous exposition of the fundamentals of the mathematical theory. It was at this time that Amiel Feinstein published his *Foundations of Information Theory*, in which he provided the single reference that had been lacking.

In this chapter we shall introduce the information measure and reveal some of its properties. With these results we shall be able to study the communication system and the factors affecting it.

2-2. A DESCRIPTION OF THE MEASURE—ENTROPY

If we were to assign numbers relating to the information carried by statements, it would be natural to assign a small number to common everyday statements such as "Hello," "Goodbye," "How are you?" For unusual items such as the announcement of the bombing of Pearl Harbor we would want to assign a large number. (Just scale the numbers to the size of the equivalent newspaper headlines!) Thus we would want to denote information content of a statement as a function that is decreasing in numerical value as the probability of occurrence is increasing.

The information measure is a logarithmic function that depends upon the uncertainty, or probability of occurrence, associated with the message symbol. Thus if a particular message symbol s_i were to occur with probability p_i, we would say that the self-information associated with this symbol is defined as

$$S_I(s_i) = -\log_2 p_i \text{ bits} \tag{2-1}$$

DEFINITION.   The *information content* of a message symbol is the negative of the logarithm of the probability that this symbol will be emitted from the source. The information content of an individual symbol is termed *self-information*, S_I.

Note.   The choice of the logarithmic base determines the *Unit* of Information content. If the chosen base is two (which is almost always the case) the unit is termed a *bit*. Thus the self-information content of a symbol from a binary source in which the symbols 0 and 1 occur with equal probability, is equal to $-\log_2(1/2) = \log_2 2 = 1$ bit. If the base chosen is 10 then the unit is termed a *hartley*; if the base chosen is the natural base the unit is termed a *nat*. In this text we shall write the $\log_2$ as log. In the appendix is a table of logarithms to the base 2 to facilitate working the problems.

From the above definition and our knowledge of logarithms we should suspect that the information measure is additive; i.e., if we have two symbols we would expect the average information of the combination to be the sum of the information of the individual symbols, weighted in accordance with their probability of occurrence. If s_1 and s_2 occur with probability p_1 and p_2 respectively, we have as the individual information content $-\log p_1$ and $-\log p_2$. The average information of the combination would then be:

$$H(s_1, s_2) = p_1(-\log p_1) + p_2(-\log p_2) \qquad (2\text{-}2)$$

where H is termed the *average information content* of the binary source consisting of symbols s_1 and s_2.

DEFINITION.   The *average information content* per symbol of a source is the weighted average of the information content per symbol emitted from the source H. The terms *entropy* and *negentropy* are sometimes used to designate the average information content. (In practice one almost always encounters the term entropy.) If we have a source with j symbols, s_j, each with probability of occurrence p_j then we have, for H,

$$H = H(s_1, \ldots, s_j) = \sum_{i=1}^{j} p_i(-\log p_i)$$

We may also see that the information measure is a symmetrical function,

$$H(s_1, s_2) = -p_1 \log p_1 - p_2 \log p_2 = -p_2 \log p_2 - p_1 \log p_1 = H(s_2, s_1)$$

and that it has an extremal value occurring for symbols with equal probability of occurrence. Thus the maximum of $H(s_1, s_2)$ occurs for the case $p_1 = p_2$.

Finally, we see that the information measure is a continuous function over the domain of allowable values for p, the probability of occurrence of the event s. We would intuitively expect this to be true, since a slight change in the probability of occurrence of a symbol would not result in a large change in the information content.

With this as background let us start with a few definitions and derive the above ideas from them.

2-3. FEINSTEIN'S AXIOMATIC APPROACH TO THE MEASURE.[†]

The author feels that a serious student should see the rigorous development of the fundamental form of the information measure.

Theorem 1. The following three conditions determine the information measure H up to a multiplicative constant, whose value serves only to determine the size of the unit of information. (Note we have expressed H as a function of the probabilities $(p_1, p_2, \ldots, p_n)$ of occurrence of corresponding symbols $(s_1, s_2, \ldots, s_n)$ and further, that H is defined only for a complete set of probabilities that are defined as a set of nonnegative numbers whose sum is unity.)

1. $H(p, 1 - p)$ is a continuous function of p for $0 < p \leqslant 1$.
2. $H(p_1, \ldots, p_n)$ is a symmetric function of all its variables.
3. If $p_n = q_1 + q_2 > 0$, then

$$H(p_1, p_2, \ldots, p_{n-1}, q_1, q_2) = H(p_1, p_2, \ldots, p_n) + p_n H\left(\frac{q_1}{p_n}, \frac{q_2}{p_n}\right)$$

Feinstein has proven the above theorem by using the three conditions to prove seven lemmas which then make the theorem almost obvious. The proof of these lemmas provides us with a series of stepping stones with which we may cross the creek with short steps rather than in one large jump. Each one builds upon the other so each must be understood before progressing.

Lemma 1. We have $H(1, 0) = 0$.

Proof. We may apply condition 3 in the following manner. Let

$$p_{n-1} = \tfrac{1}{2} = p_1 \text{ and } p_n = q_1 + q_2 = \tfrac{1}{2} + 0 = \tfrac{1}{2} = p_2.$$

Then

$$q_1/p_n = \tfrac{1}{2}/\tfrac{1}{2} = 1 \qquad q_2/p_n = 0/\tfrac{1}{2} = 0$$

and

$$H(p_1, q_1, q_2) = H(\tfrac{1}{2}, \tfrac{1}{2}, 0)$$

Also,

$$H(p_1, p_2) = H(\tfrac{1}{2}, \tfrac{1}{2}) \text{ and } p_2 H\left(\frac{q_1}{p_2}, \frac{q_2}{p_2}\right) = 1/2 \, H(1, 0)$$

[†]Sections 2-3 and 2-4 attempt to explain in detailed terms the results of Feinstein's Chapters 1 and 2 of Ref. 7. For this reason the proofs are to be considered extensions of Feinstein's proofs where desirable for clarity and in one or two rare instances the author has taken the liberty of supplying a proof in his own words.

Hence,

$$H(\tfrac{1}{2}, \tfrac{1}{2}, 0) = H(\tfrac{1}{2}, \tfrac{1}{2}) + 1/2\, H(1, 0) \qquad (2\text{-}3)$$

But from condition 2 we have

$$H(\tfrac{1}{2}, \tfrac{1}{2}, 0) = H(0, \tfrac{1}{2}, \tfrac{1}{2})$$

Applying condition 3, we have

$$H(0, \tfrac{1}{2}, \tfrac{1}{2}) = H(0, 1) + H(\tfrac{1}{2}, \tfrac{1}{2}) = H(1, 0) + H(\tfrac{1}{2}, \tfrac{1}{2}) \qquad (2\text{-}4)$$

Thus we may equate (2-3) and (2-4):

$$H(\tfrac{1}{2}, \tfrac{1}{2}) + \tfrac{1}{2}\, H(1,0) = H(\tfrac{1}{2}, \tfrac{1}{2}) + H(1, 0)$$

which implies

$$H(1,0) = 0$$

Lemma 2. We have $H(p_1, \ldots, p_n, 0) = H(p_1, \ldots, p_n)$.

Proof. Let $q_1 = p_n$, $q_2 = 0$. Then $q_1 + q_2 = p_n > 0$, and

$$H(p_1, \ldots, p_{n-1}, p_n, 0) = H(p_1, \ldots, p_{n-1}, q_1, q_2)$$
$$= H(p_1, \ldots, p_{n-1}, p_n) + p_n H(q_1/p_n, q_2/p_n)$$

by condition 3, and

$$= H(p_1, \ldots, p_n) + p_n H(1, 0) = H(p_1, \ldots, p_n)$$

by applying Lemma 1.

Lemma 3. We have

$$H(p_1, \ldots, p_{n-1}, q_1, \ldots, q_m) = H(p_1, \ldots, p_n) + p_n H(q_1/p_n, \ldots, q_m/p_n)$$

where $p_n = q_1 + q_2 + \cdots + q_m > 0$.

Proof. For $m = 2$ the above equation reduces to the condition 3 exactly and hence is true by hypothesis.

Now we will prove the lemma for general m by induction. (It is assumed that the reader is familiar with this type of mathematical proof.)

Assume the lemma is true for m. Then for $m + 1$ terms we have

$$H(p_1, \ldots, p_{n-1}, q_1, \ldots, q_{m+1})$$
$$= H(p_1, \ldots, p_{n-1}, q_1, p') + p'\, H(q_2/p', \ldots, q_{m+1}/p') \qquad (2\text{-}5)$$

by condition 3 of Theorem 1 and the assumption that the lemma is true for m. From the assumption we know that $q_1 + q_2 + \cdots + q_m > 0$. If $q_{m+1} = 0$, then we may apply Lemma 2 and thus have the case of m which is assumed true. If $q_{m+1} \neq 0$ then note that the other terms must change their value so that we still have a valid probability scheme, i.e.,

$$p_1 + p_2 + \cdots + p_{n-1} + q_1 + \cdots + q_{m+1} = 1$$

Continuing, we have, from applying condition 3,

$$H(p_1, \ldots, p_{n-1}, \ q_1, p') = H(p_1, \ldots, p_n) + p_n H(q_1/p_n, p'/p_n) \qquad (2\text{-}6)$$

where $p' = q_2 + \cdots + q_{m+1}$
and

$$H(q_1/p_n, \ldots, q_{m+1}/p_n) = H(q_1/p_n, p'/p_n) + \frac{p'}{p_n} H(q_2/p', \ldots, q_{m+1}/p') \quad (2\text{-}7)$$

where $q_1 + q_2 + \cdots + q_{m+1} = p_n$.

Substituting Eqs. 2-7 and 2-6 into Eq. 2-5, we have

$$H(p_1, \ldots, p_{n-1}, \ q_1, \ldots, q_{m+1}) = H(p_1, \ldots, p_n)$$
$$+ p_n H(q_1/p_n, \ldots, q_{m+1}/p_n) \qquad (2\text{-}8)$$

Now since the lemma is obviously true for $m = 2$ and we have proven that it is true for $m + 1$ if it is true for m, then obviously it is true for $m = 3$, and hence for $m = 4$, etc., and hence for aribtrary m.

Lemma 4. We have

$$H(q_{11}, \ldots, q_{1m_1}, \ldots, q_{n1}, \ldots, q_{nm_n})$$

$$= H(p_1, \ldots, p_n) + \sum_{i=1}^{n} p_i H(q_{i1}/p_i, \ldots, q_{im_i}/p_i)$$

where $p_i = q_{i1} + \cdots + q_{im_i} > 0$.

Proof. Let $p_1 = q_{11} + q_{12} + \cdots + q_{1m_1}$

$$p_2 = q_{21} + q_{22} + \cdots + q_{2m_2}$$
$$\vdots \qquad \vdots \qquad \vdots$$
$$p_n = q_{n1} + q_{n2} + \cdots + q_{nm_n}$$

Then we have

$$H(q_{11}, \ldots, \ q_{1m_1}, \ldots, \ q_{n1}, \ldots, q_{nm_n})$$
$$= H(p_1, \ldots, p_{n-1}, \ p_n) + p_n H(q_{n1}/p_n, \ldots, q_{nm_n}/p_n)$$

by Lemma 3.
But

$$H(p_1, \ldots, p_{n-1}, p_n) = H(p_n, p_1, \ldots, p_{n-1})$$

by condition 2, and

$$= H(p_n, p_1, \ldots, p_{n-2}, \ q_{(n-1)1}, q_{(n-1)2}, \ldots, q_{(n-1)m_{n-1}})$$
$$= H(p_n, p_1, \ldots, p_{n-1}) + p_{n-1} H\left(\frac{q_{(n-1)1}}{p_{n-1}}, \ldots, \frac{q_{(n-1)m_{n-1}}}{p_{n-1}}\right)$$

by Lemma 3.

Again shifting p_{n-1} to left, continuing the reduction, and adding the terms, we obtain the above desired result after m total steps. Now set $F(n) = H(1/n, \ldots, 1/n)$ for $n \geqslant 2$, and set $F(1) = 0$. Then if we let $m_1 = m_2 = m_3 = \ldots = m_n = m$ in Lemma 4, we would have

$$q_{11} + q_{12} + \cdots + q_{1m} = p_1$$
$$q_{21} + q_{22} + \cdots + q_{2m} = p_2$$

and finally

$$q_{n1} + q_{n2} + \cdots + q_{nm} = p_n$$

where $p_1 + p_2 + \cdots + p_n = 1$.

Further let us stipulate that all q's are equal and hence $q_{ij} = 1/mn$ for all i and j. Then we would have

$$F(mn) = H(1/mn, 1/mn, \ldots, 1/mn) = H(1/m, 1/m, \ldots, 1/m)$$
$$+ H(1/n, 1/n, \ldots, 1/n) = F(m) + F(n)$$

Now if we apply Lemma 3 we have

$$F(n) = H(1/n, \ldots, 1/n) = H[1/n, (n-1)/n]$$
$$+ [(n-1)/n] \, H[1/(n-1), \ldots, (1/(n-1)]$$

or

$$H[1/n, (n-1)/n] \equiv \eta_n \equiv F(n) - [(n-1)/n] \, F(n-1)$$

Lemma 5. As $n \longrightarrow \infty$, $\mu_n \equiv F(n)/n \longrightarrow 0$ and

$$\lambda_n \equiv F(n) - F(n-1) \longrightarrow 0$$

These statements are necessary for proofs of two following lemmas which are directly involved in determining the form of $H(p_1, \ldots, p_n)$. (Have courage, we are almost there!)

Proof. $\lim_{n \to \infty} \eta_n = \lim_{n \to \infty} H \, [1/n, (n-1)/n] \longrightarrow H(0, 1) = 0$

and

$$nF(n) = nH[1/n, (n-1)/n] + (n-1)F(n-1)$$

but

$$F(n-1) = H(1/n-1, \ldots, 1/n-1) = H[1/(n-1), (n-2)/(n-1)]$$
$$+ [(n-2)/(n-1)] \, H[1/(n-2), \ldots, 1/(n-2)]$$
$$= \eta_{n-1} + [(n-2)/(n-1)] \, F(n-2)$$

Thus

$$nF(n) = nH[1/n, (n-1)/n] + (n-1) \, [\eta_{n-1} + [(n-2)/(n-1)] \, F(n-2)]$$

or

$$nF(n) = n\eta_n + (n-1) \, \eta_{n-1} + (n-2) \, F(n-2)$$

and since in general

$$F(n - k) = \eta_{n-k} + [(n - k - 1)/(n - k)]\, F(n - k - 1)$$

we have

$$nF(n) = n\eta_n + (n - 1)\,\eta_{n-1} + (n - 2)\,\eta_{n-2} + \cdots + (n - n + 2)\,\eta_{n-n+2}$$
$$+ (n - n + 1)\, F(n - n + 1)$$

Since $F(n - n + 1) = F(1) = 0$ we may substitute for this last term the quantity $H(1, 0) = H[1/(n - n + 1), (n - n)/(n - n + 1)] = \eta_{n-n+1}$
   Thus

$$nF(n) = n\eta_n + (n - 1)\,\eta_{n-1} + (n - 2)\,\eta_{n-2}$$

$$+ \cdots + (n - n + 1)\,\eta_{n-n+1} = \sum_{K=1}^{n} K\eta_K$$

or

$$F(n)/n = (1/n^2) \sum_{K=1}^{n} K\eta_K = [(n + 1)/2n)\,(2/n\,(n + 1))] \sum_{K=1}^{n} K\eta_K$$

The term $[2/n\,(n + 1)] \sum_{K=1}^{n} K\eta_K$ is simply the arithmetic mean of the first $n(n + 1)/2$ terms of the sequence $\eta_1, \eta_2, \eta_2, \eta_3, \eta_3, \eta_3, \cdots$.
   For instance, let $n = 4$. Then

$$\frac{2}{4(5)}\,(\eta_1 + \eta_2 + \eta_2 + \eta_3 + \eta_3 + \eta_3 + \eta_4 + \eta_4 + \eta_4 + \eta_4)$$

$$= \frac{a_1 + a_2 + a_3 + a_4 + a_5 + a_6 + a_7 + a_8 + a_9 + a_{10}}{10}$$

where $a_1 = \eta_1, a_2 = a_3 = \eta_2, a_4 = a_5 = a_6 = \eta_3$, and $a_7 = a_8 = a_9 = a_{10} = \eta_4$.
   We have seen that the limit of the η_n's $\longrightarrow 0$ as $n \longrightarrow \infty$. Hence

$$\lim_{n \to \infty} [2/n\,(n + 1)] \sum_{K=1}^{n} K\eta_K \longrightarrow 0$$

from which it follows that

$$\lim_{n \to \infty} F(n)/n = \lim_{n \to \infty} \mu_n = 0$$

Now

$$\lambda_n \equiv F(n) - F(n - 1) = F(n) - F(n - 1) + 1/nF(n - 1) - 1/nF(n - 1)$$

or

$$\lambda_n = F(n) - [(n - 1)/n]\, F(n - 1) - 1/nF(n - 1) = \eta_n - 1/nF(n - 1)$$

Thus

$$\lim_{n \to \infty} \lambda_n = \lim_{n \to \infty} [\eta_n - 1/nF(n-1)] \longrightarrow 0$$

This may be shown in a similar manner as for μ_n.

The form of $F(n)$ may be determined at this point. Since $F(mn) = F(m) + F(n)$ then it is clear that we only need to know the value of $F(n)$ for prime n. (All other numbers can be factored into product of primes which we will denote by p's for convenience in the following discussion. There should not be any confusion as to when p is a prime number or a probability.) For arbitrary n we let

$$n = p_1^{\alpha_1} \, p_2^{\alpha_2} \cdots p_s^{\alpha_s}$$

be the prime factorization of n. For instance, 20 will factor into $20 = 10 \cdot 2 = 5 \cdot 2 \cdot 2 = 2^2 \cdot 5^1$. Then

$$F(n) = \alpha_1 \, F(p_1) + \alpha_2 \, F(p_2) + \cdots + \alpha_s \, F(p_s)$$

Notice that

$$F(p_1^{\alpha} \, 1) = F(\underbrace{p_1 \cdots p_1}_{\alpha_1 \text{ times}}) = \underbrace{F(p_1) + F(p_1) + \cdots + F(p_1)}_{\alpha_1 \text{ times}} = \alpha_1 \, F(p_1)$$

For all prime numbers p we define $F(p) = c_p \ln p$, where ln is natural logarithm. (Since c_p is a function of p, we have not restricted $F(p)$ to only a logarithm function.) Then

$$F(n) = \alpha_1 c_{p_1} \ln p_1 + \alpha_2 c_{p_2} \log p_2 + \cdots + \alpha_s c_{p_s} \ln p_s.$$

We shall see that the c_{p_i}'s are equal; i.e., $c_{p_1} = c_{p_2} = \cdots = c_{p_s}$.

Lemma 6. The sequence c_p; $p = 2, \ 3, \ 5, \ 7, \ 11, \ldots$ contains a largest member.

Proof. Assume the contrary; then it is possible to construct an infinite sequence of primes $p_1 < p_2 < p_3 \ldots$ such that $p_1 = 2$ and p_{i+1} is the first prime greater than p_i for which $c_{p_{i+1}} > c_{p_i}$. Then if q is a prime number less than p_i, $c_q < c_{p_i}$ by definition of the p_i's. For $i > 1$, let $p_i - 1 = q_1^{\alpha_1} \cdots q_s^{\alpha_s}$ be the prime factorization of $p_i - 1$. Then

$$\lambda_{p_i} = F(p_i) - F(p_i - 1)$$

$$= F(p_i) - \frac{F(p_i)}{\ln (p_i)} \ln (p_i - 1) + c_{p_i} \ln (p_i - 1) - F(p_i - 1)$$

since

$$c_{p_i} = \frac{F(p_i)}{\ln p_i}$$

But

$$c_{p_i} \ln (p_i - 1) = c_{p_i} \ln (q_1^{\alpha_1} \cdots q_s^{\alpha_s}) = c_{p_i} (\alpha_1 \ln q_1 + \cdots + \alpha_s \ln q_s)$$

$$= \sum_{j=1}^{s} \alpha_j c_{p_i} \ln q_j$$

and

$$F(p_i - 1) = \alpha_1 F(q_1) + \cdots + \alpha_s F(q_s) = \alpha_1 c_{q_1} \ln q_1 + \cdots + \alpha_s c_{q_s} \ln q_s$$

$$= \sum_{j=1}^{s} \alpha_j c_{q_j} \ln q_j$$

and

$$F(p_i) - \frac{F(p_i)}{\ln (p_i)} \ln (p_i - 1)$$

$$= F(p_i) \left[1 - \frac{1}{\ln (p_i)} \ln (p_i - 1) \right] = \frac{F(p_i)}{\ln (p_i)} \ln \left(\frac{p_i}{p_i - 1} \right)$$

Thus we have

$$\lambda_{p_i} = \frac{F(p_i)}{p_i} \frac{p_i}{\ln (p_i)} \ln \left(\frac{p_i}{p_i - 1} \right) + \sum_{j=1}^{s} \alpha_j (c_{p_i} - c_{q_j}) \ln q_j$$

Since $p_i - 1$ is necessarily even (remember in this case p_i is a prime number) one of the q_i must take on the value 2. Also, since $c_{p_i} > c_{q_j}$ for $j = 1, \ldots, s$, we have

$$\sum_{j=1}^{s} \alpha_j (c_{p_i} - c_{q_j}) \ln q_j \geqslant (c_{p_i} - c_2) \ln 2 \geqslant (c_{p_2} - c_2) \ln 2.$$

But as $i \longrightarrow \infty$, $p_i \longrightarrow \infty$; by Lemma 5, $\lambda_{p_i} \longrightarrow 0$ and $\dfrac{F(p_i)}{p_i} \longrightarrow 0$, while, using L'Hospital's rule, it is easily shown that

$$\lim_{p_i \to \infty} \frac{p_i}{\ln p_i} \ln \left(\frac{p_i}{p_i - 1} \right) \longrightarrow 0$$

Therefore we must have

$$\sum_{j=1}^{s} \alpha_j (c_{p_i} - c_{q_j}) \ln q_j \longrightarrow 0 \geqslant (c_{p_2} - c_2) \ln 2$$

or

$$(c_{p_2} - c_2) \leq 0 \quad \text{or} \quad c_{p_2} \leq c_2$$

which is a contradiction of the definition of p_2. Similarly we may show the existence of a smallest member of c_p, $p = 2, 3, 5, \ldots$

Lemma 7. $F(n) = c \ln n$, where c is a constant.

Proof. It suffices to show that all the c_p are equal. Suppose there is a prime, p', such that $c_{p'} > c_2$. Let p be that prime for which c_p is a maximum; then $c_p > c_2$. Let m be a positive integer and $q_1^{\alpha_1} \ldots q_s^{\alpha_s}$ be the prime factorization of $p^m - 1$. From $F(mn) = F(m) + F(n)$ we have

$$F(p^m) = \underbrace{F(p) + F(p) + \cdots + F(p)}_{m \text{ times}}$$

$$= mF(p) = mc_p \ln p = c_p \ln p^m \quad \text{or} \quad \frac{F(p^m)}{\ln (p^m)} = c_p$$

then just as in the proof of Lemma 6; we obtain $(c_p - c_2) \ln 2 \leq 0$, which contradicts $c_p > c_2$. In precisely the same way we can show the nonexistence of any prime q for which $c_q < c_2$; thus all the c_p are equal.

Note. Now that we know that $c_{p_1} = c_{p_2} = \cdots = c_{p_s} = c$ we may show

$$F(n) = \alpha_1 c_{p_1} \ln p_1 + \cdots + \alpha_s c_{p_s} \ln p_s = c(\alpha_1 \ln p_1 + \cdots + \alpha_s \ln p_s)$$

or

$$F(n) = c(\ln p_1^{\alpha_1} + \cdots + \ln p_s^{\alpha_s}) = c \ln (p_1^{\alpha_1} p_2^{\alpha_2} \cdots p_s^{\alpha_s}) = c \ln n.$$

Now let's finish the business of determining the form of $H(p_1, \ldots, p_n)$. (The p's will only represent probabilities from this point on.)

Let $p = \dfrac{r}{s}$ for integer r, s. By Lemma 4 we have

$$H\left(\frac{1}{s}, \ldots, \frac{1}{s}\right) = H\left(\frac{r}{s}, \frac{s-r}{s}\right) + \frac{r}{s} H\left(\frac{1}{r}, \ldots, \frac{1}{r}\right) + \frac{s-r}{s} H\left(\frac{1}{s-r}, \ldots, \frac{1}{s-r}\right)$$

or since

$$H\left(\frac{r}{s}, \frac{s-r}{s}\right) = H(p, 1-p)$$

we may rewrite the above equation as

$$H(p, 1-p) = F(s) - pF(r) - (1-p) F(s-r)$$

$$= c \ln s - pc \ln r - (1-p) c \ln (s-r)$$

$$= c [\ln s - p \ln r - (1-p) \ln (s-r) + p \ln s - p \ln s]$$

$$= c\left[p \ln \frac{s}{r} + (1-p) \ln \frac{s}{s-r}\right]$$

or

$$H(p, 1 - p) = c\left[p \ln \frac{1}{p} + (1 - p) \ln \left(\frac{1}{1 - p}\right)\right]$$

This extends to all irrational p's by the continuity condition.

Using condition 3 and mathematical induction on n we have

$$H(p_1, \ldots, p_n) = c\sum_{i=1}^{n} p_i \ln \frac{1}{p_i}$$

At this point the reader should have an idea of the labor involved in formally generating a simple concept. We will not undertake formal proofs of all the statements of information and coding theory as this would defeat the main objective of the text. However, it was desirable to get a firm grounding in the fundamental relation of information theory while simultaneously gaining insight in the method of making formal statements.

The constant c is so chosen that $c \ln 1/p = \log 1/p$. Thus

$$H(p_1, \ldots, p_n) = -\sum_{i=1}^{n} p_i \log p_i$$

The term *entropy* is used for H since the sum expression bears a formal resemblance to the entropy in statistical mechanics. We also define the indeterminate form for 0 (log 0) to have the value zero.

2-4. PROPERTIES OF ENTROPY

In this section we derive a few of the more useful properties of the Entropy function $H(p_1, \ldots, p_n)$. Again this section is based upon Feinstein's work, but we shall not attempt to show the formal proof of each statement. Rather the intent here will be to illustrate the useful properties in anticipation of using our new-found knowledge in the following chapters.

Let X be an abstract set of n symbols x_i, with probabilities p_i respectively. Then by $H(X)$ we shall mean $H(p_1, \ldots, p_n)$. Furthermore, we shall write

$$H(X) = -\sum_{i=1}^{n} p_{x_i} \log p_{x_i} = -\sum_{X} p(x) \log p(x)$$

Now suppose we have two abstract sets of symbols X as before, and Y a set of M symbols y_j with probabilities p_j respectively. Then by $H(X, Y)$ we shall mean

$$H(X, Y) = -\sum_{X}\sum_{Y} p(x, y) \log p(x, y)$$

From conditional probability we know that $p(x/y) = \dfrac{p(x, y)}{p(y)}$, $p(y) > 0$.

Thus we may define a *conditional information* content:

$$H(X/y) = -\sum_{i=1}^{n} p(x_i/y) \log p(x_i/y)$$

and an *average conditional information* content

$$H(X/Y) = \sum_{j=1}^{m} p(y_j) H(X/y_j) = -\sum_{j=1}^{m} \sum_{i=1}^{n} p(x_i, y_j) \log p(x_i/y_j)$$

Example 2-1.

Let a source X be the set of possible outcomes of an experiment which is the roll of a die. Thus $X = \{1, 2, 3, 4, 5, 6\}$. Assuming a fair die we have $p(1) = p(2) = p(3) = p(4) = p(5) = p(6) = \frac{1}{6}$.

(a) Find the self-entropy of a single outcome.
(b) Find the average entropy of the source X.

Solution:

(a) Since all outcomes are equally likely we have (recalling Eq. 2-1):

$$S_I(p_i) = -\log(p_i) = -\log(\tfrac{1}{6}) = -(\log 1 - \log 6) = \log 6 = 2.585$$

(b) $H(X) = -\displaystyle\sum_{i=1}^{n} p_i \log(p_i)$

$$= -[p_1 \log p_1 + p_2 \log p_2 + \cdots + p_6 \log p_6]$$
$$= -6 \left[\tfrac{1}{6} \log \tfrac{1}{6}\right] \text{ or } H(X) = -\log \tfrac{1}{6} = \log 6 = 2.585$$

For this simple example the average entropy of the source is equal to the self-entropy of each outcome. This is not the case in general.

Example 2-2.

Let a source X be a set of three possible events $\{x_1, x_2, x_3\}$ with the probability of occurrence $p_{x_1} = \frac{1}{2}, p_{x_2} = \frac{1}{4}, p_{x_3} = \frac{1}{4}$, and let Y be a set of three possible events $\{y_1, y_2, y_3\}$ related to the x's in the following manner:

$$p(y_1|x_1) = p(y_2|x_1) = p(y_3|x_1) = \tfrac{1}{3}$$
$$p(y_1|x_2) = \tfrac{1}{2} \qquad p(y_2|x_2) = p(y_3|x_2) = \tfrac{1}{4}$$
$$p(y_1|x_3) = \tfrac{1}{4} = p(y_2|x_3) \qquad p(y_3|x_3) = \tfrac{1}{2}$$

(a) Find the average entropy of Y.
(b) Find the average conditional entropy $H(X/Y)$.

Solution.

(a) Remembering $p(x_i, y_j) = p(y_j/x_i) p(x_i) = p(x_i/y_j) p(y_j)$, we must first find the probabilities $p(y_1), p(y_2), p(y_3)$.

$$p(y_1) = \sum_{i=1}^{3} p(x_i, y_1) = \sum_{i=1}^{3} p(y_1/x_i) p(x_i)$$

$$= p(y_1/x_1) p(x_1) + p(y_1/x_2) p(x_2) + p(y_1/x_3) p(x_3)$$

$$= (1/3)(1/2) + (1/2)(1/4) + (1/4)(1/4) = (1/6 + 1/8 + 1/16)$$

$$= 8/48 + 6/48 + 3/48 = 17/48$$

Similarly,

$$p(y_2) = 7/24, \quad p(y_3) = 17/48 \quad [Note: p(y_1) + p(y_2) + p(y_3) = 1]$$

Then

$$H(Y) = -\sum_{i=1}^{3} p(y_i) \log p(y_i) = -17/48 \log 17/48 - 7/24 \log 7/24$$

$$- 17/48 \log 17/48 \cong 1.5787$$

(b)

$$H(X/Y) = -\sum_{j=1}^{m}\sum_{i=1}^{n} p(x_i, y_j) \log p(x_i/y_j)$$

$$= -\sum_{j=1}^{m}\sum_{i=1}^{n} p(x_i, y_j) \log \frac{p(x_i, y_j)}{p(y_j)}$$

$$= -p(x_1, y_1) \log \frac{p(x_1, y_1)}{p(y_1)} - p(x_1, y_2) \log \frac{p(x_1, y_2)}{p(y_2)}$$

$$= -p(x_1, y_3) \log \frac{p(x_1, y_3)}{p(y_3)} - p(x_2, y_1) \log \frac{p(x_2, y_1)}{p(y_1)} - \cdots \text{etc.}$$

$$H(X/Y) = -(1/3)(1/2) \log \frac{(1/3)(1/2)}{(17/48)}$$

$$- (1/3)(1/2) \log \frac{(1/3)(1/2)}{(7/24)} - \cdots \text{etc.}$$

$$H(X/Y) = -1/6 \log 8/17 - 1/6 \log 4/7 - \ldots \text{etc.}$$

Some of the more useful properties of H are
1. $H(p)$ is nonnegative.
2. $H(p)$ is zero only for $p = 0$ or $p = 1$.

3. $H(p_1, \ldots, p_n)$ is a maximum only for $p_1 = p_2 = \cdots = p_n = 1/n$; i.e., iff the source symbols are equally likely.

4. $H(X, Y) \leqslant H(X) + H(Y)$ with equality iff $p(x, y) = p(x)\, p(y)$, i.e., X and Y are statistically independent (S.I.).

5. $H(X/Y) \leqslant H(X)$ with equality iff X and Y are S.I.

6. $H(X_1, \ldots, X_n) \leqslant H(X_1) + \cdots + H(X_n)$ with equality iff the X_i, $i = 1, \ldots, n$ are S.I.

We may obtain Property 1 from the definition of $H(p) = -p \log p$, where p is a number less than or equal to unity. The log for these values is always negative or at most zero. Hence $H(p)$ is always positive or at least zero. Property number 2 follows from the previous definition of $0\,(\log 0) = 0$, and from the defined value of $\log 1 = 0$.

The proofs of Properties 3, 4, and 5 are somewhat more involved and may be aided by first considering two properties of sequences of nonnegative numbers. The following lemmas are presented in Feinstein, Chapter 2.

Lemma 8. If $\{p_i\}$, $\{q_i\}$, $i = 1, \ldots, n$, are two sets of nonnegative numbers such that $\displaystyle\sum_{i=1}^{n} p_i = \sum_{i=1}^{n} q_i = 1$, then we have

$$-\sum_{i=1}^{n} q_i \log q_i \leqslant -\sum_{i=1}^{n} q_i \log p_i$$

with equality iff

$$p_i = q_i, \quad i = 1, \ldots, n$$

Remarks. We will not undertake the proof of Lemmas 8 and 9 but instead will discuss the implications. The set of p_i's or q_i's are suitable for probability schemes, since each element p_i and q_i is less than or at most equal to unity, and the sum of p_i's = 1 and sum of q_i's = 1. (This lemma is used several times in Chapter 3 and is worth some extra effort!)

Consider $\{p_i\} = \{1/4, 1/4, 1/2\}$ and $\{q_i\} = \{1/3, 1/3, 1/3\}$. Then from Lemma 8 we have

$$-\sum_{i=1}^{n} q_i \log q_i = -\left[1/3 \log 1/3 + 1/3 \log 1/3 + 1/3 \log 1/3\right]$$

$$\leqslant -\left[1/3 \log 1/4 + 1/3 \log 1/4 + 1/3 \log 1/2\right] = -\sum_{j=1}^{n} q_i \log p_i$$

or

$$\log 3 \leqslant 2/3 \log 4 + 1/3 \log 2$$

or

$$\frac{1}{585} < \frac{5}{3}$$

Lemma 9. Let $\{p_i\}$, $i = 1, \ldots, n$, be as in Lemma 8, and let $\sum\limits_{i=1}^{n} a_{ij} =$
$\sum\limits_{j=1}^{n} a_{ij} = 1$, with $a_{ij} \geqslant 0$; $i,j = 1, \ldots, n$. Let $p_i' = \sum\limits_{j=1}^{n} a_{ij} p_j$. Then $-\sum\limits_{i=1}^{n} p_i' \log p_i' \geqslant$
$-\sum\limits_{i=1}^{n} p_i \log p_i$, with equality if the $\{p_i'\}$ are a relabeling of the $\{p_i\}$.

Remarks. The lemma is vital in the proof of property 3 of $H(p_1, \ldots, p_n)$, thus we need to understand its implications. The set of a_{ij}'s are any arbitrary set of nonnegative numbers with the property of summation to unity over either the i or j index. The $\{p_i\}$ is a probability scheme of a set such as X of Example 2-1 or 2-2. The lemma states that we may generate a new probability scheme $\{p_i'\}$ from the original $\{p_i\}$ by constructing each $p_i' = \sum\limits_{j=1}^{n} a_{ij} p_j$. The new probability scheme based upon $\{p_i'\}$ is guaranteed to have a larger entropy (information content) than the $\{p_i\}$ by the inequality of the lemma which reads

$$H(p_i') = -\sum_{i=1}^{n} p_i' \log p_i' \geqslant -\sum_{i=1}^{n} p_i \log p_i = H(p_i)$$

with equality if and only if $\{p_i'\}$ are only a relabeling of the $\{p_i\}$. Let us consider an example.

Example 2-3.

Let $\{p_i\} = \{p_1, p_2\}$ and $[a_{ij}] = \begin{bmatrix} 1/4 & 3/4 \\ 3/4 & 1/4 \end{bmatrix}$; then we see that

$$\sum_{i=1}^{2} a_{i1} = 1/4 + 3/4 = \sum_{i=1}^{2} a_{i2} = 3/4 + 1/4 = 1$$

and

$$\sum_{j=1}^{2} a_{1j} = 1/4 + 3/4 = \sum_{j=1}^{2} a_{2j} = 3/4 + 1/4 = 1$$

We construct the $\{p_i'\} = \{p_1', p_2'\}$:

$$p_1' = \sum_{j=1}^{n} a_{1j}p_j = a_{11}p_1 + a_{12}p_2 = 1/4p_1 + 3/4p_2$$

$$p_2' = \sum_{j=1}^{n} a_{2j}p_j = a_{21}p_1 + a_{22}p_2 = 3/4p_1 + 1/4p_2$$

If $p_1 = 1/3$ and $p_2 = 2/3$, we have $p_1' = 7/12, p_2' = 5/12$, and again we see

$$-\sum_{i=1}^{2} p_i' \log p_i' = \frac{7}{12} \log \frac{12}{7} + \frac{5}{12} \log \frac{12}{5} = .97 > .925$$

$$= \frac{1}{3} \log 3 + \frac{2}{3} \log \frac{3}{2} = -\sum_{i=1}^{2} p_i \log p_i$$

Theorem 2. The maximum information content of a source having n elements is $\log n$, and is achieved only when all elements have equal probability.

Proof. Let p_i, $i = 1, 2, \ldots, n$, be the probabilities of an information source. Then the entropy of the source is $-\sum_{i=1}^{n} p_i \log p_i$. If we then apply Lemma 9, we have

$$-\sum_{i=1}^{n} p_i' \log p_i' \geqslant -\sum_{i=1}^{n} p_i \log p_i$$

where the p_i''s are constructed by the relation $p_i' = \sum_{j=1}^{n} a_{ij} p_j$ and the a_{ij} terms are of the matrix form of the lemma such that

$$\sum_{i=1}^{n} a_{ij} = \sum_{j=1}^{n} a_{ij} = 1$$

From Lemma 9 we know that the equality holds if the p_i' terms are simply the relabeling of the p_i terms. Hence the only way we can be sure that there does not exist an arbitrary selection of a_{ij} terms such that the entropy of the generated p_i' terms is larger than the original set of p_i's is to make the p_i terms such that, no matter what set of a_{ij}'s are used to make the p_i' terms, the p_i' terms are always just a relabeling of the p_i's. This leads us to state that the p_i terms must all be equal, i.e., $p_1 = p_2 = \cdots = p_n = 1/n$. For these p_i's the p_i' will always be a relabeling of the p_i and thus the entropy of the p_i' can never exceed the entropy of the $p_i = 1/n$ for all i. Thus the maximum value of the entropy function $H(p_1, \ldots, p_n)$ must be

$$H(p_1, \ldots, p_n) = -\sum_{i=1}^{n} p_i \log p_i = n(1/n \log n) = \log n$$

Continuing Example 2-3, we have

$$p_1' = 1/4p_1 + 3/4p_2$$

and

$$p_2' = 3/4p_1 + 1/4p_2$$

If $p_1 = p_2 = \frac{1}{2}$, then $p_1' = \frac{1}{2}$ and $p_2' = \frac{1}{2}$ and $H(p_i') = H(p_i)$.

In Fig. 2-1 we see a plot of the entropy of a binary source, $\{p_i\} = \{p, q\}$ versus the probability of p. The maximum of the entropy occurs at the point for which $p = q = \frac{1}{2}$.

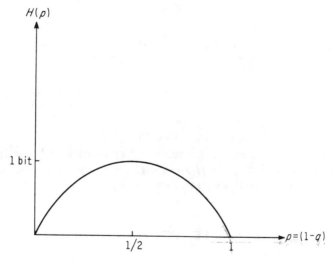

Fig. 2-1. Entropy of an independent binary source.

Now Property 4 may be proven very easily from Lemma 8:

$$H(X) + H(Y) = -\sum_{XY} p(x, y) \ [\log p(x) + \log p(y)]$$

$$= -\sum_{XY} p(x, y) \log \ [p(x)p(y)]$$

But $\sum_{XY} p(x,y) = 1$ so by Lemma 8,

$$- \sum_{XY} p(x,y) \log\left[p(x)p(y)\right] \geqslant - \sum_{XY} p(x,y) \log p(x,y) = H(XY)$$

with equality iff $p(x,y) = p(x)p(y)$ which implies x and y are statistically independent.

Property 5 may be proven using Property 4. From Property 4 we have $H(X, Y) \leqslant H(X) + H(Y)$, but this may be stated as $H(X, Y) - H(Y) \leqslant H(X)$. But

$$H(X, Y) = - \sum_{XY} p(x,y) \log p(x,y)$$

and

$$H(Y) = - \sum_{Y} p(y) \log p(y) = - \sum_{XY} p(x,y) \log p(y)$$

so

$$H(X, Y) - H(Y) = - \sum_{XY} p(x,y) \log p(x,y) + \sum_{XY} p(x,y) \log p(y)$$

$$= - \sum_{XY} p(x,y) \log \frac{p(x,y)}{p(y)} = H(X/Y)$$

Thus we have $H(X, Y) - H(Y) = H(X/Y) \leqslant H(X)$.

Property 6 may be proven by successive application of Property 4. Consider $H(X, Y, Z) \leqslant H(X, Y) + H(Z) \leqslant H(X) + H(Y) + H(Z)$ and in general, $H(X_1, X_2, \ldots, X_n) \leqslant H(X_1) + H(X_2) + \cdots + H(X_n)$.

2-5. REMARKS

At this point we have the necessary tools to discuss a communications system. In Chapter 3 we will analyze a memoryless communications system, and in doing so, we will present a physical picture of the quantities $H(X)$, $H(Y), H(X, Y), H(X/Y)$, and $H(Y/X)$ which we have developed in Chapter 2.

Let us summarize what we know at this point.

1. *Information measure* is a number which is related to the uncertainty or probability of occurrence of an event. We have the *self-information* of a single event defined as $S_I(p) = - \log p$ and the *average information* of a set of events with probabilities $\{p_i\}$ defined as

$$H(p_i) = -\sum_{i=1}^{n} p_i \log p_i$$

2. If we have X a set of events $\{x_i\}$ with probabilities $\{p_{x_i}\}$ and Y with a set of events $\{y_i\}$ with probabilities $\{p_{y_i}\}$, then the *average joint entropy* is defined as

$$H(X, Y) = -\sum_{i=1}^{n}\sum_{j=1}^{m} p(x_i, y_j) \log p(x_i, y_j)$$

The average entropy of the set X is defined as

$$H(X) = -\sum_{i=1}^{n}\left[\left(\sum_{j=1}^{m} p(x_i, y_j)\right) \log\left(\sum_{j=1}^{m} p(x_i, y_j)\right)\right]$$

The average entropy of the set Y is defined as

$$H(Y) = -\sum_{j=1}^{m}\left[\left(\sum_{i=1}^{n} p(x_i, y_j)\right) \left(\log\sum_{i=1}^{n} p(x_i, y_j)\right)\right]$$

The *average conditional entropy* of the set X with respect to Y is defined as

$$H(X/Y) = -\sum_{j=1}^{m}\sum_{i=1}^{n} p(y_j) p(x_i/y_j) \log p(x_i/y_j)$$

The *average conditional entropy* of the set Y with respect to X is defined as

$$H(Y/X) = -\sum_{i=1}^{n}\sum_{j=1}^{m} p(x_i) p(y_j/x_i) \log p(y_j/x_i)$$

In Chapter 3 we shall relate these five entropies to the communications system and draw conclusions as to their meanings and use.

3. We have seen that the entropy is a nonnegative number, i.e., $H(p) \geqslant 0$ which is equal to zero for only two cases: $p = 0$ or $p = 1$.

4. We have established several inequalities that will prove useful later on.

$$H(p_1, \ldots, p_n) \leqslant \log n \quad \text{with equality iff } p_i = 1/n$$

$$H(X, Y) \leqslant H(X) + H(Y)$$

$$H(X/Y) = H(X, Y) - H(Y) \leqslant H(X).$$

PROBLEMS

2-1.   Prove the result of substitution of Eqs. 2-7 and 2-6 into Eq. 2-5 is indeed
        Eq. 2-8.

2-2.   Construct a proof for Lemma 8. (Express p_i as $q_i + r_i$ and substitute for
        p_i in the inequality of Lemma 8. Then use the fact that for any positive
        number $\ln X \leqslant X - 1$.)

2-3.   Construct a proof for Lemma 9 using the inequality of Lemma 8.

2-4.   Prove the relation $H(Y/X) = H(XY) - H(X)$ and $H(X/Y) = H(X, Y) - H(Y)$.

2-5.   Prove the inequalities $H(X/Y) \leqslant H(X)$ and $H(Y/X) \leqslant H(Y)$. What con-
        ditions are required for the equality signs to hold?

2-6.   Show by calculation, using the probability set $\{p_1 = .1, p_2 = .2, p_3 = .3,$
        $p_4 = .1, q_1 = .1, q_2 = .2\}$, that Lemma 3 holds.

2-7.   For Example 2-2, finish part (b) and calculate $H(X, Y)$ by writing a com-
        puter program to perform the calculations. Make the program general
        and keep your program.

2-8.   A message source has three messages m_1, m_2, m_3, with probability of
        occurrence of $p_1 = .3, p_2 = .5, p_3 = .2$, respectively.
        (a). Calculate the self information of each message.
        (b). Calculate the average information per message.

2-9.   A pair of dice are thrown and the sum of their faces is 5. What is the in-
        formation content of this message?

2-10.   Let a source X be a set of two possible events x_1 and x_2, with probability
        of occurrence $p_1 = .25$ and $p_2 = .75$. Let a source Y be a set of three
        possible events related to the X's by the following relations: (Why not
        check your program on this problem?)

$$p(y_1/x_1) = .25 \quad p(y_1/x_2) = .10$$
$$p(y_2/x_1) = .35 \quad p(y_2/x_2) = .70$$
$$p(y_3/x_1) = .40 \quad p(y_3/x_2) = .20$$

        (a). Find the average information (entropy) of Source X.
        (b). Find the average information of Source Y.
        (c). Find the average conditional information $H(X|Y)$.
        (d). Find the average joint information $H(X, Y)$.
        (e). Compare your results of part (c) with part (a) and comment.

2-11.   A message source consists of the same messages and probabilities of oc-
        currence of the source of Prob. 2-8. In order to increase the probability
        of correct reception of the message, the message is transmitted three
        times. What does this do to the rate at which the information is trans-
        mitted? How would you define the term *information rate?* What is the
        probability of correct reception?

CHAPTER 3

Communication Systems without Memory

3-1. INTRODUCTION

In this chapter we endeavor to apply the developments of the previous chapters, and in so doing we must strive for a physical understanding of the terms developed axiomatically in Chapter 2.

The application of information theory to communication systems requires a simplification of the actual description of the system that is manageable yet accurate in its statements of the generation, transmission, and reception of information. This will be a hard task, for we will in effect be simplifying away our problem in order to make a mathematical study of the system. Naturally one has as a goal the minimum simplification necessary to achieve a mathematical model that is usable.

Our mathematical study will yield upper bounds on system performance which will give us something to strive for, but unfortunately will not provide a method or procedure by which we can achieve the optimum system performance. Even so, information theory will yield insights into system performance and from this better understanding of what effects each part of the system has on overall performance we may make more intelligent adjustments of system parameters.

In keeping with our simplification for mathematical modeling purposes we shall discuss the basic communication system shown in Fig. 3-1.

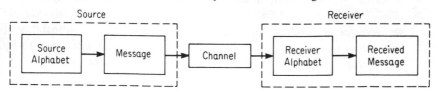

Fig. 3-1. Basic communication system.

First we will consider the source and its information content, then we will consider the channels and their effect upon the received information.

At this point the reader is reminded that this chapter deals with memoryless (zero-memory) systems, hence all results should be tagged as pertaining to memoryless systems. We will investigate memory processes later on.

3-2. SOURCE ENTROPY AND EXTENSIONS OF SOURCES

DEFINITION. A *source* may be considered to consist of an alphabet from which messages are constructed using the source alphabet symbols in accordance with our definition of *message* in Chapter 1. For instance, we may consider a source with the twenty-six lowercase letters of the English language as the alphabet. Our messages could then be words of the English language.

Let us consider several examples of sources.

Example 3-1

Consider a source whose alphabet consists of the binary digits $x_1 = 0$ and $x_2 = 1$, thus $A = \{x_1, x_2\}$. Let the messages consist of three digit sequences. The possible messages could then be tabulated as

a	b	c	Decimal Equivalent
0	0	0	0
0	0	1	1
0	1	0	2
0	1	1	3
1	0	0	4
1	0	1	5
1	1	0	6
1	1	1	7

Note that we have a total possible number of messages $M = 2^n = 2^3 = 8$, where n is the number of binary digits per message. (What would M be if we had three trinary digits per message? The answer is on page 27 of any book!) If we choose the value of each binary digit a, b, and c by the toss of an honest coin, then each message would be equally likely to occur. For this type of source, termed an *equally likely memoryless source*, we may calculate several quantities of interest.

First let us consider individual letters of the alphabet 0 and 1. Each letter carries some information content which is termed the *self-information* of the letter as defined on page 6. For the source of this example we have the probability of occurrence of a zero equal to the probability of occurrence of a one, equal to one-half, since we are picking 0's and 1's by the tossing of an honest coin. Thus the self-information of a zero is

$$S_I(x_1) = -\log p(x_1) = -\log \tfrac{1}{2} = 1$$

where $p(x_1)$ = probability of a zero, and the self-information of a one is

$$S_I(x_2) = -\log p(x_2) = -\log \tfrac{1}{2} = 1.$$

Now let us calculate the average information content per symbol emitted from the source as opposed to the above self-information content of a single letter. This quantity is often termed the *entropy* of the source alphabet as we have defined on page 6. The entropy of this source alphabet is

$$H(A) = \sum_{i=1}^{2} -p(x_i) \log p(x_i) = -p(x_1) \log p(x_1) - p(x_2) \log p(x_2)$$

$$= +\tfrac{1}{2}(1) + \tfrac{1}{2}(1) = 1 \text{ bits}$$

Finally we shall calculate the entropy of the source on a message basis. For this source each message is equally likely, and hence

$$H(M) = -\sum_{j=0}^{7} p(m_j) \log p(m_j)$$

$$= -1/8 \log 1/8 - 1/8 \log 1/8 - 1/8 \log 1/8 - 1/8 \log 1/8$$
$$ -1/8 \log 1/8 - 1/8 \log 1/8 - 1/8 \log 1/8 - 1/8 \log 1/8$$
$$= +\log 8 = 3 \text{ bits per message}$$

The entropy of the source message $H(M)$ on a per symbol (letter) basis is seen to be

$$H(M) \text{ per source symbol} = \tfrac{3}{3} = 1 \text{ bit}$$

If we had encoded the eight messages with four symbols each, then

$$H(M) = -\tfrac{1}{8} \log \tfrac{1}{8} - \tfrac{1}{8} \log \tfrac{1}{8} - \cdots - \tfrac{1}{8} \log \tfrac{1}{8} = 3 \text{ bits per message}$$

and

$$H(M) \text{ per source symbol} = \tfrac{3}{4} = .75 \text{ bit}$$

Several points are apparent from this example and we should consider them now; later we will note the difference between this example and the next example.

First observe that for this source $S_I(x_i)$ and $H(A)$ are equal. This is not universally true, as we shall see in the next example. Secondly, the entropy of the source on a per message basis is different from that of the entropy of the source on a per letter (symbol) basis when we encode with four digits. This tells us that encoding (construction of words or messages from source-alphabet letters or symbols by a procedure termed *encoding*) is a give-and-take situation. We shall discover later that the reliability of transmission may be increased by encoding but, as we can see, the entropy of the encoded messages per symbol will generally be different from the entropy of the original messages per symbol. Now let us consider a second example.

Example 3-2

Consider a source whose alphabet consists of the twenty-six lowercase letters of the English alphabet: $A = \{a, b, c, \cdots, x, y, z\}$. We need the probability of occurrence of each letter in the typical English text. Below is a table (see also Ref. 14, p. 183) of the letters and their frequency of occurrence assuming each successive letter is transmitted independently.[8,14] (We know this to be false, but we will wait for memory-type sources to consider the true case. Give an example of a letter that is not transmitted independently of the preceding letter.)

TABLE 3-1.   Frequency of Occurrence of Letters
in English Language, Percent

a	7.81	n	7.28
b	1.28	o	8.21
c	2.93	p	2.15
d	4.11	q	0.14
e	13.05	r	6.64
f	2.88	s	6.46
g	1.39	t	9.02
h	5.85	u	2.77
i	6.77	v	1.00
j	0.23	w	1.49
k	0.42	x	0.30
l	3.60	y	1.51
m	2.62	z	0.09

For this source the self-information of each symbol is of course different. For instance,

$$S_I(e) = -\log .1305 = 2.94$$
$$S_I(z) = -\log .0009 = 10.00$$

Thus the most common letter, e, carries the least self-information and the least common letter, z, carries the most self-information. This is consistent with our intuitive ideas as stated earlier. The source entropy of this source alphabet, A, may be computed by

$$H(A) = \sum_{i=1}^{26} p(x_i)S_I(x_i) = -p(a)S_I(a) - p(b)S_I(b) - \cdots - p(z)S_I(z).$$

Rather than perform this laborious calculation, show that the lower bound of the answer must be greater than .991 by using the three most significant terms. (Which, by the way, are which terms?) Note also that not only are the self-information terms not in general equal but also that they are not in general equal to the source entropy.

Before we investigate channels and their properties let us treat one other aspect of sources which we will find useful in our study of coding; the extension of a source.

Let us compare two sources:

Source 1: $A = \{0, 1\}$
Source 2: $B = \{00, 01, 10, 11\}$

We see that source A consists of two symbols and that source B consists of four symbols (00 is considered a symbol for source B). Now take note that source B can be generated from source A by letting $B = A \otimes A$, where $\otimes$ is the symbol for *product space*.

A product space has the following operational properties: given two sets $A = \{a_1, a_2, \ldots, a_q\}$ and $B = \{b_1, b_2, \ldots, b_q\}$ the set $A \otimes B = \{a_1 b_1, a_1 b_2, \ldots, a_1 b_q, a_2 b_1, a_2 b_2, \ldots, a_2 b_q, \ldots, a_q b_1, a_q b_2, \ldots, a_q b_q\}$.

Thus if $A = \{0, 1\}$, then $A \otimes A = \{00. 01, 10, 11\}$. (Note that $\otimes$ and $\oplus$ are different symbols and that we will use $\oplus$ operation later in the book, so keep them separated in your mind.)

Having seen above that source $B = A \otimes A$, we may state that B is an extension of A. We could make another extension of source A and create a source $C = A \otimes A \otimes A = \{000, 001, 010, 011, 100, 101, 110, 111\}$. Now we have a source with eight symbols. Let us generalize these results in a formal statement about source extensions.

DEFINITION. The *n*th *extension* of a source $A = \{a_1, a_2, \ldots, a_q\}$ is $A^n = A \otimes A \otimes \ldots \otimes A$, where the product operation is performed $n - 1$ times. Thus the third extension is written as $A^3 = A \otimes A \otimes A$ (an easy way to keep this straight is to count the number of times the source appears on the right). The *n*th extension of a q symbol source will have q^n symbols each corresponding to some sequence of n of the original symbols, and if the probabilities of the original source symbols are p_i corresponding to the symbols a_i, then the probabilities of the *n*th extension's symbols are the probabilities of the corresponding sequences of original symbols.

If we have $A = \{a_1, a_2\}$ with the probability of a_1 being p_1 and of a_2 being p_2, then the 2nd extension is $A^2 = A \otimes A = \{a_1 a_1, a_1 a_2, a_2 a_1, a_2 a_2\}$ where the 2nd extension symbols have the following probabilities:

2nd Extension Symbols	Associated Probabilities
$a_1 a_1$	$p_1 p_1$
$a_1 a_2$	$p_1 p_2$
$a_2 a_1$	$p_2 p_1$
$a_2 a_2$	$p_2 p_2$

What is the first extension of any source?

Now we need to calculate the entropy of the nth extension of a source. Consider the source A^2. The entropy of A^2 may be written

$$H(A^2) = -p(a_1, a_1) \log p(a_1, a_1) - p(a_1, a_2) \log p(a_1, a_2)$$
$$-p(a_2, a_1) \log p(a_2, a_1) - p(a_2, a_2) \log p(a_2, a_2)$$

But

$$p(a_1, a_1) = p(a_1) p(a_1); \quad p(a_1, a_2) = p(a_1) p(a_2)$$
$$p(a_2, a_1) = p(a_2) p(a_1); \quad p(a_2, a_2) = p(a_2) p(a_2)$$

and

$$p(a_1) + p(a_2) = 1$$

Therefore, since $\log p^2(a_1) = 2 \log p(a_1)$,

$$H(A^2) = -2p(a_1) p(a_1) \log p(a_1) - p(a_1) p(a_2) [\log p(a_1) + \log p(a_2)]$$
$$- p(a_2) p(a_1) [\log p(a_1) + \log p(a_2)] - 2p(a_2) p(a_2) \log p(a_2)$$

or

$$H(A^2) = -2p(a_1) [p(a_1) + p(a_2)] \log p(a_1) - 2p(a_2)$$
$$[p(a_1) + p(a_2)] \log p(a_2)$$

or

$$H(A^2) = 2H(A)$$

We can generalize this interesting and useful result of the nth extension in the following manner:

We have a^n symbols in the nth extension with each symbol a sequence of n of the original source symbols. Thus a symbol in the extension, σ_j, may be written as $\sigma_j = a_{i1}, a_{i2}, \ldots, a_{in}$ with probability $p_j = p_{i1} p_{i2} \cdots p_{in}$ thus

$$\left.\begin{array}{l} H(A^n) = -(p_1 p_1 p_1 \cdots p_1) \log (p_1 p_1 p_1 \cdots p_1) \\ -(p_1 p_1 p_1 \cdots p_2) \log (p_1 p_1 p_1 \cdots p_2) \\ -(p_n p_n p_n \cdots p_n) \log (p_n p_n p_n \cdots p_n) \end{array}\right\} q^n \text{ terms}$$

We may combine these terms just as in our 2nd extension above, resulting in

$$H(A^n) = -n \sum_{j=1}^{q} p_j \sum_{i=1}^{q} p_i \log p_j, \quad \text{but} \sum_{i=1}^{q} p_i = 1$$

Thus

$$H(A^n) = -n \sum_{j=1}^{q} p_j \log p_j = nH(A)$$

or

$$H(A^n) = nH(A) \tag{3-1}$$

Example 3-3

Consider a binary source $A = \{x_1, x_2\}$ where $x_1 = 0, x_2 = 1$ and $p(x_1) = 1/4, p(x_2) = 3/4$. The entropy of this source is:

$$H(A) = -p(x_1) \log p(x_1) - p(x_2) \log p(x_2)$$

$$= +1/4 \log 4 + 3/4 \log 4/3 = .500 + .311 = .811 \text{ bit}$$

The 2nd extension $A^2 = \{x_1x_1, x_1x_2, x_2x_1, x_2x_2\}$ and $p(x_1x_1) = 1/16$, $p(x_1x_2) = p(x_2x_1) = 3/16$, $p(x_2x_2) = 9/16$. The entropy of the 2nd extension is:

$$H(A^2) = -1/16 \log 1/16 - 3/16 \log 3/16 - 3/16 \log 3/16 - 9/16 \log 9/16$$

or

$$H(A^2) = 1.622 = 2H(A)$$

Now consider the binary source $A = \{x_1, x_2\}$ with $p(x_1)$ and $p(x_2)$ as the symbol probabilities. In Chapter 2 we proved that the entropy function has a maximum when all the symbols have equal probabilities. It is also easy to show that the binary source entropy has a maximum, that it is a broad maximum, and that it reaches that maximum for the case of equally likely source symbols. The entropy is expressible as

$$H(A) = -p(x_1) \log p(x_1) - p(x_2) \log p(x_2)$$

where $p(x_2) = 1 - p(x_1)$.

The first derivative is

$$\frac{dH(A)}{dp(x_1)} = -\ln 2 - \log p(x_1) + \ln 2 + \log p(x_2)$$

Setting the derivative equal to zero, we have

$$\log p(x_1) = \log p(x_2)$$

which implies $p(x_1) = p(x_2) = 1/2$.

The second derivative is

$$\frac{d^2 H(A)}{dp(x_1)^2} = -\frac{1}{p(x_1)} - \frac{1}{p(x_2)}$$

which is less than zero showing that $H(A)$ does indeed have a maximum at $p(x_1) = p(x_2)$. A plot of the entropy of a binary source has been illustrated in Fig. 2-1.

3-3. INFORMATION CHANNELS

In Chapter 1 we defined the term *channel*. We will now define a somewhat more restrictive term that will be more useful, the *information channel*.

DEFINITION. An *information channel* accepts symbols from a source alphabet and yields output symbols from an output alphabet. The probability matrix that indicates the probability of any output symbol occurring for any given input symbol completely describes the information channel.

The information channel bears the same relationship to its input and output symbols as a network does to its input and output voltages. Just as we use impedance matrices to characterize networks we use a channel matrix to characterize the channel's transmission characteristics. Figure 3-2 shows a typical channel and its associated channel matrix.

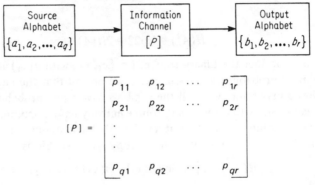

Fig. 3-2. Typical information channel.

The elements of the channel matrix, characterized by the conditional probability symbol, p_{ij}, represent the probability of an output symbol occurring for a particular input symbol. Thus p_{34} is the probability that the output symbol b_4 will be received when the input symbol a_3 is transmitted. Sometimes when the input and output alphabets are small in number a channel is represented by a line drawing, as shown in Fig. 3-3 for a binary input source and trinary output source. (That's right—the number of output symbols does not

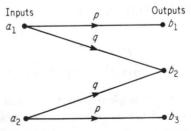

Fig. 3-3. Binary erasure channel (BEC).

have to equal the number of input symbols. Give an example of a system for which the number of input symbols far exceeds the number of output symbols.)

The channel shown in Fig. 3-3 is termed a binary erasure channel. If the symbol b_2 is received it is usually not displayed, and no decision is made as to whether a_1 or a_2 was transmitted. Later, in our study of coding, we shall see the merit of this type of channel also termed a single-error-detecting channel.

For any channel the input is picked from the source with a specified probability scheme. Thus if the channel matrix is specified one may calculate the output symbol probability, the source entropy, and the entropy at the receiver. In addition, two mutual entropy terms which are of much interest may be calculated. Let us illustrate these procedures by considering a general source and system and then working through an example. In actuality there is nothing new here, but simply a putting together of many isolated facts already learned.

In Fig. 3-2 a typical information channel with its source was shown. The source alphabet consists of q symbols each occurring in a message with some probability p_i. This set of source symbol probabilities may be written in matrix form. This will be termed the source matrix $P[A]$. The source matrix may be written as either a diagonal matrix or a row matrix, depending upon what one desires to calculate.

The channel matrix, a conditional probability matrix, has been described already. Using the source matrix $P[A]$ and the channel matrix $P[B/A]$ we may calculate two other quantities of interest, the joint probability matrix $P[A,B]$ and the output alphabet probability matrix $P[B]$.

When we write the source matrix as a diagonal matrix and multiply by the channel matrix the result is the joint probability matrix:

$$P[A]_D \times P[B/A] = P[A,B] \tag{3-2}$$

This is seen best by considering a ternary source alphabet and a ternary output alphabet. Let $A = \{a_1, a_2, a_3\}$ and $B = \{b_1, b_2, b_3\}$. Then we have

$$\begin{bmatrix} p(a_1) & 0 & 0 \\ 0 & p(a_2) & 0 \\ 0 & 0 & p(a_3) \end{bmatrix} \begin{bmatrix} p(b_1/a_1) & p(b_2/a_1) & p(b_3/a_1) \\ p(b_1/a_2) & p(b_2/a_2) & p(b_3/a_2) \\ p(b_1/a_3) & p(b_2/a_3) & p(b_3/a_3) \end{bmatrix}$$

$$= \begin{bmatrix} p(a_1,b_1) & p(a_1,b_2) & p(a_1,b_3) \\ p(a_2,b_1) & p(a_2,b_2) & p(a_2,b_3) \\ p(a_3,b_1) & p(a_3,b_2) & p(a_3,b_3) \end{bmatrix}$$

Note that each element of $P[A,B]$ is easily found by the matrix multiplication on the left, i.e., $p(a_3,b_2) = p(a_3) p(b_2/a_3)$, and the relation obeys our notions of conditional probability. The elements of the joint probability matrix express the probability of the joint occurrence of a source symbol, say a_3, and an output symbol, say b_2. Please notice that Eq. 3-2 may be used to find any one of the matrices provided the other two matrices are known. The reader is reminded to use the correct form for the source matrix.

If we write the source matrix as a row matrix we may calculate the output probability matrix, $P[B]$.

$$P[A]_R \times P[B/A] = P[B] \qquad (3-3)$$

Again consider a ternary source and a ternary output. Then we have

$$[p(a_1) \quad p(a_2) \quad p(a_3)] \begin{bmatrix} p(b_1/a_1) & p(b_2/a_1) & p(b_3/a_1) \\ p(b_1/a_2) & p(b_2/a_2) & p(b_3/a_2) \\ p(b_1/a_3) & p(b_2/a_3) & p(b_3/a_3) \end{bmatrix} = [P(B)]$$

Note that the $p(b_2)$ is easily found by multiplying the left row matrix by the second column of the channel matrix,

$$p(b_2) = p(a_1) p(b_2/a_1) + p(a_2) p(b_2/a_2) + p(a_3) p(b_2/a_3)$$

One other item of interest is the conditional probability, $p(a_i/b_j)$, which will be useful for calculating the entropy $H(A/B)$. This quantity is easily obtained by the relation

$$p(a_i/b_j) = \frac{p(a_i, b_j)}{p(b_j)} \qquad (3-4)$$

At this point it is desirable to recount our achievements. We have discussed five basic probabilities which will be useful to us.

$P[A]$	Source probability matrix
$P[B]$	Output probability matrix
$P[A/B]$	Conditional probability matrix
$P[B/A]$	Channel (conditional probability) matrix
$P[A, B]$	Joint (input-output) probability matrix

Generally speaking, the source matrix and the channel matrix are knowns from which the others may be obtained. On the other hand, one could certainly derive a source matrix from a given output matrix and desired channel matrix. Other combinations are also possible and used when needed.

Now let us use these results to obtain those quantities with which we analyze information systems—that is, our tools with which we work in this area. These quantities are five in number also.

$H(A)$	*Source entropy* (average information per character of the source). Units are bits.
$H(B)$	*Receiver entropy* (average information per character at the receiver (output). Units are bits.
$H(A, B)$	*System entropy* (average information per pairs of transmitted and received characters). Units are bits.

$H(A/B)$ *Noise entropy* (average uncertainty about the transmitted symbol, average over all received signals). Units are bits per symbol.

$H(B/A)$ *Channel entropy* (a measure of the uncertainty of the received symbol where it is known which a_i was transmitted). Units are bits per symbol.

The source and receiver entropies tell us about the nature of the source and output. These terms we want to be large, indicating an uncertainty as to what symbols are to be sent or received, thus carrying a large amount of information relatively speaking.

The noise entropy yields a measure of information lost in the transmission of a symbol from noise in the channel. This quantity (often termed *equivocation*) we want to be small, thereby minimizing the loss of information in the channel.

The channel entropy gives us a measure of the information lost in transmitting a symbol through a channel. This term we would also like to be small.

A schematic analogy of these quantities is shown in Fig. 3-4.

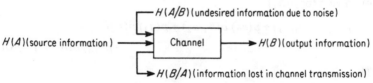

Fig. 3-4. System entropies.

We need to state the relations between the above entropies and the previously stated probabilities derived in matrix form. These entropies have been defined in Sec. 2-5 under (2) of the remarks.

Example 3-4

Consider a source with four letters $\{a_1, a_2, a_3, a_4\}$ and a receiver with three letters $\{b_1, b_2, b_3\}$. Let us suppose that the probabilities of the source letters being transmitted are $p(a_1) = .30$, $p(a_2) = .40$, $p(a_3) = .20$, $p(a_4) = .10$. Furthermore let us suppose that the probabilities of receiving an output given a specific input are given by the channel matrix

$$\begin{array}{c} \\ a_1 \\ a_2 \\ a_3 \\ a_4 \end{array} \begin{bmatrix} b_1 & b_2 & b_3 \\ .5 & .3 & .2 \\ .1 & .6 & .3 \\ 0.0 & .1 & .9 \\ 0.0 & 0.0 & 1.0 \end{bmatrix}$$

(Note that the probability assignments for both source and receiver could be approximated by counting the number of occurrences of each letter sent or received. The relative frequency of occurrence or approximate probability of occurrence may be estimated in this manner.)

From this information we shall calculate the quantities discussed above.

Expressing the source probabilities as a row matrix we may find the output probability matrix from Eq. 3-3.

$$P[A]_R \times P[B/A] = P[B]$$

or

$$[p(a_1) \quad p(a_2) \quad p(a_3) \quad p(a_4)] \begin{bmatrix} p(b_1/a_1) & p(b_2/a_1) & p(b_3/a_1) \\ p(b_1/a_2) & p(b_2/a_2) & p(b_3/a_2) \\ p(b_1/a_3) & p(b_2/a_3) & p(b_3/a_3) \\ p(b_1/a_4) & p(b_2/a_4) & p(b_3/a_4) \end{bmatrix}$$

$$= [p(b_1) \quad p(b_2) \quad p(b_3)]$$

or solving for $p(b_1)$,

$$p(a_1)p(b_1/a_1) + p(a_2)p(b_1/a_2) + p(a_3)p(b_1/a_3)$$
$$+ p(a_4)p(b_1/a_4) = p(b_1)$$

Therefore

$$p(b_1) = (.3)(.5) + (.4)(.1) + (.2)(0) + (.1)(0) = .15 + .04 = .19$$

Similarly, we have $p(b_2) = .35$ and $p(b_3) = .46$.

Note that $p(b_1) + p(b_2) + p(b_3) = 1.0$ as it should, and how easy it is to use this as a check on numerical mistakes.

The joint matrix may now be obtained from Eq. 3-2.

$$P[A]_D \times P[B/A] = P[A, B]$$

or

$$\begin{bmatrix} p(a_1) & 0 & 0 & 0 \\ 0 & p(a_2) & 0 & 0 \\ 0 & 0 & p(a_3) & 0 \\ 0 & 0 & 0 & p(a_4) \end{bmatrix} \begin{bmatrix} p(b_1/a_1) & p(b_2/a_1) & p(b_3/a_1) \\ p(b_1/a_2) & p(b_2/a_2) & p(b_3/a_2) \\ p(b_1/a_3) & p(b_2/a_3) & p(b_3/a_3) \\ p(b_1/a_4) & p(b_2/a_4) & p(b_3/a_4) \end{bmatrix}$$

$$= \begin{bmatrix} p(a_1, b_1) & p(a_1, b_2) & p(a_1, b_3) \\ p(a_2, b_1) & p(a_2, b_2) & p(a_2, b_3) \\ p(a_3, b_1) & p(a_3, b_2) & p(a_3, b_3) \\ p(a_4, b_1) & p(a_4, b_2) & p(a_4, b_3) \end{bmatrix}$$

or solving for $p(a_1, b_1)$,

$$p(a_1)p(b_1/a_1) = p(a_1, b_1)$$

Therefore

$$p(a_1, b_1) = (.3)(.5) = .15$$

and we have,

$$P[A, B] = \begin{bmatrix} .15 & .09 & .06 \\ .04 & .24 & .12 \\ 0 & .02 & .18 \\ 0 & 0 & .1 \end{bmatrix}$$

We may now proceed to calculate the desired entropies. (The value of a digital computer program for matrix calculation becomes clear, doesn't it?)

$$H(A, B) = -\sum_{i=1}^{4}\sum_{j=1}^{3} p(a_i, b_j) \log p(a_i, b_j)$$

or

$$\begin{aligned} H(A, B) = &-p(a_1, b_1) \log p(a_1, b_1) - p(a_2, b_1) \log p(a_2, b_1) \\ &-p(a_3, b_1) \log p(a_3, b_1) - p(a_4, b_1) \log p(a_4, b_1) \\ &-p(a_1, b_2) \log p(a_1, b_2) - p(a_2, b_2) \log p(a_2, b_2) \\ &-p(a_3, b_2) \log p(a_3, b_2) - p(a_4, b_2) \log p(a_4, b_2) \\ &-p(a_1, b_3) \log p(a_1, b_3) - p(a_2, b_3) \log p(a_2, b_3) \\ &-p(a_3, b_3) \log p(a_3, b_3) - p(a_4, b_3) \log p(a_4, b_3) \\ = &-(.15) \log (.15) - (.04) \log (.04) - 0 \log 0 - 0 \log 0 \\ &-(.09) \log (.09) - (.24) \log (.24) - (.02) \log (.02) \\ &-0 \log 0 - (.06) \log (.06) - (.12) \log (.12) \\ &-(.18) \log (.18) - (.1) \log (.1) \end{aligned}$$

Therefore $H(A, B) = 2.7036$.

$$H(A) = -\sum_{i=1}^{4} p(a_i) \log p(a_i) = -p(a_1) \log p(a_1) - p(a_2) \log p(a_2)$$
$$-p(a_3) \log p(a_3) - p(a_4) \log p(a_4)$$

or

$$H(A) = -(.3) \log (.3) - (.4) \log (.4) - (.2) \log (.2) - (.1) \log (.1)$$
$$= .521 + .528 + .464 + .332$$

or

$$H(A) = 1.846$$

$H(B)$ is found in a similar manner:

$$H(B/A) = - \sum_{i=1}^{4} \sum_{j=1}^{3} p(a_i, b_j) \log p(b_j/a_i)$$

After more lengthy calculation which the student should do for familiarity and practice, we have (use your program)

$$H(B/A) = 1.058 \text{ bits/symbols}$$

3-4. MUTUAL INFORMATION AND CHANNEL CAPACITY

As mentioned earlier, we are developing tools with which one may analyze the information capacity of communication systems. Perhaps the most useful tool and certainly one used quite often is that of *channel capacity*. For our development of this quantity we must first develop a quantity directly related to channel capacity, that of mutual information.

DEFINITION. Mutual information is defined mathematically by:

$$I(A, B) = H(A) - H(A/B) \text{ bits/symbol} \tag{3-5}$$

The physical interpretation of this quantity then involves the two terms $H(A)$ and $H(A/B)$. Let's look at these two terms again.

$H(A)$ is the source entropy and thus is the average amount of information per source symbol and hence is the average amount of information transmitted over the channel per source symbol (assuming the source symbol is put directly into the channel with no coding changes in between). Now we know that $H(A/B)$ is the noise entropy and gives us an indication of the loss of information in its transmission through the channel.

Another viewpoint of the noise entropy is obtained from the conditional probability from which it is calculated. The quantity $p(a_i/b_j)$ is the conditional probability that a_i was transmitted when b_j is received. The quantity $\log 1/p(a_i/b_j)$ is then the uncertainty about the transmitted symbol a_i when b_j is received; that is, how sure are we that it was a_i that was indeed transmitted? Thus we could interpret $\log 1/p(a_i/b_j)$ as the loss of information due to channel noise. The noise entropy then becomes the average loss of information per symbol due to channel noise. For an ideal, noiseless channel we would expect to know without a doubt which source symbol a_i was transmitted when we receive an output symbol b_j. Thus $p(a_i/b_j)$ would be either a zero or a one, resulting in $H(A/B)$ being zero in either case.

Now we may see that the mutual information $I(A, B)$ must be the average amount of information received per symbol transmitted and is equal to the average amount of information transmitted in the ideal, noiseless case. This quantity thus is a measure of the system's effectiveness from the source to the output of the channel. It is also termed a measure of the information transmitted through the channel, or the *transinformation* of the channel.

There are several properties of mutual information of interest to us:

1. Symmetry with respect to a_i and b_j.
2. Nonnegative function.
3. A maximum for an ideal channel.
4. Various mathematical expressions for $I(A, B)$.

The mutual information may be written as

$$I(A, B) = H(A) - H(A/B) = \sum_{i=1}^{q} p(a_i) \log \frac{1}{p(a_i)} - \sum_{i=1}^{q}\sum_{j=1}^{r} p(a_i, b_j) \log \frac{1}{p(a_i/b_j)}$$

But

$$p(a_i) = \sum_{j=1}^{r} p(a_i, b_j)$$

and hence

$$I(A, B) = \sum_{i=1}^{q}\sum_{j=1}^{r} p(a_i, b_j) \log \frac{1}{p(a_i)} - \sum_{i=1}^{q}\sum_{j=1}^{r} p(a_i, b_j) \log 1/p(a_i/b_j)$$

$$= \sum_{i=1}^{q}\sum_{j=1}^{r} p(a_i, b_j) \log \frac{p(a_i/b_j)}{p(a_i)}$$

However, we may write $p(a_i, b_j) = p(a_i/b_j) p(b_j)$ so that

$$I(A, B) = \sum_{i=1}^{q}\sum_{j=1}^{r} p(a_i, b_j) \log \frac{p(a_i, b_j)}{p(a_i) p(b_j)} \tag{3-6}$$

From Eq. 3-6 we may easily prove properties one and two. Since $p(a_i, b_j) = p(b_j/a_i) p(a_i)$ we see that

$$I(A, B) = \sum_{i=1}^{q}\sum_{j=1}^{r} p(a_i, b_j) \log \frac{p(b_j/a_i)}{p(b_j)} = I(B, A) \tag{3-7}$$

proving Property 1.

Property 2 is proven by applying Lemma 8 of Chapter 2 to Eq. 3-6 resulting in $I(A, B) \geqslant 0$. This is left as an exercise for the student.

Since $H(A)$ and $H(A/B)$ are both nonnegative, the maximum $I(A, B)$ occurs for $H(A/B)$ equal to 0.

From Eq. 3-7 we may write $I(A, B)$ as

$$I(A, B) = \sum_{i=1}^{q} \sum_{j=1}^{r} p(a_i, b_j) \log 1/p(b_j) - \sum_{i=1}^{q} \sum_{j=1}^{r} p(a_i, b_j) \log 1/p(b_j/a_i)$$

or

$$I(A, B) = H(B) - H(B/A) = H(A) - H(A/B) \tag{3-8}$$

From (4) of Sec. 2-5 we have the relation $H(A/B) = H(A, B) - H(B)$ from which we may state,

$$I(A, B) = H(A) - H(A, B) + H(B) = H(A) + H(B) - H(A, B) \tag{3-9}$$

From the mutual information quantity we may seek the conditions for which $I(A, B)$ reaches a maximum value (not necessarily *the* maximum value ideally possible). This maximum value of $I(A, B)$ for a certain set of conditions is termed the Channel Capacity per symbol transmitted. Thus

DEFINITION. The *channel capacity* is defined as

$$C = \max I(A, B) \tag{3-10}$$

From Eq. 3-8 we see that $I(A, B)$ is a function of the channel's statistical characteristics and the input symbol probabilities. For a given channel matrix, then, we can maximize $I(A, B)$ by varying the input symbol probabilities.

In general the quantities $H(A)$, $H(A/B)$, and $H(B/A)$ depend on the input symbol probabilities. Thus in general it is not a simple matter to maximize $I(A, B)$. There are some specialized channels that can be analyzed fairly easily and that are of much interest to the engineer.

3-5. SPECIAL CHANNELS AND THEIR CAPACITIES

As mentioned in Sec. 3-4, it is generally very difficult to find the channel capacity of an arbitrary channel. Yet for some specific channels it is fairly easy to find the channel capacity. In this section we will look at these simple-to-analyze but useful channels.

We shall treat seven types of channels in detail. Some of these types, such as the BSC and BEC channels, bear a similarity but are useful enough to deserve special mention. These seven channel types are listed below:

1. Lossless channel
2. Deterministic channel
3. Ideal channel
4. Uniform channel
5. Binary symmetric channel

6. Binary erasure channel
7. General binary channel

DEFINITION. A *lossless channel* is one whose channel matrix has only one nonzero element in each column.

A lossless channel has a channel diagram and a corresponding channel matrix as shown in Fig. 3-5.

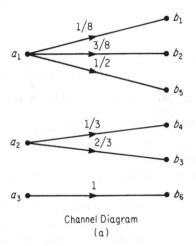

Channel Diagram
(a)

Inputs   Outputs

$$
\begin{array}{c c}
 & \begin{array}{cccccc} b_1 & b_2 & b_3 & b_4 & b_5 & b_6 \end{array} \\
\begin{array}{c} a_1 \\ a_2 \\ a_3 \end{array} &
\left[\begin{array}{cccccc}
1/8 & 3/8 & 0 & 0 & 1/2 & 0 \\
0 & 0 & 2/3 & 1/3 & 0 & 0 \\
0 & 0 & 0 & 0 & 0 & 1
\end{array} \right]
\end{array}
$$

Channel Matrix

(b)

Fig. 3-5. Lossless channel.

The mutual information of a lossless channel is calculated from the general expression of Eq. 3-5. We have

$$H(A/B) = - \sum_{i=1}^{q} \sum_{j=1}^{r} p(a_i, b_j) \log p(a_i/b_j)$$

But from the channel matrix or from the channel diagram we see that for every b_j received we know with complete certainty which a_i was transmitted. Hence $p(a_i/b_j)$ is a one or zero for every case.

Thus for a lossless channel,

$$H(A/B) = 0$$

This being the case, the resulting expression for the mutual information is reduced to the source entropy:

$$I(A, B) = H(A) \quad \text{(for lossless channel)}$$

The channel capacity is then found by maximizing this mutual information term as

$$C = \max H(A) \quad \text{(for lossless channel)}$$

In Sec. 2-4 theorem 2 we learned that the entropy of a source is maximum only when all the source symbols have equal probabilities. Thus

$$C = \max H(A) = \log q \quad \text{(for lossless channel)}$$

where q equals the number of source symbols.

DEFINITION. A *deterministic channel* is one whose channel matrix has only one nonzero element in each row.

The channel diagram and channel matrix of a deterministic channel are shown in Fig. 3-6.

Since each row may have only one nonzero element, this element must be unity. This is obvious, as each row represents all the possible outputs for a given input and we know that one output must result. Because only one is allowed this must have probability of unity. The result is a simplification of a calculation for $H(B/A)$.

$$H(B/A) = -\sum_{i=1}^{q} \sum_{j=1}^{r} p(a_i, b_j) \log p(b_j/a_i)$$

but $p(b_j/a_i)$ is either 0 or 1. Thus

$$H(B/A) = 0$$

Hence

$$I(A, B) = H(B) \quad \text{(for deterministic channel)}$$

The channel capacity is then

$$C = \max H(B) = \log r \quad \text{(for deterministic channel)} \qquad (3\text{-}12)$$

where r is the number of output symbols. This means the maximum channel capacity occurs when the output symbols are equally likely. From this information and the channel matrix probabilities one may calculate the required source symbol probabilities to achieve equally likely output symbol probabilities and hence maximum channel capacity. (In the chapters on coding theory we shall see how to take an existing source with prespecified probabilities and transform these into a coded source with the desired probabilities, while still maintaining a semblance of efficiency.)

DEFINITION. An *ideal channel* is one whose channel matrix has only one nonzero element in each row and each column, i.e., a diagonal matrix. (An ideal channel is obviously both lossless and deterministic.) The channel diagram and channel matrix of an ideal channel are shown in Fig. 3-7.

The student should show that for an ideal channel

$$C = \max H(B) = \max H(A) = \log q = \log r \quad \text{(for ideal channel)} \quad (3\text{-}13)$$

DEFINITION. A *uniform channel* is one whose channel matrix has identical rows except for permutations and identical columns except for permutations. If the channel matrix is square, then every row and every column are simply permutations of the first row.

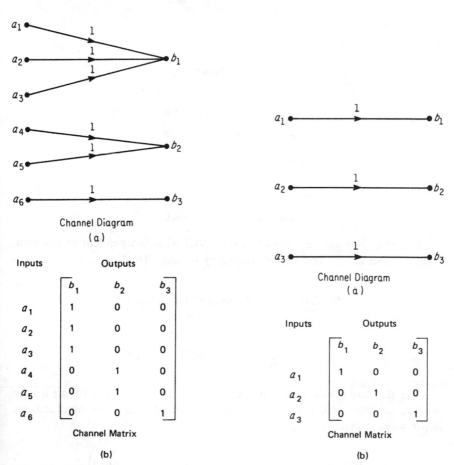

Channel Diagram
(a)

Inputs	Outputs		
	b_1	b_2	b_3
a_1	1	0	0
a_2	1	0	0
a_3	1	0	0
a_4	0	1	0
a_5	0	1	0
a_6	0	0	1

Channel Matrix

(b)

Fig. 3-6. Deterministic channel.

Channel Diagram
(a)

Inputs	Outputs		
	b_1	b_2	b_3
a_1	1	0	0
a_2	0	1	0
a_3	0	0	1

Channel Matrix

(b)

Fig. 3-7. Ideal channel.

A channel diagram and channel matrix of a uniform channel are shown in Fig. 3-8.

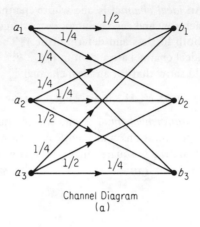

Channel Diagram
(a)

Inputs		Outputs	
	b_1	b_2	b_3
a_1	1/2	1/4	1/4
a_2	1/4	1/4	1/2
a_3	1/4	1/2	1/4

Channel Matrix

(b)

Fig. 3-8. Uniform channel.

For this channel the channel entropy $H(B/A)$ is independent of the input symbol probabilities. This is easily shown by writing $H(B/A)$ as

$$H(B/A) = -\sum_{i=1}^{q} \sum_{j=1}^{r} p(a_i, b_j) \log p(b_j/a_i)$$

$$= -\sum_{i=1}^{q} p(a_i) \sum_{j=1}^{r} p(b_j/a_i) \log p(b_j/a_i)$$

But the summation over j of the conditional probabilities $p(b_j/a_i)$ is independent of the i index, since each row is identical except for permutations. Hence we may write $H(B/A)$ as

$$H(B/A) = \left(-\sum_{j=1}^{r} p(b_j/a_i) \log p(b_j/a_i)\right) \left(\sum_{i=1}^{q} p(a_i)\right)$$

or

$$H(B/A) = -\sum_{j=1}^{r} p\,(b_j/a_i)\,\log p\,(b_j/a_i)$$

Thus the mutual information is

$$I(A,B) = H(B) + \sum_{j=1}^{r} p\,(b_j/a_i)\,\log p\,(b_j/a_i)$$

The maximum of the mutual information then occurs for equally likely output symbols, which for a uniform channel also occurs for equally likely input symbols. Thus the channel capacity for a uniform channel is

$$C = H(B) - H(B/A) = H(A) - H(B/A)$$

$$= \log q + \sum_{j=1}^{r} p\,(b_j/a_i)\,\log p\,(b_j/a_i) \qquad \text{(for a uniform channel)} \quad (3\text{-}14)$$

DEFINITION. The *binary symmetric channel* (BSC) is defined by the channel matrix shown in Fig. 3-9. Note that the BSC is a uniform channel.

The channel capacity is easily calculated from Eq. 3-14:

$$C = \log 2 + p \log p + q \log q \qquad \text{(for BSC channel)}$$

DEFINITION. The *binary erasure channel* (BEC) is defined by the channel diagram and channel matrix shown in Fig. 3-10. Note that there is an output symbol y used to detect an error in transmission. The BEC channel is a single-error-detecting channel.

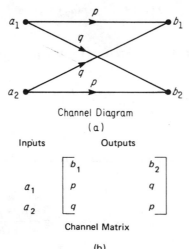

Channel Diagram

(a)

Inputs Outputs

Channel Matrix

(b)

Fig. 3-9. Binary symmetric channel.

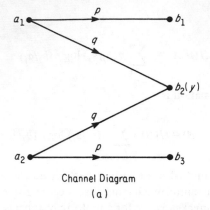

Channel Diagram
(a)

Inputs   Outputs

$$\begin{array}{c} \\ a_1 \\ a_2 \end{array} \begin{bmatrix} b_1 & b_2 & b_3 \\ p & q & 0 \\ 0 & q & p \end{bmatrix}$$

Channel Matrix

(b)

Fig. 3-10. Binary erasure channel.

The mutual information $I(A, B)$ is easily caclulated from

$$I(A, B) = H(A) - H(A/B)$$

Let the source symbols have the following probabilities:

$$p(a_1) = \alpha, \quad p(a_2) = 1 - \alpha$$

Then

$$H(A) = - \alpha \log \alpha - (1 - \alpha) \log (1 - \alpha)$$

$$H(A/B) = - \sum_{i=1}^{q} \sum_{j=1}^{r} p(b_j) \, p(a_i/b_j) \log p(a_i/b_j)$$

We may find $p(a_i/b_j)$ from the relationship

$$p(a_i/b_j) \, p(b_j) = p(a_i, b_j) = p(b_j/a_i) \, p(a_i)$$

Thus,

$$H(A/B) = - \sum_{i=1}^{q} \sum_{j=1}^{r} p(b_j/a_i) \, p(a_i) \log \frac{p(b_j/a_i) \, p(a_i)}{p(b_j)}$$

$$= -\sum_{i=1}^{2}\sum_{j=1}^{3} p(b_j/a_i)\, p(a_i)\, \log \frac{p(b_j/a_i)\, p(a_i)}{p(b_j)}$$

$$= -p(b_1/a_1)\, p(a_1)\, \log \frac{p(b_1/a_1)\, p(a_1)}{p(b_1)}$$

$$-p(b_1/a_2)\, p(a_2)\, \log \frac{p(b_1/a_2)\, p(a_2)}{p(b_1)}$$

$$-p(b_2/a_1)\, p(a_1)\, \log \frac{p(b_2/a_1)\, p(a_1)}{p(b_2)}$$

$$-p(b_2/a_2)\, p(a_2)\, \log \frac{p(b_2/a_2)\, p(a_2)}{p(b_2)}$$

$$-p(b_3/a_1)\, p(a_1)\, \log \frac{p(b_3/a_1)\, p(a_1)}{p(b_3)}$$

$$-p(b_3/a_2)\, p(a_2)\, \log \frac{p(b_3/a_2)\, p(a_2)}{p(b_3)}$$

The quantity

$$p(b_1) = p(b_1/a_1)\, p(a_1) + p(b_1/a_2)\, p(a_2)$$

and

$$p(b_2) = p(b_2/a_1)\, p(a_1) + p(b_2/a_2)\, p(a_2)$$

$$p(b_3) = p(b_3/a_1)\, p(a_1) + p(b_3/a_2)\, p(a_2)$$

Thus

$$p(b_1) = p(\alpha) + 0(1 - \alpha) = p\alpha$$

$$p(b_2) = q(\alpha) + q(1 - \alpha) = q$$

$$p(b_3) = 0(\alpha) + p(1 - \alpha) = (1 - \alpha)p$$

Substituting for $H(A/B)$,

$$H(A/B) = -\alpha p \log \frac{\alpha p}{\alpha p} - (0)(1 - \alpha) \log \frac{(0)(1 - \alpha)}{\alpha p}$$

$$-q\alpha \log \frac{q\alpha}{q} - q(1 - \alpha) \log \frac{q(1 - \alpha)}{q}$$

$$-(0)(\alpha) \log \frac{(0)(\alpha)}{(1 - \alpha)p} - p(1 - \alpha) \log \frac{p(1 - \alpha)}{(1 - \alpha)p}$$

or

$$H(A/B) = -\alpha p \log 1 - 0 \log 0$$

$$-\alpha q \log \alpha - q(1 - \alpha) \log (1 - \alpha)$$

$$- 0 \log 0 - p(1 - \alpha) \log 1$$

$$H(A/B) = q\left[- \alpha \log \alpha - (1 - \alpha) \log (1 - \alpha)\right] = qH(A)$$

Therefore the mutual information is:

$$I(A, B) = H(A) - H(A/B) = H(A) - qH(A)$$
$$= (1 - q)H(A) = pH(A)$$

The channel capacity is then:

$$C = \max I(A, B) = \max (pH(A)) = p \max H(A)$$

Since the source is binary, the maximum value of $H(A)$ occurs for equally probable source symbols; thus for $p(a_1) = p(a_2) = \frac{1}{2}$. The maximum of $H(A)$ is therefore

$$\max H(A) = -\frac{1}{2} \log \frac{1}{2} - \frac{1}{2} \log \frac{1}{2} = +\frac{1}{2} + \frac{1}{2} = 1$$

and the channel capacity is:

$$C = p \quad \text{(for BEC channel)}$$

DEFINITION. The *general binary channel* (GBC) is defined by the channel matrix and channel diagram shown in Fig. 3-11. It would be wise to note the

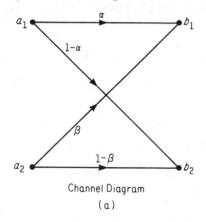

Channel Diagram

(a)

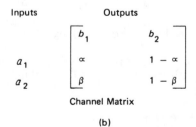

Channel Matrix

(b)

Fig. 3-11. General binary channel.

differences between the GBC and the BSC channel. (By the way, what are the differences?)

For this channel we might write the expression for the mutual information to get a feeling for the difficulty in maximizing the expression to obtain the channel capacity.

Let

$$p(a_1) = p$$

and

$$p(a_2) = q$$

We then would have

$$H(A) = -p \log p - q \log q$$

$$H(A/B) = - \alpha p \log \frac{\alpha p}{\alpha p + \beta q} - \beta q \log \frac{\beta q}{\alpha p + \beta q}$$

$$- (1 - \alpha)p \log \frac{(1 - \alpha)p}{(1 - \alpha)p + (1 - \beta)q} - (1 - \beta)q \log \frac{(1 - \beta)q}{(1 - \alpha)p + (1 - \beta)q}$$

$$I(A, B) = H(A) - H(A/B)$$

It is obvious from the above expressions for $H(A)$ and $H(A/B)$ that maximization of $I(A, B)$ is dependent upon the relations between α and β which we wish to treat as unknowns. Thus we will need to use a different approach to maximize $I(A, B)$.

S. Muroga[9] has presented a method of maximizing the expression for $I(A, B)$ by use of Lagrangian multipliers, and R. Silverman[10] has presented the solution for the channel capacity and the input symbol probabilities in terms of the channel matrix elements.

Before discussing the results of Muroga and Silverman it would be advantageous to present briefly the use of Lagrangian multipliers.

If we have a constraining surface

$$G(x,y,z) = K = \text{const.}$$

then the extremal values of a function $F(x,y,z)$ may be found with respect to this constraining surface in the following manner:

1. Form the function U, where

$$U(x,y,z) = F(x,y,z) + \lambda G(x,y,z),$$

and λ is an undetermined constant.

2. Since the function $F(x,y,z)$ is to have an extremal value then its total derivative is zero, and from the statement of $G(x,y,z)$ we know its total is zero. This implies the function $U(x,y,z)$ also has a zero derivative. Thus

$$\frac{\partial U}{\partial x} = \frac{\partial U}{\partial y} = \frac{\partial U}{\partial z} = 0$$

3. Solve these three equations along with the equation of constraint $G(x, y, z) = K$ to find values of the four quantities x, y, z, and λ that satisfy the equations.

More than one point (x, y, z) may be found, but among the points so found will be the points of the *extremal values* of $F(x, y, z)$ with respect to the constraining function $G(x, y, z)$.

Now let us find the maximum value of $I(A, B)$ for a general $m \times m$ channel by the procedure of Muroga.

Consider a channel with an $m \times m$ matrix consisting of elements p_{ij}. Then the term $H(B/A)$ may be written

$$H(B/A) = -\sum_{i=1}^{m} p(a_i) \sum_{j=1}^{m} p(b_j/a_i) \log p(b_j/a_i)$$

where a_i is the ith input symbol, and we will write $p(b_j/a_i) = p_{ij}$ and $p(a_i) = p_i$.

We may rewrite the right-hand summation as a set of equations with unknown auxiliary quantities X_i's as:

$$p_{11} X_1 + \cdots + p_{1m} X_m = \sum_{j=1}^{m} p(b_j/a_1) \log p(b_j/a_1) = \sum_{j=1}^{m} p_{1j} \log p_{1j}$$

$$\vdots \qquad\qquad\qquad\qquad\qquad\qquad \vdots \qquad (3\text{-}15)$$

$$p_{m1} X_1 + \cdots + p_{mm} X_m = \sum_{j=1}^{m} p(b_j/a_m) \log (b_j/a_m) = \sum_{j=1}^{m} p_{mj} \log p_{mj}$$

The quantity $H(B/A)$ may then be written in a form involving the X_i's as:

$$H(B/A) = -p_1 (p_{11} X_1 + \cdots + p_{1m} X_m) - p_2 (p_{21} X_1 + \cdots + p_{2m} X_m)$$
$$- \cdots - p_m (p_{m1} X_1 + \cdots + p_{mm} X_m)$$

where $p_1 = p(a_1), p_2 = p(a_2)$, and $p_i = p(a_i)$.

Regrouping the terms so we may factor out the common X_i's we have:

$$H(B/A) = -(p_1 p_{11} + p_2 p_{21} + \cdots + p_m p_{m1}) X_1$$
$$-(p_1 p_{12} + p_2 p_{22} + \cdots + p_m p_{m2}) X_2$$
$$\vdots$$
$$-(p_1 p_{1m} + p_2 p_{2m} + \cdots + p_m p_{mm}) X_m$$

However, the quantity $p_1 p_{11} + p_2 p_{21} + \cdots + p_m p_{m1} = p'_1$ where $p'_1 = p(b_1)$, is the probability of the occurrence of the output symbol b_1 and in general:

$$p(b_j) = p(a_1)p(b_j/a_1) + p(a_2)p(b_j/a_2) + \cdots + p(a_m)p(b_j/a_m) = p'_j$$

Thus we may write $H(B/A)$ as:

$$H(B/A) = -p'_1 X_1 - p'_2 X_2 - \cdots - p'_m X_m$$

In turn we may write the mutual information as:

$$I(A,B) = H(B) - H(B/A)$$

$$= -(p'_1 \log p'_1 + p'_2 \log p'_2 + \cdots + p'_m \log p'_m)$$
$$+ (p'_1 X_1 + p'_2 X_2 + \cdots + p'_m X_m)$$

or

$$I(A,B) = -\sum_{i=1}^{m} p'_i \log p'_i + \sum_{i=1}^{m} p'_i X_i \tag{3-16}$$

Equation 3-16 corresponds to the function $F(x,y,z)$ but is a function of the p_i variables rather than x, y, or z. We now form the function $U \equiv U(p'_i)$ as:

$$U = -\sum_{i=1}^{m} p'_i \log p'_i + \sum_{i=1}^{m} p'_i X_i + \lambda \sum_{i=1}^{m} (p'_i)$$

Thus

$$\frac{\partial U}{\partial p'_i} = -(1 + \log p'_i) + X_i + \lambda = 0 \tag{3-17}$$

From Eq. 3-17 we may write a set of equations which must be simultaneously true:

$$-1 + X_1 - \log p'_2 + \lambda = 0$$
$$-1 + X_2 - \log p'_2 + \lambda = 0$$
$$\vdots \qquad\qquad \vdots$$
$$-1 + X_m - \log p'_m + \lambda = 0$$

From these equations, which we see must be true simultaneously, we have the relationship

$$X_i - \log p'_i = X_j - \log p'_j \qquad i \neq j$$

Now if we multiply Eq. 3-17 by p'_i and sum over i, we have:

$$-\sum_{i=1}^{m} p'_i + \sum_{i=1}^{m} p'_i (X_i - \log p'_i) + \lambda \sum_{i=1}^{m} p'_i = 0$$

or, since $X_i - \log p_i'$ is constant over the index i, and since $\displaystyle\sum_{i=1}^{m} p_i' = 1$,

$$-1 + X_i - \log p_i' + \lambda = 0$$

or,

$$X_i - \log p_i' = 1 - \lambda \tag{3-18}$$

Our function $U(p_i')$ is now a maximum for the set of p_i' and X_i that satisfy Eq. 3-18, and thus if we substitute these values for $I(A,B)$ we obtain the maximum of $I(A,B)$ and hence the channel capacity.

Thus,

$$I(A,B) = \sum_{i=1}^{m} p_i'(X_i - \log p_i') = \sum_{i=1}^{m} p_i'(1 - \lambda) = 1 - \lambda = C$$

Hence,

$$C = 1 - \lambda = X_i - \log p_i'$$

We still need to express C in terms of the variables X_i and eliminate the dependence upon the output symbols p_i':

$$p_i' = 2^{(X_i - C)}$$

and from $\displaystyle\sum_{i=1}^{m} p_i' = 1$ we have

$$\sum_{i=1}^{m} p_i' = 1 = \sum_{i=1}^{m} 2^{(X_i - C)} = \frac{\displaystyle\sum_{i=1}^{m} 2^{X_i}}{2^C}$$

Hence,

$$2^C = \sum_{i=1}^{m} 2^{X_i}$$

or,

$$C = \log \sum_{i=1}^{m} 2^{X_i} = \log\left(2^{X_1} + 2^{X_2} + \cdots + 2^{X_m}\right) \tag{3-19}$$

The X_i's are found from the set of simultaneous equations (3-15), where we must remember that for a channel with a known matrix the right-hand summations, $\sum_{j=1}^{m} p_{ij} \log p_{ij}$ for specific i, are knowns and in fact are expressible as real numbers.

We have, in Eq. 3-19, the channel capacity of a general channel with m input symbols and m output symbols. (Muroga also derives the capacity of a general channel with r input symbols and m output symbols.)

Before continuing our discussion of a general binary channel it would be appropriate to consider an example.

Example 3-5

Find the capacity of a channel with the channel matrix given below (remember all logs are base 2):

$$
\begin{array}{cc}
\text{Input} & \text{Output} \\
\end{array}
$$

$$
\begin{array}{c}
 \\
a_1 \\
a_2 \\
a_3 \\
a_4 \\
\end{array}
\begin{array}{cccc}
b_1 & b_2 & b_3 & b_4 \\
\end{array}
\left[
\begin{array}{cccc}
1/4 & 1/2 & 1/4 & 0 \\
0 & 0 & 1 & 0 \\
0 & 1/3 & 0 & 2/3 \\
0 & 1 & 0 & 0 \\
\end{array}
\right]
$$

First we find the X_i's.

$$(1/4)X_1 + (1/2)X_2 + (1/4)X_3 + (0)X_4$$
$$= 1/4 \log 1/4 + 1/2 \log 1/2 + 1/4 \log 1/4 + 0 \log 0$$

$$(0)X_1 + (0)X_2 + (1)X_3 + (0)X_4$$
$$= 0 \log 0 + 0 \log 0 + 1 \log 1 + 0 \log 0$$

$$(0)X_1 + (1/3)X_2 + (0)X_3 + (2/3)X_4$$
$$= 0 \log 0 + 1/3 \log 1/3 + 0 \log 0 + 2/3 \log 2/3$$

$$(0)X_1 + (1)X_2 + (0)X_3 + (0)X_4$$
$$= 0 \log 0 + 1 \log 1 + 0 \log 0 + 0 \log 0$$

Thus,

$$X_1 + 2X_2 + X_3 = -6$$
$$X_3 = 0$$
$$X_2 + 2X_4 = -2.75$$
$$X_2 = 0$$

Solving for each X_i, we have

$$X_1 = -6 \quad X_2 = 0$$
$$X_3 = 0 \quad X_4 = -1.375$$

Therefore

$$C = \log(2^{-6} + 2^0 + 2^0 + 2^{-1.375})$$
$$= \log(2.4016) = 1.26 \text{ bits}$$

The general binary channel is easily analyzed now that we have developed the results for a general $m \times m$ channel.

First we will develop the channel capacity expression in terms of α and β, elements of the channel matrix as shown in Fig. 3-11.

Writing the set of equations for this channel corresponding to Eqs. 3-15, we have:

$$\alpha X_1 + (1-\alpha)X_2 = -H(\alpha) = \alpha \log \alpha + (1-\alpha)\log(1-\alpha)$$
$$\beta X_1 + (1-\beta)X_2 = -H(\beta) = \beta \log \beta + (1-\beta)\log(1-\beta)$$

Solving for X_1,

$$\alpha X_1 + \frac{(1-\alpha)}{(1-\beta)}[-H(\beta) - \beta X_1] = -H(\alpha)$$

Thus,

$$X_1 = \frac{\beta H(\alpha) - \alpha H(\beta) - H(\alpha) + H(\beta)}{\alpha - \beta}$$

and

$$X_2 = \frac{\beta H(\alpha) - \alpha H(\beta)}{\alpha - \beta}$$

The channel capacity becomes (using Eq. 3-19)

$$C = \log(2^{X_1} + 2^{X_2})$$
$$= \log \left\{ 2^{[\beta H(\alpha) - \alpha H(\beta) - H(\alpha) + H(\beta)]/(\alpha - \beta)} \right.$$
$$\left. + 2^{[\beta H(\alpha) - \alpha H(\beta)]/(\alpha - \beta)} \right\}$$
$$= \log \left\{ 2^{[\alpha H(\beta) - \beta H(\alpha)]/(\alpha - \beta)} \right\} + \log \left\{ 1 + 2^{[-H(\alpha) + H(\beta)]/(\alpha - \beta)} \right\}$$

$$C = \frac{-\beta H(\alpha) + \alpha H(\beta)}{\beta - \alpha} + \log \left\{ 1 + 2^{[H(\alpha) - H(\beta)]/(\beta - \alpha)} \right\} \qquad (3\text{-}20)$$

Equation 3-20 is the channel capacity of a general binary channel in terms of the channel matrix elements only.

The input probability for which zeros should be chosen if the channel is to be operated at maximum capacity may also be derived in terms of parameters α and β.

Let P be the vector representing the transmitted symbol distribution which achieves capacity, and P' be the vector representing the corresponding received symbol distribution. Then

$$P = \begin{bmatrix} P_0 \\ 1 - P_0 \end{bmatrix} \quad \text{and} \quad P' = \begin{bmatrix} P_0' \\ 1 - P_0' \end{bmatrix}$$

where P_0 is the probability of a zero being transmitted and P_0' is the probability of a zero being received if the channel achieves capacity.

P and P' are related by the relation[†]

$$P' = P[B/A]^T P$$

In terms of the auxiliary variables, X_i, P_0 is equal to*:

$$P = \frac{2^{-C}}{\det \begin{bmatrix} \alpha & 1 - \alpha \\ \beta & 1 - \beta \end{bmatrix}} \det \begin{bmatrix} 2^{X_1} & 2^{X_2} \\ \beta & 1 - \beta \end{bmatrix}$$

But

$$2^{-C} = 2^{-\log(2^{X_1} + 2^{X_2})} = (2^{X_1} + 2^{X_2})^{-1}$$

Therefore,

$$P_0 = \frac{(2^{X_1} + 2^{X_2})^{-1}}{\alpha - \beta} (2^{X_1} - \beta 2^{X_1} - \beta 2^{X_2})$$

$$= \frac{2^{X_1}(2^{X_1} + 2^{X_2})^{-1}}{\alpha - \beta} - \frac{\beta}{\alpha - \beta}$$

or, since

$$X_2 - X_1 = \frac{H(\alpha) - H(\beta)}{\alpha - \beta}$$

we may express P_0 as

$$P_0 = \frac{\beta}{\beta - \alpha} - \frac{(1 + 2^{X_2 - X_1})^{-1}}{\beta - \alpha}$$

or

$$P_0 = \beta(\beta - \alpha)^{-1} - (\beta - \alpha)^{-1} \{1 + 2^{[H(\beta) - H(\alpha)]/(\beta - \alpha)}\}^{-1} \quad (3\text{-}21)$$

Equation 3-21 allows us to calculate the required probability of a zero being transmitted if the channel is to be operated at the maximum capacity.

[†]See Ref. 10, p. 17.

3-6. CASCADED CHANNELS

A natural extension of a single channel is that of *cascaded channels*, Fig. 3-12. The fact that information often propagates through a series of

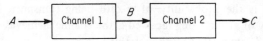

Fig. 3-12. Two channels in cascade.

electronic devices which comprise a channel, and then through a medium such as the atmosphere which comprises a different channel, gives a practical reason for investigating cascaded channels. Richard Silverman[10] presents a detailed analysis of cascaded binary channels in which the question of which type of channel would produce the largest end-to-end capacity in a cascade if the cascade is comprised of a chain of identical channels is posed. (Why not look up the reference, page 24, for the answer to the question?)

A more general result which is easily shown is the tendency of channels to lose information as they transmit information.

Let us assume that the alphabets A, B, and C in Fig. 3-12 consist of m, n, and r symbols respectively. The loss of information in a cascade may be shown by proving the increase of the equivocations when cascading channels. (The following results were first proven by Woodward[11].

$$H(A/C) - H(A/B) = -\sum_{i=1}^{m} \sum_{k=1}^{r} p(a_i, c_k) \log p(a_i/c_k)$$

$$+ \sum_{i=1}^{m} \sum_{j=1}^{n} p(a_i, b_j) \log p(a_i/b_j)$$

However,

$$\sum_{j=1}^{n} p(b_j) = \sum_{k=1}^{r} p(c_k) = 1$$

Hence,

$$H(A/C) - H(A/B) = -\sum_{i=1}^{m} \sum_{j=1}^{n} \sum_{k=1}^{r} p(a_i, b_j, c_k) \log p(a_i/c_k)$$

$$+ \sum_{i=1}^{m} \sum_{j=1}^{n} \sum_{k=1}^{r} p(a_i, b_j, c_k) \log p(a_i/b_j)$$

$$= \sum_{i=1}^{m} \sum_{j=1}^{n} \sum_{k=1}^{r} p(a_i, b_j, c_k) \log \frac{p(a_i/b_j)}{p(a_i/c_k)} \qquad (3\text{-}22)$$

Now we must realize that when an output symbol c_k is received it is dependent only upon which b_j was transmitted to channel two and not upon which a_i was originally transmitted. This may be stated as:

$$p(c_k/b_j, a_i) = p(c_k/b_j)$$

Applying Bayes' theorem to the above equation we have

$$p(a_i/b_j, c_k) = p(a_i/b_j) \qquad (3\text{-}23)$$

Equation 3-22 may then be written as

$$H(A/C) - H(A/B) = \sum_{i=1}^{m} \sum_{j=1}^{n} \sum_{k=1}^{r} p(a_i, b_j, c_k) \log \frac{p(a_i/b_j, c_k)}{p(a_i/c_k)}$$

But $p(a_i, b_j, c_k) = p(b_j, c_k) \, p(a_i/b_j, c_k)$ by the probability multiplication theorem. Thus,

$$H(A/C) - H(A/B) = \sum_{j=1}^{n} \sum_{k=1}^{r} p(b_j, c_k) \left(\sum_{i=1}^{m} p(a_i/b_j, c_k) \log \frac{p(a_i/b_j, c_k)}{p(a_i/c_k)} \right) (3\text{-}24)$$

From Lemma 8, Sec. 2-4, we know that

$$-\sum_{i=1}^{n} q_i \log q_i \leqslant -\sum_{i=1}^{n} q_i \log p_i$$

or

$$\sum_{i=1}^{n} q_i \log \frac{q_i}{p_i} \geqslant 0$$

The parenthesis of Eq. 3-24 is thus a positive quantity, and therefore the complete equation is a nonnegative quantity. Thus,

$$H(A/C) - H(A/B) \geqslant 0 \qquad (3\text{-}25)$$

But

$$I(A, B) = H(A) - H(A/B)$$

and

$$I(A, C) = H(A) - H(A/C)$$

Hence

$$I(A,B) - I(A,C) \geqslant 0$$

from Eq. 3-25, and we have

$$I(A,B) \geqslant I(A,C) \tag{3-26}$$

From Eq. 3-26 we see that as we cascade channels the final output cannot yield a greater amount of information than the input. The case of a "lossless" cascade is achieved for the condition $p(a_i/b_j, c_k) = p(a_i/c_k)$ and $p(b_j, c_k) \neq 0$ for which the equality of Eq. 3-26 holds.

Example 3-6

Calculate the difference between the mutual information of channel 1 and the mutual information of the cascaded channel combination shown below:

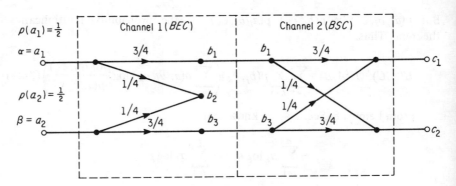

From the equation for $H(A/B)$ developed in the discussion of the BEC channel we have

$$H(A/B) = qH(A) = q[-\alpha \log \alpha - \beta \log \beta] = .25$$

From the equation for $H(A/B)$ developed in the discussion of the general binary channel we have for the cascade from A to C

$$H(A/C) \cong \frac{9.815}{16} \cong .62$$

(Note that the channel matrix from input to output may be written as

$$
\begin{array}{cc}
 & \begin{array}{cc} c_1 & c_2 \end{array} \\
\begin{array}{c} a_1 \\ a_2 \end{array} & \begin{bmatrix} p^2 & pq \\ pq & p^2 \end{bmatrix}
\end{array}
$$

Hence $I(A,B) - I(A,C) = H(A/C) - H(A/B) = .37$

Consider now the cascade of n BSC channels.[†] The binary symmetric channel has a channel matrix given by

$$P[B/A] = \begin{bmatrix} p & q \\ q & p \end{bmatrix}$$

If this channel is cascaded n times the resultant channel matrix is

$$P[B/A]^n$$

This problem may be approached by direct calculation of this matrix. Let

$$P[B/A] = P$$

Now P is a real symmetric matrix. Matrix algebra tells us that there is some orthogonal matrix Q such that

$$D = Q^T P Q$$

where D is a diagonal matrix with the elements on the diagonal being the eigenvalues of P. These eigenvalues may be calculated as

$$|P - \lambda I| = 0$$

$$\begin{vmatrix} p - \lambda & q \\ q & p - \lambda \end{vmatrix} = 0$$

$$(p - \lambda)^2 - q^2 = 0$$

$$(p - \lambda - q)(p - \lambda + q) = 0$$

The roots of this are

$$\lambda_1 = p - q$$

$$\lambda_2 = p + q$$

$$D = \begin{bmatrix} p + q & 0 \\ 0 & p - q \end{bmatrix}$$

and

$$D^n = \begin{bmatrix} (p + q)^n & 0 \\ 0 & (p - q)^n \end{bmatrix}$$

The matrix Q is made up of the eigenvectors of P. For

$$\lambda = p - q$$

$$Px - \lambda x = 0$$

gives

$$\begin{bmatrix} p - (p - q) & q \\ q & p - (p - q) \end{bmatrix} \begin{bmatrix} q_{11} \\ q_{21} \end{bmatrix} = \begin{bmatrix} 0 \\ 0 \end{bmatrix}$$

[†]Courtesy of Mr. A. C. Watts, Mississippi State University graduate student.

$$q_{11}x_1 + q_{21}x_2 = 0$$

$$x_1 = -x_2$$

$$q_1 = \frac{1}{\sqrt{2}}\begin{bmatrix} 1 \\ -1 \end{bmatrix}$$

For

$$\lambda = p + q$$

$$Px - \lambda x = 0$$

gives

$$\begin{bmatrix} p - (p+q) & q \\ q & p - (p+q) \end{bmatrix} \begin{bmatrix} q_{12} \\ q_{22} \end{bmatrix} = \begin{bmatrix} 0 \\ 0 \end{bmatrix}$$

$$-qq_{12} + qq_{22} = 0$$

$$q_{12} = q_{22}$$

$$q = \frac{1}{\sqrt{2}}\begin{bmatrix} 1 \\ 1 \end{bmatrix}$$

The matrix which will transform P to D is

$$Q = \frac{1}{\sqrt{2}}\begin{bmatrix} 1 & 1 \\ -1 & 1 \end{bmatrix}$$

Note now that

$$Q^T Q = I$$

Now consider

$$D^n = [Q^T P Q]^n$$
$$= Q^T P Q Q^T P Q Q^T P Q \cdots Q^T P Q$$

But since

$$Q^T Q = Q Q^T = I$$
$$D^n = Q^T P^n Q$$

and

$$P^n = Q D^n Q^T$$

This then gives

$$P^n = \frac{1}{\sqrt{2}}\begin{bmatrix} 1 & 1 \\ -1 & 1 \end{bmatrix}\begin{bmatrix} (p-q)^n & 0 \\ 0 & (p+q)^n \end{bmatrix}\begin{bmatrix} 1 & -1 \\ 1 & 1 \end{bmatrix}\frac{1}{\sqrt{2}}$$

Carrying out the indicated matrix multiplications give

$$P^n = \begin{bmatrix} \dfrac{(p+q)^n + (p-q)^n}{2} & \dfrac{(p+q)^n - (p-q)^n}{2} \\[3mm] \dfrac{(p+q)^n - (p-q)^n}{2} & \dfrac{(p+q)^n + (p-q)^n}{2} \end{bmatrix}$$

This result gives several interesting facts.

1. Cascading a binary symetric channel n times gives a binary symetric channel.
2. An ideal channel $(p = 1, q = 0)$ cascaded n times gives an ideal channel.

The mutual information can be written directly as we still have a BSC channel.

$$I(A, C) = H(C) + \left[\frac{(p+q)^n + (p-q)^n}{2} \right] \log \left[\frac{(p+q)^n + (p-q)^n}{2} \right]$$
$$+ \left[\frac{(p+q)^n - (p-q)^n}{2} \right] \log \left[\frac{(p+q)^n - (p-q)^n}{2} \right]$$

Noting that $(p + q) = 1$ this may be written

$$I(A, C) = H(C) + \left[\frac{1 + (p-q)^n}{2} \right] \log \left[\frac{1 + (p-q)^n}{2} \right]$$
$$+ \left[\frac{1 - (p-q)^n}{2} \right] \log \left[\frac{1 - (p-q)^n}{2} \right]$$

The channel capacity is then

$$C = \log 2 + \left[\frac{1 + (p-q)^n}{2} \right] \log \left[\frac{1 + (p-q)^n}{2} \right]$$
$$+ \left[\frac{1 - (p-q)^n}{2} \right] \log \left[\frac{1 - (p-q)^n}{2} \right]$$

Several things which are intuitively obvious may be derived from this. Note that if

$$q > 0$$
$$p - q < 1$$
$$\lim_{n \to \infty} (p - q)^n = 0$$

$$\lim_{n \to \infty} = C = \log 2 + \tfrac{1}{2} \log \tfrac{1}{2} + \tfrac{1}{2} \log \tfrac{1}{2} = 0; q > 0$$

But if

$$q = 0; p = 1$$

$$\lim_{n \to \infty} (p - q)^n = 1$$

$$\lim_{n \to \infty} C = \log 2 + 1 \log 1 + 0 \log 0 = \log 2$$

As one would expect for any BSC channel which is not ideal, the channel capacity approaches 0 as the channel is cascaded an increasing number of times.

3-7. REMARKS

In this chapter we have developed the majority of the basic tools with which we may analyze and compare communication systems. These tools are the concepts of sources and channels and the various forms of mathematics used to describe them.

We have learned that a source is an alphabet from which we construct messages. Sources have an information content which is expressed in terms of our information measure and which we have termed *source entropy*. Source entropy is the *average* information content per source symbol as opposed to the self-information per source symbol, which is the information content of an individual source symbol.

We may generate larger sources from an original source by the extension of a source. For memoryless sources—the only kind treated so far—the source entropy of the nth extension is equal to n times the original source entropy.

Information channels are characterized by their channel matrix, which tells us the probability of receiving a specific output symbol when a specific input symbol is transmitted. This matrix completely describes the information channel. An information channel includes the statistical description of the physical path the signals are transmitted through, the kind of signals used (binary, trinary, orthogonal, etc.), and the type of receiver-detection scheme used. The channel matrix is necessarily altered by changes in signal structure, propagation path, or in receiver types.

A method of comparing information transmission schemes has been developed using the channel capacity as a basis for comparison. The channel capacity is derived from the mutual information of a system, which is the average amount of information received per symbol transmitted. Thus the mutual information is an indication of the efficiency of the information channel and the maximum mutual information achievable by a channel, termed the *channel capacity*, is a function of the channel matrix. If the channel is fixed, that is the physical path and the receiver type, then we may maximize the mutual information for the channel, hence achieving the channel capacity by varying the signal structure and hence the input-symbol probabilities.

Correspondingly, if we have two information transmission schemes to choose from we may compute the channel capacity for each scheme and compare. (This does not include consideration of cost, complexity of equipment, size, power required, etc.)

We know the channel capacity to be the maximum value of $H(A) - H(A/B)$ and as a result we know the channel capacity is always less than or at best equal to the maximum source entropy, which is of course the value obtained for equally likely source symbols.

Channel capacity may be expressed in bits per symbol, as we have in this chapter, or in bits per second, thus indicating the maximum rate of transmission of information through the channel. To see this, let us consider an example.

Example 3-7

Consider a BSC channel with $p = .75$ and $q = .25$. Furthermore let the input symbols be transmitted at a rate of one per microsecond, and let each symbol be 1 microsec wide in time duration. A series of binary ones and zeros are illustrated to show their time relationship.

For a BSC channel with these probabilities the channel capacity is

$$C = \log 2 + p \log p + q \log q = .189 \text{ bit per binary digit (binit)}$$

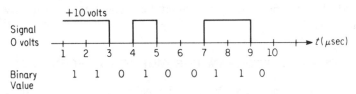

Since each binit has the same time duration of t sec, the channel capacity may be expressed as

$$C_t = \frac{1}{t} C \text{ bits/sec}$$

For this example, then

$$C_t = \frac{1}{10^{-6}} \times .189 = 189,000 \text{ bits/sec}$$

Thus the maximum rate of transmission of this channel is 189,000 bits/sec and would be attained only if the input symbols were equally likely to occur. If the input symbol probabilities were $p(1) = 2/3$, $p(0) = 1/3$ then the actual rate of transmission would be found from the equation for $I(A, B)$ as follows:

$$I_t(A, B) = \frac{1}{t} I(A, B)$$

$$I(A, B) = H(B) - H(B/A)$$

But

$$H(B) = -p(b_1) \log p(b_1) - p(b_2) \log p(b_2)$$

and

$$p(b_1) = p(b_1/a_1) \, p(a_1) + p(b_1/a_2) \, p(a_2) = (\tfrac{3}{4}) \, (\tfrac{2}{3}) + (\tfrac{1}{4}) \, (\tfrac{1}{3}) = \tfrac{7}{12}$$

$$p(b_2) = p(b_2/a_1) \, p(a_1) + p(b_2/a_2) \, p(a_2) = (\tfrac{1}{4}) \, (\tfrac{2}{3}) + (\tfrac{3}{4}) \, (\tfrac{1}{3}) = \tfrac{5}{12}$$

Therefore

$$H(B) \cong .981$$

$$H(B/A) = -\sum_{j=1}^{2} p(b_j/a_i) \log p(b_j/a_i) = -p \log p - q \log q = +.811$$

$$\therefore I_t \, (A, B) = \frac{1}{10^{-6}} \, (.981 - .811) = 170{,}000 \text{ bits/sec}$$

When channels are in cascade we have seen that they tend to leak (or lose) information, and that the mutual information of the overall cascade is less than or at best equal to that of an individual channel. This implies the channel capacity of the cascade is less than or at best equal to the capacity of an individual channel.

COMPUTER PROGRAM FOR MUROGA'S TECHNIQUE[†]

The channel capacity of an N by N channel is calculated when the channel matrix is specified. Entry into the program requires a reordering of the rows of the channel matrix so the diagonal of the matrix has no zero elements. In addition a small number, designated *EPS*, must be supplied for checking the matrix for singularity. This number, *EPS*, is usually chosen as a very small number such as 10^{-12}.

The output of the program prints three items, the augmented channel matrix, the solution matrix for the X's, and the channel capacity.

Example
Calculate the channel capacity for the following channel:

$$P[B/A] = \begin{bmatrix} 0 & 1.0 & 0 & 0 \\ .25 & .5 & .25 & 0 \\ 0 & 0 & 1.0 & 0 \\ 0 & .333 & 0 & .667 \end{bmatrix}$$

The channel is 4 × 4 and hence the dimension N is 4.
The *EPS* is arbitrarily chosen to be 10^{-10}.
Since the channel matrix has a zero in one of the diagonal matrix

[†]Courtesy of Mr. Tommy Shumpert, Mississippi State University graduate student.

elements the matrix will be reordered by rows by interchanging the first and second rows. This does not alter the final answer.

On the third page of the program the input data is presented. Note that N and EPS are written in as 41.00000-10 which is a suitable format for $N = 4$ and $EPS = 10^{-10}$.

The augmented channel matrix printed out consists of the channel matrix and, as an added column, the computed values of

$$\sum_{j=1}^{N} p(b_j/a_i) \log p(b_j/a_i)$$

for each row.

The solution matrix for the X's is printed out next showing for this example

$$X_1 = -6.0$$
$$X_2 = 0.0$$
$$X_3 = 0.0$$
$$X_4 = -1.377$$

The channel capacity is printed out last and for this example we have

$$C = 1.263$$

```
C
C
C     THIS PROGRAM COMPUTES THE CHANNEL CAPACITY OF AN NXN CHANNEL WHEN
C     THE CHANNEL (CONDITIONAL PROBABILITY) MATRIX P(B/A) IS KNOWN.
C
C
C     THE CHANNEL CAPACITY IS DETERMINED USING MUROGA'S TECHNIQUE.
C
C     THE SYSTEM OF LINEAR EQUATIONS THAT IS GENERATED BY THIS TECHNIQUE
C     IS SOLVED BY MEANS OF A GAUSS-JORDAN REDUCTION.
C
C
C
C     ************************** WARNING **************************
C
C     ONE MUST ARRANGE THE ROWS OF THE CHANNEL (CONDITIONAL PROBABILITY)
C     MATRIX P(B/A) SO THAT THE MAIN DIAGONAL ELEMENTS ARE NON-ZERO.
C     REARRANGING THE ROWS DOES NOT AFFECT THE VALUE OF THE CHANNEL
C     CAPACITY AND HELPS TO INSURE THAT THE GAUSS-JORDAN REDUCTION
C     WILL YIELD THE PROPER SOLUTION TO THE SYSTEM OF LINEAR EQUATIONS.
C
C     *****************************************************************
C
C
C     THE CHANNEL (CONDITIONAL PROBABILITY) MATRIX P(B/A) IS READ IN BY
C     ROWS,I.E.,A(1,1),A(1,2),....,A(1,N),A(2,1),A(2,2),....,A(N,N).
C
C
C                 DEFINITION OF VARIABLES
C
C
C     N           DIMENSION(N) OF THE NXN CHANNEL MATRIX P(B/A)
C
C     EPS         PARAMETER FOR CHECKING THE SINGULARITY OF THE
C                 COEFFICIENT MATRIX
C
```

```
C     A(I,J)          ELEMENT IN THE ITH ROW AND JTH COLUMN OF THE CHANNEL
C                     MATRIX
C
C     SUM             ELEMENT IN THE (J+1)TH COLUMN OF THE AUGMENTED CHANNEL
C                     MATRIX.(SUM = (1.0/ALOG(2.))*(A(I,1)*ALOG(A(I,1)) +
C                     A(I,2)*ALOG(A(I,2)) + ... + A(I,N)*ALOG(A(I,N)))
C
C     MAGIC           FACTOR FOR CONVERTING LOGARITHMS TO THE BASE 2 TO
C                     LOGARITHMS TO THE BASE E.(MAGIC = ALOG(2.))
C
C     C               CHANNEL CAPACITY (C = MAGIC*ALOG(2**X(1) + 2**X(2) + ...
C                     + 2**X(N)))WHERE X(I) IS THE ELEMENT IN THE ITH ROW
C                     &(J+1)TH COLUMN OF THE SOLUTION MATRIX
C     DIMENSION A(50,51)
      REAL MAGIC
      MAGIC = (1./0.69315)
C  THE MATRIX WHICH IS READ IS THE CHANNEL MATRIX AND THE ELEMENTS ARE
C  READ IN BY ROWS
      WRITE(6,398)
 398  FORMAT('1')
      READ(5,100)N,EPS
 100  FORMAT(I4,E10.5)
      NP1 = N + 1
      WRITE(6,509)
 509  FORMAT(/)
      WRITE(6,405)
 405  FORMAT(15X,'***',34X,'***',/15X,'*',38X,'*',/15X,'*',38X,'*')
      DO 2 I=1,N
      SUM = 0.0
      READ(5,101)(A(I,J),J=1,N)
      DO 3 J=1,N
 101  FORMAT(4E20.8)
      IF(A(I,J))4,3,4
   4  SUM = A(I,J)*MAGIC*ALOG(A(I,J)) + SUM
   3  CONTINUE
      A(I,N+1) = SUM
      WRITE(6,201)(A(I,J),J = 1,NP1)
 201  FORMAT(17X,5F7.3/)
   2  CONTINUE
      WRITE(6,417)
 417  FORMAT(15X,'*',38X,'*'/15X,'*',38X,'*'/15X,'***',34X,'***')
      WRITE(6,509)
      WRITE(6,411)
 411  FORMAT(23X,'AUGMENTED CHANNEL MATRIX')
      WRITE(6,209)
 209  FORMAT(///)
C  BEGIN GAUSS-JORDAN REDUCTION
      DETER = 1.0
      DO 9 K=1,N
      DETER = DETER*A(K,K)
      IF(DABS(A(K,K)).GT.EPS) GO TO 5
      WRITE(6,202)
      GO TO 111
 202  FORMAT( 8X,'PIVOT ELEMENT SMALL - MATRIX MAY BE SINGULAR')
   5  KP1 = K+1
      DO 6 J =KP1,NP1
   6  A(K,J) = A(K,J)/A(K,K)
      A(K,K) = 1.
      DO 9 I = 1,N
      IF(I.EQ.K.OR.A(I,K).EQ.0.) GO TO 9
      DO 8 J = KP1,NP1
   8  A(I,J)= A(I,J) - A(I,K)*A(K,J)
      A(I,K)=0.
   9  CONTINUE
      WRITE(6,405)
      DO 10 I = 1,N
  10  WRITE(6,201)(A(I,J),J=1,NP1)
      WRITE(6,417)
      WRITE(6,509)
      WRITE(6,412)
 412  FORMAT(25X,'SOLUTION MATRIX FOR X')
      WRITE(6,209)
```

```
  203 FORMAT(E20.8,10X,I4,10X,I4)
C     CALCULATION OF CHANNEL CAPACITY
      SUMX=0.0
      DO 12 I=1,N
      SUMX = 2.**A(I,NP1)+ SUMX
   12 CONTINUE
      IF(SUMX)14,15,14
   15 C=0.0
      GO TO 16
   14 C = MAGIC*ALOG(SUMX)
   16 CONTINUE
      WRITE(6,413) C
  413 FORMAT( 8X,'C = LOG2 (   2**X(1) + 2**X(2) + ... + 2**X(N)   ) =
     1',F6.3)
  111 STOP
      END
C
C
C               INPUT DATA FOR EXAMPLE PROBLEM
C
   41.00000-10
C
        .25000000+00         .50000000+00         .25000000+00
                             1.0
                                                  1.0
                             .33333333+00                              .66666667
C
```

```
         ***                                    ***
         *                                        *
         *                                        *
             .250    .500    .250    .000  -1.500

             .000   1.000    .000    .000    .000

             .000    .000   1.000    .000    .000

             .000    .333    .000    .667   -.918

         *                                        *
         *                                        *
         ***                                    ***
```

AUGMENTED CHANNEL MATRIX

```
         ***                                    ***
         *                                        *
         *                                        *
           1.000    .000    .000    .000  -6.000

            .000   1.000    .000    .000    .000

            .000    .000   1.000    .000    .000

            .000    .000    .000   1.000  -1.377

         *                                        *
         *                                        *
         ***                                    ***
```

SOLUTION MATRIX FOR X

```
     C = LOG2 (   2**X(1) + 2**X(2) + ... + 2**X(N)   )  =    1.263
```

PROBLEMS

3-1.   Find the 3rd extension of the trinary source $A = \{0, 1, 2\}$ with source symbol probabilities of p_0, p_1, p_2 respectively.

3-2.   Find the probabilities associated with the 3rd extension symbols of Prob. 3-1.

3-3.   If the symbol probabilities of Prob. 3-1 are .3, .5, .2 respectively, show by calculation that $H(A^3) = 3H(A)$.

3-4.   A source has four symbols $\{a_1, a_2, a_3, a_4\}$ and the output of the channel has three symbols $\{b_1, b_2, b_3\}$. The joint probability matrix $P[A, B]$ is

$$
P[A, B] = \begin{array}{c} \\ a_1 \\ a_2 \\ a_3 \\ a_4 \end{array} \begin{array}{ccc} b_1 & b_2 & b_3 \\ \begin{bmatrix} .25 & 0 & .10 \\ 0 & .30 & .05 \\ .10 & .05 & 0 \\ 0 & 0 & .15 \end{bmatrix} \end{array}
$$

(a) Construct the channel matrix $P[B|A]$

(b) Find the set of source probabilities and construct the source probability matrix both in row matrix form and diagonal matrix form.

(c) Show the validity of Eq. 3-2.

(d) Using the row matrix of part (b) and the channel matrix of part (a) find the set of output symbol probabilities.

(e) Determine the different entropies $H(A, B)$, $H(A)$, $H(B)$, $H(B|A)$, $H(A|B)$ for this channel.

3-5.   Calculate the mutual information of the channel of Prob. 3-4.

3-6.   Prove that $I(A, B) = I(B, A)$ by rewriting Eq. 3-7.

3-7.   Prove property two of Sec. 3-4 by applying Lemma 8 of Chapter 2 to Eq. 3-6.

3-8.   Find the capacity of the channel shown below,

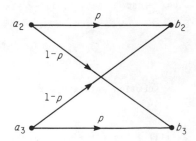

3-9. Compute the channel capacity using Muroga's technique for the channel with the following matrix,

$$\begin{bmatrix} \frac{3}{4} & \frac{1}{4} & 0 \\ \frac{1}{8} & \frac{3}{4} & \frac{1}{8} \\ \frac{1}{4} & 0 & \frac{3}{4} \end{bmatrix}$$

3-10. Two BSC's each with channel matrix

$$\begin{bmatrix} p & p' \\ p' & p \end{bmatrix}$$

are cascaded as

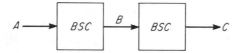

If the two inputs have equal probability, calculate $I(A, B)$ and $I(A, C)$.

3-11. If another identical BSC with output set D is added to the end of the chain of Prob. 3-10, find $I(A, D)$. Compare $I(A, D), I(A, C)$ and $I(A, B)$ and explain.

3-12. Find the capacity of the channel with matrix

$$P[B|A] = \begin{bmatrix} 1 & 0 \\ 1 & 0 \\ 0 & 1 \end{bmatrix}$$

For what input distribution is this capacity achieved?

3-13. The BEC has two inputs 0, 1 and three outputs 0, e, 1. Using the channel matrix below find the channel capacity.

$$P[B|A] = \begin{bmatrix} \frac{1}{4} & \frac{3}{4} & 0 \\ 0 & \frac{3}{4} & \frac{1}{4} \end{bmatrix}$$

3-14. A BSC has source symbol probabilities and channel matrix as shown below.

$$P[B|A] = \begin{bmatrix} \frac{2}{3} & \frac{1}{3} \\ \frac{1}{3} & \frac{2}{3} \end{bmatrix}$$

$$p(a_1) = \frac{3}{4} \qquad p(a_2) = \frac{1}{4}$$

Compare the channel capacity with the mutual information for this channel and source. Explain the difference.

3-15. The channel shown below is termed a binary multiplicative channel, BMC. This channel may be modeled as a zero memory channel with four possible input combinations making up the input alphabet, $A' = \{00, 01, 10, 11\}$.

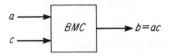

(a) Write the channel matrix for the channel with A' as the input alphabet and B as the output alphabet.

(b) Assuming input symbol probabilities for a zero and one as p and q derive the expression for $I(A, B)$.

(c) Can you determine the channel capacity?

3-16. Write a computer program using matrix calculations routines to solve Example 3-4. Calculate $H(A, B)$, $H(A)$, $H(B)$, $H(B/A)$. Keep your program.

CHAPTER 4

Communication Systems with Memory

4-1. INTRODUCTION

Previously we have restricted ourselves to sources whose outputs were independent of previous outputs. This is an unrealistic restriction in many cases and certainly one can see this in the case of English where many letters and even words are not independent of the previous transmissions.

In this chapter we will study *Markov processes*, which are dependent processes in which the output symbol is dependent upon a finite number of the preceding symbols. Stationary and ergodic Markov processes and Markov sources will be of interest also. Here also we will develop the transition matrix and the state diagram which are useful in describing the Markov process.

4-2. MARKOV PROCESSES

A Markov process is a type of characterization of a series of dependent trials. The dependency arises from the fact that the result of an event depends upon the state of past events. The English language is an example of a Markov process. In particular consider the occurrence of the letter T. We usually find an H after T, and very rarely a Z. This could be expressed in the form of a probability notation as follows:

$$P(H|T) > P(Z|T)$$

This is a simple case for which we have only considered the immediately preceding state in determining the next state. A more practical example is obtained by considering the old adage "I before E except after C." This could be expressed in probability notation as follows:

$$P(E|IC') > P(E|IC)$$

This simply states the probability of an E occurring after an I which is not

71

preceded by a C is greater than the probability of an E occurring after an I which is preceded by a C.

In general, if we have a set of mutually exclusive, collectively exhaustive states $a_1, a_2 \ldots, a_q$, and if we write $a_i(k)$ as the event that the process is in state a_i after k trials, then the process may be described by transition probabilities of the form:

$$P[a_i(k)/a_1(k-1) a_2(k-2) a_3(k-3) \cdots a_m(k-m)]; \quad k = 1, 2, 3, \ldots,$$

where the states $a_1, a_2, a_3 \ldots, a_m$ are arbitrary states in general.

This quantity is a statement of the conditional probability that the system will be in state a_i immediately after the kth trial, given that the previous state history of the process is as described by the series of events $a_1(k-1) a_2(k-2) a_3(k-3) \cdots a_m(k-m)$. If the transition probabilities for a series of trials are only dependent upon the immediately proceeding trial then we have a first-order Markov process.†

$$P[a_i(k)/a_1(k-1) a_2(k-2) a_3(k-3) \ldots a_m(k-m)]$$
$$= P[a_i(k)/a_1(k-1)] \quad (4\text{-}1)$$

If we assume the transition probabilities, Eq. 4-1, are independent of the trial number n, we may write the probability of progressing to state j from state i in one trail for a first-order Markov process as:

$$P[a_j(k)/a_i(k-1)] = p_{ij}^{(1)}(1) = p_{ij} \quad (4\text{-}2)$$

A transition matrix is used to express the probabilities of progressing from state i to state j in one trial. A typical transition matrix is shown in Fig. 4-1.

$$[P] = \begin{bmatrix} p_{11} & p_{12} & \cdots & p_{1q} \\ p_{21} & p_{22} & \cdots & p_{2q} \\ \vdots & \vdots & & \vdots \\ p_{q1} & p_{q2} & \cdots & p_{qq} \end{bmatrix}$$

Fig. 4-1. Typical transition matrix.

Since the process must be in one of the q possible states after a trial, we have the relation

$$\sum_{j=1}^{q} p_{ij} = 1 \quad \text{for } i = 1, 2, 3, \ldots, q$$

†The number of previous states that the transition probabilities are dependent upon determine the order of the Markov process. Thus for a third-order process we have, $P[a_j(k)/a_1(k-1) a_2(k-2) a_3(k-3)] = p_{3j}^{(3)}(k)$.

We are also interested in the conditional probability that the process will progress from state i to state j in k trials (or steps), called the *k-step transition probability* $p_{ij}(k)$,

$$p_{ij}(k) = P[a_j(n + k)/a_i(n)] \tag{4-3}$$

For a step of zero we have

$$p_{ij}(0) = \begin{cases} 1 & i = j \\ 0 & i \neq j \end{cases}$$

whereas for a step of 1 we have

$$p_{ij}(1) = p_{ij}$$

Now for any step l such that $0 \leqslant l \leqslant k$,

$$p_{ij}(k) = P[a_j(n + k)/a_i(n)] = \sum_{x=1}^{q} P[a_j(n + k) \, a_x(n + k - l)/a_i(n)] \tag{4-4}$$

Equation 4-4 simply states that the process was in at least one state after the $(n + k - l)$th step.

By applying the theorem of conditional probability and then using Eq. 4-1 for a first-order Markov process, it is easily shown that

$$p_{ij}(k) = \sum_{x=1}^{q} p_{ix}(k - l) \, p_{xj}(l)$$

$$k = 1, 2, 3, \ldots,; \quad 0 \leqslant l \leqslant k; \quad 1 \leqslant i, j \leqslant q$$

If $l = 1$,

$$p_{ij}(k) = \sum_{x=1}^{q} p_{ix}(k - 1) \, p_{xj} \tag{4-5}$$

Use of Eq. 4-5 allows the calculation of the k-step transition probabilities.

Example 4-1

Consider a handball player with a psychological hang-up about returning the serve. If he returned the serve the previous time he will be successful in returning the next serve with probability $2/3$. If he failed to return the serve the previous time he will be unsuccessful in returning the next serve with probability $3/4$. The transition probability matrix is

$$[P] = \begin{bmatrix} 2/3 & 1/3 \\ 1/4 & 3/4 \end{bmatrix}$$

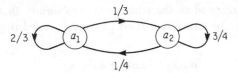

Fig. 4-2. State transition diagram.

We are calling a successful serve state 1 and an unsuccessful serve state 2. A state-transition diagram is shown in Fig. 4-2.

Using Eq. 4-5 we may calculate the probability that if the player has returned the last serve successfully he will have returned the kth serve from then successfully. The results for $k = 1, 2, 3, 4, 5, 6, 7, 8$ are shown below. The student should confirm the numbers presented (rounded off to three places). (A computer program of this example is presented at the end of this chapter.[†])

k	1	2	3	4	5	6	7	8
$p_{11}(k)$	.667	.528	.477	.449	.437	.432	.430	.430
$p_{12}(k)$	.333	.472	.523	.551	.563	.568	.570	.570
$p_{21}(k)$	.250	.354	.398	.416	.423	.426	.427	.428
$p_{22}(k)$	.750	.646	.602	.584	.577	.574	.573	.572

From the table we see by the circled entry that if the player has returned the last serve successfully he will have returned the fifth serve from then successfully with a probability of only .437. (Will he most likely win the game? Why?)

Notice the limiting values of $p_{ij}(k)$ which are reached for increasing k's. This is an important and useful property that is not true of *all* Markov processes but only of *some* Markov processes.

Before progressing further some basic terms will be defined.

DEFINITION. A *chain* consists of a sequence of states where the probability of moving from any state to the immediately succeeding state is prescribed by the elements of the transition probability matrix, $[p_{ij}]$. If we have a process with q states, a possible chain is:

$$\ldots a_2 a_1 a_3 a_5 a_2 a_2 \ldots$$

DEFINITION. If the elements of the transition probability matrix are not dependent upon time, but instead remain constant with time, then the chain is said to be *stationary.* Our work will concern stationary chains.

DEFINITION. A state a_i is a *transient* state of a Markov chain if from at least one state which may be reached from a_i (directly or indirectly) the chain can never return to a_i. In Fig. 4-3 is shown the state diagram of a Markov process. The states a_2, a_3, a_4, and a_5 are transient states.

†Courtesy of Mr. Keith Hall, graduate student of Mississippi State University.

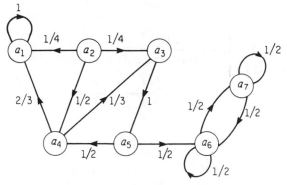

Fig. 4-3. Markov process state diagram.

DEFINITION. A state a_i is *recurrent* if from every state which may be reached from a_i (directly or indirectly), the chain may eventually return to a_i. In Fig. 4-3 the states a_1, a_6, and a_7 are recurrent states.

DEFINITION. A *periodic* state a_i is one for which there exists an integer, d, with $d > 1$, such that $p_{ii}(k)$ is zero for all values of k other than $d, 2d, 3d, \ldots,$. In Fig. 4-3 the states a_3, a_4 and a_5 are periodic states.

DEFINITION. A state a_i is an *absorbing* state if it is impossible to leave that state. Thus $p_{ii}(k) = 1$. In Fig. 4-3 the state a_1 is an absorbing state.

We have shown how to calculate the transition probability of progressing from state a_i to a_j in k steps, $p_{ij}(k)$, by Eq. 4-5. If we make the transition probability matrix for k steps using as the elements $p_{ij}(k)$ then we shall denote this matrix as:

$$[P]^k = \begin{bmatrix} p_{11}(k) \ldots \ldots p_{1q}(k) \\ \vdots \qquad\qquad \vdots \\ \vdots \qquad\qquad \vdots \\ \vdots \qquad\qquad \vdots \\ p_{q1}(k) \ldots \ldots p_{qq}(k) \end{bmatrix}$$

This matrix is useful enough to warrant some extra explanation.

If we have $[P]$ for one step as

$$[P] = \begin{bmatrix} p_{11} & p_{12} \\ p_{21} & p_{22} \end{bmatrix}$$

then

$$[P]^2 = \begin{bmatrix} \overbrace{p_{11}(2)}^{} & \overbrace{p_{12}(2)}^{} \\ (p_{11}p_{11} + p_{12}p_{21}) & (p_{11}p_{12} + p_{12}p_{22}) \\ \underbrace{p_{21}(2)}_{} & \underbrace{p_{22}(2)}_{} \\ (p_{21}p_{11} + p_{22}p_{21}) & (p_{21}p_{12} + p_{22}p_{22}) \end{bmatrix}$$

and,

$$[P]^3 = [P]^2 [P] = \begin{bmatrix} \overbrace{(p_{11}p_{11}(2) + p_{21}p_{12}(2)}^{p_{11}(3)} & \overbrace{p_{12}p_{11}(2) + p_{22}p_{12}(2)}^{p_{12}(3)} \\ \overbrace{(p_{11}p_{21}(2) + p_{21}p_{22}(2)}^{p_{21}(3)} & \overbrace{p_{12}p_{21}(2) + p_{22}p_{22}(2)}^{p_{22}(3)} \end{bmatrix}$$

In general,

$$[P]^k = \begin{bmatrix} p_{11}(k) & p_{12}(k) \\ p_{21}(k) & p_{22}(k) \end{bmatrix}$$

where we may calculate $p_{ij}(k)$ from Eq. 4-5.

In particular, let us show that $p_{21}(3)$ is easily calculated from Eq. 4-5:

$$p_{21}(3) = \sum_{x=1}^{2} p_{2x}(3\text{-}1)\, p_{x1} = p_{21}(2)\, p_{11} + p_{22}(2)\, p_{21}$$

$$p_{21}(3) = p_{11}p_{21}p_{11} + p_{11}p_{22}p_{21} + p_{21}p_{21}p_{12} + p_{21}p_{22}p_{22}$$

Another form of Eq. 4-5 is given below since it is often more useful due to direct calculation of $p_{ij}(k)$ in terms of the one-step probabilities. (Does your program do it this way?)

$$p_{ij}(k) = \sum_{x_1=1}^{q} \cdots \sum_{x_{k-1}=1}^{q} p_{ix_1}\, p_{x_1 x_2} \cdots p_{x_{k-1}j} \qquad (4\text{-}5b)$$

Thus

$$p_{21}(3) = \sum_{x_1=1}^{2} \sum_{x_2=1}^{2} p_{2x_1}\, p_{x_1 x_2}\, p_{x_2 1}$$

$$= \sum_{x_2=1}^{2} p_{21}p_{1x_2}p_{x_2 1} + \sum_{x_2=1}^{2} p_{22}p_{2x_2}p_{x_2 1}$$

$$= p_{21}p_{11}p_{11} + p_{21}p_{12}p_{21} + p_{22}p_{21}p_{11} + p_{22}p_{22}p_{21}$$

Now for illustration of the difference between the step and the order of the process, let us consider a second-order Markov process by considering a binary source. Thus we have as the number of possible states

$$q = n^m = 2^2 = 4$$

These states are listed below in a table with the associated transition probabilities which have been assumed:

State	Second-Order History $a_1(k-1)\, a_2(k-2)$	Next Digit Probability 0 1
1	00	¼ ¾
2	10	⅓ ⅔
3	01	1 0
4	11	½ ½

The state diagram for this process is illustrated below and the one-step, $k = 1$, transition matrix P is as shown:

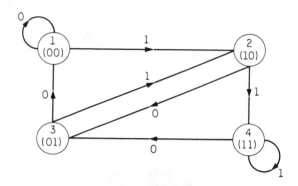

$$[P] = \begin{bmatrix} \frac{1}{4} & \frac{3}{4} & 0 & 0 \\ 0 & 0 & \boxed{\frac{1}{3}} & \frac{2}{3} \\ 1 & 0 & 0 & 0 \\ 0 & 0 & \frac{1}{2} & \frac{1}{2} \end{bmatrix}$$

The encircled entry in the transition matrix is the transitional probability of being in state 3 in one step, given that the process was in state 2 initially:

$$P[\%_{10}] = p_{23}^{(2)}(1) = \frac{1}{3}$$

If we want the two-step transitional probability of being in state 3 given that the process was in state 4 initially we would calculate the two-step Matrix as shown and find the 4, 3 entry (again encircled):

$$[P]^2 = [P]\,[P] = \begin{bmatrix} \frac{1}{16} & \frac{3}{16} & \frac{1}{4} & \frac{1}{2} \\ \frac{1}{3} & 0 & \frac{1}{3} & \frac{1}{3} \\ \frac{1}{4} & \frac{3}{4} & 0 & 0 \\ \frac{1}{2} & 0 & \boxed{\frac{1}{4}} & \frac{1}{4} \end{bmatrix}$$

where we have

$$p_{43}^{(2)}(2) = \frac{1}{4}$$

We could also have used Eq. 4-5b to calculate $p_{43}^{(2)}$ (2) in the following manner:

$$p_{43}^{(2)} (2) = \sum_{x_1=1}^{4} p_{4x_1} p_{x_1 5} = p_{41} p_{13} + p_{42} p_{23} + p_{43} p_{33} + p_{44} p_{43}$$

$$= (0)(0) + (0)(1/3) + (0)(0) + (1/2)(1/2) = 1/4$$

Now there is an important property concerning the k-step transition probability matrix which we will develop below.

DEFINITION. A chain is termed a *regular chain* if for some positive integer k_0 the matrix $[P]^{k_0}$ has no zero elements. (Of course if $[P]^{k_0}$ has no zero elements then $[P]^k, k > k_0$ will have no zero elements also.) Show that for $k = 2$ the matrix $[P]$ in Fig. 4-4 has no zero elements and hence is regular.

$$[P] = \begin{bmatrix} 1/2 & 1/2 & 0 \\ 0 & 3/4 & 1/4 \\ 1/2 & 0 & 1/2 \end{bmatrix}$$

Fig. 4-4. One-step matrix of a regular
and ergodic chain.

DEFINITION. A Markov chain is termed *ergodic* if the chain can progress from any one state to any other state in a finite number of steps. The matrix in Fig. 4-4 corresponds to an ergodic chain. It should be obvious that a regular chain is always ergodic, but an ergodic chain is not necessarily regular. The differences between a regular chain and an ergodic chain should be understood. Figure 4-5 shows the state diagram of a chain that is ergodic but not regular. Note that one may always progress from any state to any other state in at most two moves, but one cannot derive a transition probability matrix with all non-zero elements no matter how many steps are considered. (Note that $[P]^4$ is identical to $[P]$.)

Figure 4-3 illustrates a chain that is neither regular nor ergodic. The chain will arrive at either state a_1 or a_6 with nonzero probability, and once in either of these states the chain will never emit an a_2, a_3, a_4, or a_5 again, thus ruling out the possibilities of the chain being regular or ergodic.

Regular chains (and hence ergodic chains) are the subject of an important and useful theorem which is discussed next.

Theorem. If $[P]$ is a regular transition matrix, then
(a) The elements of $[P]^k$ approach a probability matrix S as k grows large.
(b) Each row of $[S]$ is the same probability vector $\alpha = \{s_1, s_2, \ldots, s_q\}$. ($[S]$ is termed the stationary distribution matrix.)
(c) The components of α are positive.

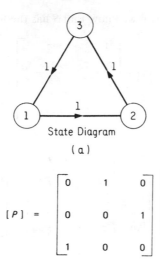

State Diagram

(a)

$$[P] = \begin{bmatrix} 0 & 1 & 0 \\ 0 & 0 & 1 \\ 1 & 0 & 0 \end{bmatrix}$$

Transition Probability Matrix

(b)

Fig. 4-5. An ergodic but not regular chain.

This theorem[13] states that for regular (and hence ergodic~~ FALSE~~) chains the probability transition matrix becomes independent of the initial probability with which the states are chosen after a large number of steps, say k steps. Thus after k steps we would have $[P]^k = [P]^{k+1} = [P]^{k+2} = \cdots = [S]$; that is, the transition matrix becomes a constant. Furthermore the rows of the matrix S are identical and each element is a positive number. The proof of this theorem is not complicated and may be found in several texts,[†] hence it will not be presented here.

The matrix S is easily found from the original transition probability matrix P in the following manner.

Since for steps greater than k the matrix is a constant we may state the following:

$$\lim_{k=\infty} [P]^{k+1} = \lim_{k \to \infty} [P]^k [P] = (\lim_{k=\infty} [P]^k) [P] = [S][P]$$

but

$$\lim_{k=\infty} [P]^{k+1} = [S]$$

hence

$$[S] = [S][P]$$

[†]The proof may be found in Feller,[12] Kemeny and Snell,[13] Reza.[14]

From the theorem part b we know that S has the form

$$[S] = \begin{bmatrix} s_1 & s_2 & \cdots & s_q \\ s_1 & s_2 & \cdots & s_q \\ \cdot & \cdot & & \cdot \\ \cdot & \cdot & & \cdot \\ \cdot & \cdot & & \cdot \\ s_1 & s_2 & \cdots & s_q \end{bmatrix}$$

Thus

$$\begin{bmatrix} s_1 & s_2 & \cdots & s_q \\ s_1 & s_2 & \cdots & s_q \\ \cdot & \cdot & & \cdot \\ \cdot & \cdot & & \cdot \\ \cdot & \cdot & & \cdot \\ s_1 & s_2 & \cdots & s_q \end{bmatrix} \begin{bmatrix} p_{11} & p_{12} & \cdots & p_{1q} \\ p_{21} & p_{22} & \cdots & p_{2q} \\ \cdot & \cdot & & \cdot \\ \cdot & \cdot & & \cdot \\ \cdot & \cdot & & \cdot \\ p_{q1} & p_{q2} & \cdots & p_{qq} \end{bmatrix} = \begin{bmatrix} s_1 & s_2 & \cdots & s_q \\ s_1 & s_2 & \cdots & s_q \\ \cdot & \cdot & & \cdot \\ \cdot & \cdot & & \cdot \\ \cdot & \cdot & & \cdot \\ s_1 & s_2 & \cdots & s_q \end{bmatrix}$$

or

$$s_1 p_{11} + s_2 p_{21} + \cdots + s_q p_{q1} = s_1$$
$$s_1 p_{12} + s_2 p_{22} + \cdots + s_q p_{q2} = s_2 \qquad\qquad (4\text{-}6a)$$
$$\vdots \qquad \vdots \qquad\qquad \vdots \qquad \vdots$$
$$s_1 p_{1q} + s_2 p_{2q} + \cdots + s_q p_{qq} = s_q$$

and since each row vector of $[S]$ is a probability vector,

$$s_1 + s_2 + \cdots + s_q = 1 \qquad\qquad (4\text{-}6b)$$

If the original transition matrix of a regular chain is known then the stationary distribution matrix S may be found by simultaneous solution of Eq. 4-6.

What comments concerning regular chains and ergodic chains can be made concerning the chain with the transition matrix of Example 4-1? Note how the values of the S matrix are illustrated by the values in the table of Example 4-1. The S matrix is approximately equal to $[P]^8$ and hence

$$[S] \cong [P]^8 = \begin{bmatrix} .430 & .570 \\ .428 & .572 \end{bmatrix}$$

4-3. MARKOV SOURCE ENTROPY

In this section we will develop the entropy of a single-step chain, an adjoint source, and a k-step chain.

For a single-step chain with q possible states the transition matrix indicates the individual probabilities of moving from any one state to any other state. For each state the amount of information gained when the chain moves one step ahead from an initial state a_i would be

$$H(a_i) = -\sum_{j=1}^{q} p_{ij} \log p_{ij} = -\sum_{j=1}^{q} p(a_j/a_i) \log p(a_j/a_i) \qquad (4\text{-}7)$$

Equation 4-7 is the average amount of information gained when the chain moves ahead one step starting from a single state, namely a_i. If we now average $H(a_i)$ over all possible starting states we will have the average amount of information gained when the chain moves ahead one step. (Note that Eq. 4-8 is the source entropy of a single-step first-order Markov chain. Reread the above paragraph to insure understanding of the difference between Eqs. 4-7 and 4-8.)

$$H(A) = \overline{H(a_i)} = \sum_{i=1}^{n} p(a_i) H(a_i) = -\sum_{i=1}^{n}\sum_{j=1}^{q} p(a_i) p_{ij} \log p_{ij} \qquad (4\text{-}8)$$

Before we continue we should note a few properties of the entropies of Eqs. 4-7 and 4-8.

The entropy of Eq. 4-7 is reminiscent of our entropy of a simple zero-memory source, since the quantity p_{ij} is a probability distribution on the symbols a_j. While it is true that p_{ij} is a conditional probability it is still true that

$$p_{ij} = p(a_j/a_i) \geqslant 0 \qquad j = 1, 2, \ldots, q$$

and,

$$\sum_{j=1}^{q} p(a_j/a_i) = 1$$

Thus $H(a_i)$ must have the properties developed for the zero-memory source, and hence

$$H(a_i) \leqslant \log n \qquad (4\text{-}9)$$

where n is the number of symbols in the source alphabet and is also equal to the number of possible states, 8, for a first-order chain. The quantity $\log n$ is often termed the *capacity* of the alphabet, C_a.

From Eq. 4-9 we see that the entropy of Eq. 4-7 is a maximum of $\log n$ and achieves this value only when the number of source symbols are equally likely so that $p(a_j/a_i) = 1/n$ for all i, j.

We may write Eq. 4-8 in the form

$$H(A) = -\left(\sum_{i=1}^{n} p(a_i) \sum_{j=1}^{q} p_{ij} \log p_{ij} \right) \leqslant (\log n) \sum_{i=1}^{n} p(a_i) = \log n$$

or,

$$H(A) \leqslant \log n \tag{4-10}$$

Thus we see that the entropy of Eq. 4-8 is also bounded by $\log n$ and achieves this maximum for equally likely source-alphabet symbols.

If we are dealing with a regular k-step Markov chain we may calculate the stationary distribution matrix S for the chain. For one-step regular chains this matrix is identical with the set of source-alphabet symbols, and hence $[S]$ yields the probability distribution of the source symbols for a one-step regular chain. For k-step Markov chains the stationary distribution matrix S may be used to determine the one-step probability distribution which is equal to the source-alphabet symbol probabilities.

The adjoint source is defined in terms of the one-step (first-order) distribution as follows:

DEFINITION. The *adjoint source* A^a of an mth order Markov source with a source alphabet $A = \{a_1, a_2, \ldots, a_n\}$ with first-order source symbol probabilities $p(a_1), p(a_2), \ldots p(a_n)$ is the zero-memory source with source alphabet $A = \{a_1, a_2, \ldots, a_n\}$ and with source symbol probabilities $p(a_1), p(a_2), \ldots, p(a_n)$.

The entropy of the adjoint source is simply that of zero-memory source with source symbol probabilities as stated. Hence,

$$H(A^a) = -\sum_{i=1}^{n} p(a_i) \log p(a_i) \leqslant \log n \tag{4-11}$$

It is easily shown that the entropy $H(A)$ is not only bounded by $\log n$ but also bounded by $H(A^a)$, its adjoint entropy.

From Lemma 8, Chapter 2 we know that if p_i and q_i are two sets of probabilities, then,

$$-\sum_{i=1}^{n} q_i \log q_i \leqslant -\sum_{i=1}^{n} q_i \log p_i$$

with equality iff $p_i = q_i$; $i = 1, 2, \ldots, n$, or,

$$\sum_{i=1}^{n} q_i \log \frac{p_i}{q_i} \leqslant 0$$

We may then write

$$\sum_{i=1}^{n} \sum_{j=1}^{q} p(a_i, a_j) \log \frac{p(a_i) \, p(a_j)}{p(a_i, a_j)} \leqslant 0$$

or, since $p(a_i, a_j) = p(a_i/a_j) \, p(a_j) = p(a_j/a_i) \, p(a_i)$, rearranging

$$\sum_{i=1}^{n}\sum_{j=1}^{q} p(a_i/a_j)\, p(a_j) \log\frac{1}{p(a_i/a_j)} \leqslant \sum_{i=1}^{n}\sum_{j=1}^{q} p(a_i, a_j) \log\frac{1}{p(a_i)}$$

But the right-hand side is equal to

$$\sum_{i=1}^{n} p(a_j) \log\frac{1}{p(a_i)} = H(A^a)$$

and the left-hand side is equal to $H(A)$.

Hence we have

$$H(A) \leqslant H(A^a) \leqslant \log n \qquad (4\text{-}12)$$

Next we consider the entropy of a k-step regular Markov Chain. If we use the transition matrix for a k-step chain then the individual elements of the matrix represent the probability of the system progressing from state a_i to a_j in k steps $p_{ij}(k)$. The amount of information obtained when the given chain progresses k steps, starting from the state a_i, would be

$$H(a_i(k)) = -\sum_{j=1}^{q} p_{ij}(k) \log p_{ij}(k) \qquad (4\text{-}13)$$

Averaging over all the possible starting states, each with state probability $p(a_i)$, we then obtain the average amount of information given by moving ahead k steps in the given regular Markov chain. This entropy, termed the k-step entropy of the chain, is

$$H(A(k)) = \overline{H(a_i(k))} = -\sum_{i=1}^{n}\sum_{j=1}^{q} p(a_i)\, p_{ij}(k) \log p_{ij}(k) \qquad (4\text{-}14)$$

An interesting property of k-step entropies for regular chains is the property of additivity. This property is proven by Khinchin[15] and his proof is outlined below. (Use of equation 4-14 is illustrated in Example 4-2.)

DEFINITION. The *additivity property* of the k-step entropies of a regular Markov chain with initial probabilities equal to those of the stationary distribution matrix S; i.e.,

$$p(a_1) = s_1, \quad p(a_2) = s_2, \ldots, p(a_n) = s_n$$

is defined as

$$H(k + m) = H(k) + H(m)$$

where $H(k) = H(A(k))$ and $H(m) = H(A(m))$.

To illustrate the additivity we shall compute the entropy of a $(k + 1)$-step chain by considering this as a one-step move and then a k-step move starting from state a_i.

$$H(a_i(k+1)) = H(a_i) + \sum_{j=1}^{q} p_{ij} H(a_j(k))$$

The average entropy for a $k+1$ step move is then

$$H(A(k+1)) = \overline{H(a_i(k+1))} = \sum_{i=1}^{n} p(a_i) H(a_i(k+1))$$

$$= \sum_{i=1}^{n} p(a_i) H(a_i) + \sum_{i=1}^{n} \sum_{j=1}^{q} p(a_i) p_{ij} H(a_j(k))$$

$$= H(A) + \sum_{j=1}^{q} H(a_j(k)) \sum_{i=1}^{n} p(a_i) p_{ij}$$

$$= H(A) + \sum_{j=1}^{q} p(a_j) H(a_j(k))$$

$$H(A(k-1)) = H(A) + H(A(k)) \tag{4-15}$$

Using the result of Eq. 4-14 we may show the following.

$$k = 1; \quad H(A(1+1)) = H(A(2)) = H(A) + H(A(1)) = 2H(A)$$
$$k = 2; \quad H(A(2+1)) = H(A(2)) + H(A) \quad = \quad 3H(A)$$

or in general

$$H(A(k+1)) = (k+1)H(A)$$

and,

$$H(A(k)) = kH(A) \tag{4-16}$$

From Eq. 4-16 we see that the entropy of a k-step regular Markov chain equals k times the entropy for the chain moving ahead one step.

The following example sums up the developments of this section.

Example 4-2
Let us consider a first-order Markov source with alphabet

$$A = \{a_1 = a, a_2 = b, a_3 = c\}$$

and initial source symbol probabilities

$$p(a_1) = 1/3 \qquad p(a_2) = 1/2 \qquad p(a_3) = 1/6$$

and transition matrix

$$[P]^1 = \begin{bmatrix} p_{11} & p_{12} & p_{13} \\ p_{21} & p_{22} & p_{23} \\ p_{31} & p_{32} & p_{33} \end{bmatrix} = \begin{bmatrix} 0 & 2/5 & 3/5 \\ 1/4 & 3/4 & 0 \\ 1/2 & 2/5 & 1/10 \end{bmatrix}$$

For this example we have the number of source symbols as

$$n = 3$$

and the Markov process as a first-order memory single-step process so that

$$k = 1, \text{ and } m = 1$$

this leaves us with the number of possible states as

$$q = n^m = 3$$

The state diagram is shown in Fig. 4-6 along with a typical sequence which might be produced by this source.

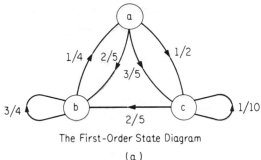

The First-Order State Diagram

(a)

bbbbacabbacacbabbacac

A Typical Sequence

(b)

Fig. 4-6. First-order state diagram.

Let us determine whether this Markov chain is ergodic and regular, and compute the first-step entropy, the adjoint source entropy, the capacity of the alphabet, and, if the source is ergodic, the stationary distribution matrix S, and the second-step entropy.

(a) If the chain is regular and ergodic there will be a k-step matrix with all nonzero elements. If the chain is only ergodic then we will be able to progress from any state to any other state in some finite number of steps.

It is obvious that this chain is first-step ergodic but not first-step regular.

To determine the number of steps required to achieve regularity, if any, let us calculate as many of the $[P]^k$ matrices as needed:

$$[P]^2 = [P] \, [P] = \begin{bmatrix} 2/5 & 27/50 & 3/50 \\ 3/16 & 53/80 & 3/20 \\ 3/20 & 27/50 & 31/100 \end{bmatrix}$$

Thus this source is second-step regular and first-step ergodic.

(b) The first-step entropy is calculated from Eq. 4-8.

$$H(A) = \overline{H(a_i)} = - \sum_{i=1}^{n} \sum_{j=1}^{q} p(a_i) p_{ij} \log p_{ij}.$$

$$H(A) = -p(a_1) [p_{11} \log p_{11} + p_{12} \log p_{12} + p_{13} \log p_{13}]$$
$$-p(a_2) [p_{21} \log p_{21} + p_{22} \log p_{22} + p_{23} \log p_{23}]$$
$$-p(a_3) [p_{31} \log p_{31} + p_{32} \log p_{32} + p_{33} \log p_{33}]$$
$$= -\tfrac{1}{3} [0 \log 0 + \tfrac{2}{5} \log \tfrac{2}{5} + \tfrac{3}{5} \log \tfrac{3}{5}]$$
$$- \tfrac{1}{2} [\tfrac{1}{4} \log \tfrac{1}{4} + \tfrac{3}{4} \log \tfrac{3}{4} + 0 \log 0]$$
$$- \tfrac{1}{6} [\tfrac{1}{2} \log \tfrac{1}{2} + \tfrac{2}{5} \log \tfrac{2}{5} + \tfrac{1}{10} \log \tfrac{1}{10}].$$

$$\therefore H(A) = .9560$$

(c) The adjoint source entropy is

$$H(A^a) = - \sum_{i=1}^{n} p(a_i) \log p(a_i)$$

$$= -p(a_1) \log p(a_1) - p(a_2) \log p(a_2) - p(a_3) \log p(a_3)$$
$$= -\tfrac{1}{3} \log \tfrac{1}{3} - \tfrac{1}{2} \log \tfrac{1}{2} - \tfrac{1}{6} \log \tfrac{1}{6}$$
$$\therefore H(A^a) = 1.4588$$

(d) The capacity of the alphabet is

$$C_a = \log n = \log 3 = 1.5849$$

Note: $H(A) < H(A^a) < C_a$.

(e) The matrix S is found from Eqs. 4-6.

$$s_1 p_{11} + s_2 p_{21} + s_3 p_{31} = s_1$$
$$s_1 p_{12} + s_2 p_{22} + s_3 p_{32} = s_2$$
$$s_1 p_{13} + s_2 p_{23} + s_3 p_{33} = s_3$$
$$s_1 + s_2 + s_3 = 1$$

or

$$s_1(0) + s_2(\tfrac{1}{4}) + s_3(\tfrac{1}{2}) = s_1$$
$$s_1(\tfrac{2}{5}) + s_2(\tfrac{3}{4}) + s_3(\tfrac{2}{5}) = s_2$$
$$s_1(\tfrac{3}{5}) + s_2(0) + s_3(\tfrac{1}{10}) = s_3$$
$$s_1(\tfrac{3}{5}) + s_2(0) + s_3(\tfrac{1}{10}) = s_3$$
$$s_1 + s_2 + s_3 = 1$$

Thus

$$s_1 = {}^3/_{13} \qquad s_2 = {}^8/_{13} \qquad s_3 = {}^2/_{13}$$

$$[S] = \begin{bmatrix} {}^3/_{13} & {}^8/_{13} & {}^2/_{13} \\ {}^3/_{13} & {}^8/_{13} & {}^2/_{13} \\ {}^3/_{13} & {}^8/_{13} & {}^2/_{13} \end{bmatrix}$$

(f) The second-step entropy may be calculated from either Eq. 4-14 or Eq. 4-16.

1. From Eq. 4-16,

$$H(A(2)) = 2H(A) = 2(.9560) = 1.912$$

2. From Eq. 4-14,

$$H(A(2)) = - \sum_{i=1}^{3} \sum_{j=1}^{3} p(a_i)\, p_{ij}(2) \log p_{ij}(2)$$

where

$$p_{ij}(2) = \sum_{x_1=1}^{3} p_{ix_1} p_{x_1 j}$$

from Eq. 4-5b, and $p_{ij}(2) \log p_{ij}(2)$ is defined as follows.
Consider $p_{12}(2)$; then

$$p_{12}(2) = p_{11}p_{12} + p_{12}p_{22}$$

and

$$p_{12}(2) \log p_{12}(2) = p_{11}p_{12} \log p_{11}p_{12} + p_{12}p_{22} \log p_{12}p_{22}$$

Thus,

$H(A(2)) =$

$-p(a_1)\, [p_{11}(2) \log p_{11}(2) + p_{12}(2) \log p_{12}(2) + p_{13}(3) \log p_{13}(3)]$
$-p(a_2)\, [p_{21}(2) \log p_{21}(2) + p_{22}(2) \log p_{22}(2) + p_{23}(2) \log p_{23}(2)]$
$-p(a_3)\, [p_{31}(2) \log p_{31}(2) + p_{32}(2) \log p_{32}(2) + p_{33}(2) \log p_{33}(2)]$

or,

$H(A(2)) =$

$-p(a_1)\, [p_{11}p_{11} \log p_{11}p_{11} + p_{12}p_{21} \log p_{12}p_{21} + p_{13}p_{31} \log p_{13}p_{31}$
$+p_{11}p_{12} \log p_{11}p_{12} + p_{12}p_{22} \log p_{12}p_{22} + p_{13}p_{32} \log p_{13}p_{32}$
$+p_{11}p_{13} \log p_{11}p_{13} + p_{12}p_{23} \log p_{12}p_{23} + p_{13}p_{33} \log p_{13}p_{33}]$
$-p(a_2)\, [p_{21}p_{11} \log p_{21}p_{11} + p_{22}p_{21} \log p_{22}p_{21} + p_{23}p_{31} \log p_{23}p_{31}$

$$+p_{21}p_{12} \log p_{21}p_{12} + \cdots + p_{23}p_{33} \log p_{23}p_{33}]$$

$$-p(a_3) [p_{31}p_{11} \log p_{31}p_{11} + \cdots + p_{33}p_{33} \log p_{33}p_{33}]$$

$$H(A(2)) = -\tfrac{1}{3} [0 \log 0 + \tfrac{1}{10} \log \tfrac{1}{10} + \tfrac{3}{10} \log \tfrac{3}{10} + \tfrac{3}{10} \log \tfrac{3}{10}$$
$$+ \tfrac{6}{25} \log \tfrac{6}{25} + 0 \log 0 + \tfrac{3}{50} \log \tfrac{3}{50}]$$
$$- \tfrac{1}{2} [0 \log 0 + \tfrac{3}{16} \log \tfrac{3}{16} + 0 \log 0 + \tfrac{1}{10} \log \tfrac{1}{10}$$
$$+ \tfrac{9}{16} \log \tfrac{9}{16} + 0 \log 0 + \tfrac{3}{20} \log \tfrac{3}{20} + 0 \log 0 + 0 \log 0]$$
$$- \tfrac{1}{6} [0 \log 0 + \tfrac{1}{10} \log \tfrac{1}{10} + \tfrac{1}{20} \log \tfrac{1}{20} + \tfrac{1}{5} \log \tfrac{1}{5}$$
$$+ \tfrac{3}{10} \log \tfrac{3}{10} + \tfrac{1}{25} \log \tfrac{1}{25} + \tfrac{3}{10} \log \tfrac{3}{10} + 0 \log 0 + \tfrac{1}{100} \log \tfrac{1}{100}]$$
$$= \tfrac{1}{3} [2.1118] + \tfrac{1}{2} [1.6615] + \tfrac{1}{6} [2.3066] = 1.919$$

The reader should note the small difference between the results of $H(A(2))$ by Eq. 4-14 versus Eq. 4-16. If $H(A)$ and $H(A(2))$ are calculated using the initial probabilities as given by the S matrix rather than the initial probabilities originally specified the resulting values of $H(A(2))$ would be identical. Using the S matrix initial probabilities we have

$$H(A(2)) = \tfrac{3}{13} [2.1118] + \tfrac{8}{13} [1.6615] + \tfrac{2}{13} [2.3066] = 1.865$$

and

$$2H(A) = 2 [\tfrac{3}{13} [.9708] + \tfrac{8}{13} [.8112] + \tfrac{2}{13} [1.3608]] = 1.865$$

hence,

$$H(A(2)) = 2H(A) = 1.865$$

4-4. APPLICATION OF THE ENTROPY CONCEPT

One of the simplest ways of applying the entropy concept is that of the coding of a source. This will serve as an example of the interrelation between the use of information theory as a tool for analyzing system performance and as an exercise in mathematics.

Consider a source A with n symbols, and suppose the source emits different sequences of these symbols as different messages. We will assume this source to be a Markov chain and assume that its statistical nature is known, including its entropy $H(A)$ which may be calculated from its statistical nature.

Now let us try coding the source messages with its same symbols but assigning the original messages to the coded sequences in a manner that enhances system performance. In doing so, however, we must also consider several factors—the cost function of the system, the relation between the coded message sequence and the cost function, and the practicality of implementing the desired coding scheme.

The cost function of a system varies with the desired use of the system. If the system is to handle commercial communication traffic, then the cost functions are most likely the time required to send the message, message transmission reliability, and system maintenance—in that order of importance. On the other hand, if the system is a Presidential communications system for the transmission of national policy instructions and information important to national security, then the cost functions are most likely the message security and the message transmission reliability, in that order of importance. If the system is a command destruct communication link with a missile, then the cost functions would be the message transmission reliability and the message security, in that order of importance. And it continues with as many different cost functions and priorities as there are different systems.

For this example we will consider a commercial communications system for which the time required to send the message is of utmost importance. The longer it takes to send a message the fewer number of messages can be sent, resulting in a higher monetary cost for longer messages.

We must encode the original source so that the coded source is shorter in length than the original source. It is not a simple matter of transcribing the longer sequences into shorter sequences, since one must also take into account the frequency of occurrence of the sequence.

The average length of a sequence of symbols S may be computed as

$$L_s = \sum_{s_i} p(s_i)\, s_i$$

For a particular source sequence length S the ratio of the coded-message length C, to the original-message length S is an indication of the coding efficiency. Naturally we would like the ratio to approach zero, indicating a coded word sequence that is negligibly small in length compared to the original word-sequence length.

The average of this ratio is termed the *average compression for sequences of length S*:

$$\mu_s = \frac{\displaystyle\sum_{c_i} p(c_i)\, c_i}{S}$$

By considering longer and longer sequences we arrive at a limiting value for the average compression, termed the *compression coefficient*:

$$\mu = \lim_{s \to \infty} \mu_s$$

An important property of the quantity μ is given by the following statement:

Given a message source with entropy H; the greatest lower bound of the compression coefficient is $H/\log n$, where n has been defined as the number of source symbols and the code must be such that the original message may be recovered.

This statement implies that no matter how good our coding technique, we shall never produce a code for which the limiting value of the average compression is less than the entropy of the original source divided by the maximum entropy of the original source which has been shown to be log n in Sec. 4-3, Eq. 4-10. To determine this lower bound we need only the number of source symbols n and the source entropy H, and we do not need detailed statistical information.

A simple example illustrating the above principles follows:

Example 4-3

Consider a four-message binary source with message probabilities as shown:

Message	Message Probability	Code A	Length	Code B	Length
m_1	$1/4$	00	2	01	2
m_2	$1/8$	01	2	011	3
m_3	$1/2$	10	2	0	1
m_4	$1/8$	11	2	0111	4

The average lengths of code A and code B are:

$$L_A = \sum_{i=1}^{4} p(m_i)\, l_{a_i} = (1/4)\,(2) + (1/8)\,(2) + (1/2)\,(2) + (1/8)\,(2)$$

$$= 2 \text{ bits/message}$$

$$L_B = \sum_{i=1}^{4} p(m_1)\, l_{b_i} = (1/4)\,(2) + (1/8)\,(3) + (1/2)\,(1) + (1/8)\,(4)$$

$$= 1.875 \text{ bits/message}$$

Thus code B is on the average shorter than code A. Now let us see what the theoretical lower bound would be:

$$H = -\sum_{i=1}^{4} p(m_i) \log p(m_i) = (1/4) \log 4 + (1/8) \log 8 + (1/2) \log 2$$

$$+ (1/8) \log 8 = 1.750$$

and

$$\log 2 = 1.0$$

Thus the theoretical lower bound would be 1.750 bits per message. There exist other simple codes with shorter average length than code B, but we shall see later that code B has a property of interest to us—that of unique and instantaneous decodability.

4-5. THE CONTINUOUS CHANNEL

Previously we have only been concerned with sources which could be modeled by discrete-amplitude probability density functions. The consideration of sources which are modeled by continuous-amplitude probability density functions is worthwhile, even though it is usually feasible to approximate these systems with a many discrete-amplitude analogy. However, we will see that there are several interesting facets of the entropy function developed for the continuous-amplitude system which are well to know if for no other reason than to avoid their pitfalls.

Consider the continuous curve which is to be approximated by small discrete samples in Fig. 4-7. It is obvious that the probability that we will lie in

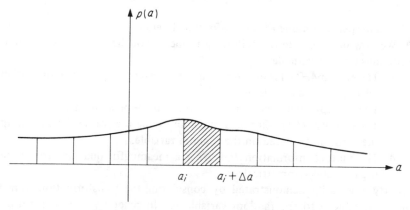

Fig. 4-7. Approximation by discrete sampling.

the interval $(a_i, a_i + \Delta a)$ is approximately $p(a_i) \Delta a$. In the limit as $\Delta a \longrightarrow 0$ the error of our approximation will also tend to zero. The average entropy of the continuous random variable A is therefore

$$H(A) = \lim_{\Delta a \to o} \left[- \sum_{i=-\infty}^{\infty} p(a_i) \Delta a \, \log\!\left[p(a_i) \Delta a \right] \right]$$

$$= \lim_{\Delta a \to o} \left[- \sum_{i=-\infty}^{\infty} [p(a_i) \log p(a_i)] \, \Delta a - \sum_{i=-\infty}^{\infty} [p(a_i) \Delta a \, \log \Delta a \,] \right]$$

$$= - \int_{-\infty}^{\infty} p(a) \log p(a) \, da - \lim_{\Delta a \to o} \left[\log \Delta a \int_{-\infty}^{\infty} p(a) \, da \right]$$

or

$$H(A) = - \int_{-\infty}^{\infty} p(a) \log p(a)\, da - \lim_{\Delta a \to o} \log \Delta a \qquad (4\text{-}17)$$

We see that the entropy of a continuous source has two terms—one which is similar to the definition of entropy for a discrete source and one which, in the limit, approaches minus infinity. The overall entropy of a continuous random variable has magnitude of infinity—a logical outcome because the probability of taking on any single value of a continuous random variable is zero, and this represents a maximum uncertainty and hence a large (infinite) entropy. The entropy expression is useful, however, if we consider the integral term as the relative entropy of the source and the logarithmic term as the reference from which we measure the relative entropy.

DEFINITION. The entropy of a continuous amplitude source is defined as

$$H(A) = - \int_{-\infty}^{\infty} p(a) \log p(a)\, da$$

with the properties unique to itself as outlined below.

We now demonstrate the following properties of the entropy function for a continuous random variable.

1. The entropy $H(A)$ is dependent upon transformation in random variables (change in base coordinates).
2. The entropy $H(A)$ takes on values that can be positive, negative, or zero.
3. The entropy $H(A)$ takes on a maximum value that varies dependent upon the constraints placed on the random variable.
4. The mutual information $I(A, B)$ is a meaningful quantity that is non-negative and symmetrical.

Property 1 is easily demonstrated by considering the transformation from the random variable a to the random variable b. In general we know from probability theory or from theory of calculus that a change in variables is related by the Jacobian of the transformation. Thus we have the general relation

$$p(B) = p(A)|J(A/B)| \qquad (4\text{-}18)$$

where

$$J(A/B) = \begin{vmatrix} \dfrac{\partial a_1}{\partial b_1} & \dfrac{\partial a_1}{\partial b_2} & \cdots & \dfrac{\partial a_1}{\partial b_n} \\[2mm] \dfrac{\partial a_2}{\partial b_1} & \dfrac{\partial a_2}{\partial b_2} & \cdots & \dfrac{\partial a_2}{\partial b_n} \\[2mm] \vdots & & & \\[2mm] \dfrac{\partial a_n}{\partial b_1} & \dfrac{\partial a_n}{\partial b_2} & \cdots & \dfrac{\partial a_n}{\partial b_n} \end{vmatrix}$$

and A and B are sets of n random variables with joint probability distribution

$$p(A) = p(a_1, a_2, \ldots, a_n)$$
$$p(B) = p(b_1, b_2, \ldots, b_n)$$

The entropy for A is

$$H(A) = - \int_{a_1}^{(\infty)} \int_{a_2} \cdots \int_{a_n} p(A) \log p(A)\, d(A)$$

$$(-\infty)$$

where $d(A) = da_1\, da_2 \cdots da_n$.

The entropy for B is

$$H(B) = - \int_{b_1}^{(\infty)} \int_{b_2} \cdots \int_{b_n} p(B) \log p(B)\, d(B)$$

$$(-\infty)$$

$$= - \int_{-\infty}^{\infty} \int_{-\infty}^{\infty} \cdots \int_{-\infty}^{\infty} (p(A)|J(A/B)|) \log (p(A)|J(A/B)|)\, d(B)$$

But,

$$d(B) = J(B/A)\, d(A)^\dagger$$

Hence,

$$H(B) = - \int_{-\infty}^{\infty} \int_{-\infty}^{\infty} \cdots \int_{-\infty}^{\infty} [(p(A)|J(A/B)|) \log (p(A)|J(A/B)|)] J(B/A) d(A)$$

$$= - \int_{-\infty}^{\infty} \int_{-\infty}^{\infty} \cdots \int_{-\infty}^{\infty} p(A)|J(A/B)||J(B/A)| \log p(A)\, d(A)$$

$$- \int_{-\infty}^{\infty} \int_{-\infty}^{\infty} \cdots \int_{-\infty}^{\infty} p(A)|J(A/B)||J(B/A)| \log |J(A/B)| d(A)$$

We now make use of the fact that

$$|J(A/B)||J(B/A)| = \pm 1$$

and have

$$H(B) = H(A) - \int_{-\infty}^{\infty} \int_{-\infty}^{\infty} \cdots \int_{-\infty}^{\infty} p(A) \log |J(A/B)| d(A) \qquad (4\text{-}19)$$

The integral in Eq. 4-19 is seen to be the expected value of the quantity

†See any text on advanced calculus.

$\log |J(A/B)|$ with respect to the variable A, and hence we may write

$$H(B) = H(A) - E_A \left(\log |J(A/B)|\right) \tag{4-20}$$

From Eq. 4-20 we see that the entropy is a function of the transformation and hence may be expected to change when we change variables. The following example illustrates the relationship between two variables as indicated by Eq. 4-20.

Example 4-4

Consider the transformation from the random variable $A = \{a\}$ to the random variable $B = \{b\}$ by multiplication by a constant c. We then have

$$B = cA$$

and

$$|J(A/B)| = \left\| \frac{\partial A}{\partial B} \right\| = \left| \frac{1}{c} \right|$$

and

$$H(B) = H(A) - \int_{-\infty}^{\infty} p(a) \log \left(\frac{1}{c}\right) da$$

or

$$H(B) = H(A) + \log |c|$$

Example 4-5

Consider the transformation from the random variable $A = \{a\}$ to the random variable $B = \{b\}$ by addition of a constant c. Then we have

$$B = A + c$$

and

$$|J(A/B)| = \left\| \frac{\partial A}{\partial B} \right\| = 1$$

and

$$H(B) = H(A) - \int_{-\infty}^{\infty} p(a) \log (1) \, da$$

or

$$H(B) = H(A)$$

Thus we see that for the special case of transformation by translation we have no change in entropy. The point to remember is that one should in general expect a change.

Property 2 becomes evident if we consider a uniformly distributed random variable over the interval $(0, 1/C)$. Then we have

$$p(a) = \begin{cases} C & 0 \leqslant a \leqslant 1/C \\ 0 & \text{elsewhere} \end{cases}$$

Then

$$H(A) = - \int_0^{1/C} C \log C \, da$$

or

$$H(A) = - \log C$$

Now if C is greater than one we have $H(A)$ negative, if C is less than one we have $H(A)$ positive, and if C is 1 we have $H(A)$ as zero. Thus the entropy of a continuous source is unlike that of a discrete source which always has a positive entropy.

For the discrete random variable we found that the maximum entropy occurred for a source with equally likely letters. For the continuous random variable the probability distribution of the source that maximizes the source entropy is dependent upon constraints applied to the random variable. In general the maximization problem, Property 3, may be stated as follows.

Given a source A with entropy

$$H(A) = - \int_{-\infty}^{\infty} p(A) \log p(A) \, d(A) = \int_{-\infty}^{\infty} F(A,p) \, d(A) \tag{4-21}$$

find the probability distribution which maximizes $H(A)$ subject to the following constraints:

$$\int_{-\infty}^{\infty} F_1 (A,p) \, d(A) = \lambda_1$$

$$\int_{-\infty}^{\infty} F_2 (A,p) \, d(A) = \lambda_2$$

$$\vdots \tag{4-22}$$

$$\int_{-\infty}^{\infty} F_K (A,p) \, d(A) = \lambda_K$$

where the λ_K's are given constants. This is a problem of calculus of variations and the form of the probability density function that results in a maximum for $H(A)$ is determined from the solution of the equation

$$\frac{\partial F}{\partial p} + \alpha_1 \frac{\partial F_1}{\partial p} + \alpha_2 \frac{\partial F_2}{\partial p} + \cdots + \alpha_K \frac{\partial F_K}{\partial p} = 0 \tag{4-23}$$

where the α's are undetermined constants which are found by substituting the solution found for F in terms of the α's and A's into the constraint Eqs. 4-22.

The following example illustrates the use of the above technique and the stipulation of the constraint equations. Note that the first constraint equation is always a constant.

Example 4-6

Find the probability density function $p(a)$ that maximizes the entropy of the source $A = \{a\}$ if the mean-square value of the source is to be a constant σ^2. In this case we have

$$H(A) = \int_{-\infty}^{\infty} F(a, p)\, da$$

with

$$F(a, p) = -p(a) \log p(a)$$

and the constraint equations

1.

$$\int_{-\infty}^{\infty} p(a)\, da = 1$$

2.

$$\int_{-\infty}^{\infty} a^2\, p(a)\, da = \sigma^2$$

Thus

$$F_1\,(a, p) = p(a)$$
$$F_2\,(a, p) = a^2 p(a)$$

and using Eq. 4-23 we have

$$\frac{\partial\,[-p(a)\ln p(a)]}{(\ln 2)\,\partial p(a)} + \alpha_1\,\frac{\partial p(a)}{\partial p(a)} + \alpha_2\,\frac{\partial a^2 p(a)}{\partial p(a)} = 0$$

or

$$-\frac{[1 + \log p(a)]}{(\ln 2)} + \alpha_1 + \alpha_2\, a^2 = 0$$

Solving for $p(a)$, we have

$$p(a) = e^{(\alpha_1 - 1)\,\ln 2}\, e^{\alpha_2 a^2 \ln 2}$$

Now substitute the expression for $p(a)$ into the constraint equations

$$\int_{-\infty}^{\infty} e^{(\alpha_1 - 1)\ln 2} \, e^{\alpha_2 a^2 \ln 2} \, da = 1$$

$$\int_{-\infty}^{\infty} a^2 \, e^{(\alpha_1 - 1)\ln 2} \, e^{\alpha_2 a^2 \ln 2} \, da = \sigma^2$$

resulting in

$$e^{(\alpha_1 - 1)\ln 2} = \sqrt{-\frac{\ln 2 \, \alpha_2}{\pi}}$$

from the first, and

$$\ln 2 \, \alpha_2 = -\frac{1}{2\sigma^2}$$

from the second. The resulting expression for $p(a)$ is

$$p(a) = \frac{e^{-a^2/2\sigma^2}}{\sigma \sqrt{2\pi}} \tag{4-24}$$

We should recognize Eq. 4-24 as the expression for a zero mean gaussian random variable. Note that this does not imply that we started with a zero mean variable, since we did not specify a constraint on the mean value. Remember also that the entropy function for continuous random variables is independent of translation by a constant! We will see later that this is a very significant result.

Finally we shall derive the mutual information $I(A, B)$ and show it to be a nonnegative and symmetric quantity, Property 4. When a particular value of the source is transmitted, with probability $p(a)\,(\Delta a)$, it is sent through a channel that may introduce a disturbance and cause some uncertainty as to what value was actually transmitted. This uncertainty as to what was transmitted when a certain value was received is expressed as

$$p(a/b)\,\Delta a \tag{4-25}$$

where b is the received value. Equation 4-25 is read as the probability that when value b is received the value transmitted was in the interval $(a, a + \Delta a)$. This uncertainty arises because of channel noise, and is loss of information. The net received self-information must then be the self-information transmitted, $-\log p(a)\Delta a$, minus the self-information lost, $-\log p(a/b)\Delta a$ or the net self-information received is

$$S(A, B) = \log \frac{p(a/b)\Delta a}{p(a)\Delta a} = \log \frac{p(a/b)}{p(a)}$$

The average self-information, the mutual information is thus

$$I(A, B) = \int_{-\infty}^{\infty} \int_{-\infty}^{\infty} p(a, b) \log \left(\frac{p(a/b)}{p(a)} \right) da\,db$$

$$= - \int_{-\infty}^{\infty} \int_{-\infty}^{\infty} p(a, b) \log p(a) \, da\,db + \int_{-\infty}^{\infty} \int_{-\infty}^{\infty} p(a, b) \log p(a/b) \, da\,db$$

$$= - \int_{-\infty}^{\infty} p(a) \log p(a) \, da \int_{-\infty}^{\infty} p(b/a) \, db$$

$$+ \int_{-\infty}^{\infty} \int_{-\infty}^{\infty} p(a, b) \log p(a/b) \, da\,db$$

or

$$I(A, B) = H(A) - \int_{-\infty}^{\infty} \int_{-\infty}^{\infty} p(a, b) \log \frac{1}{p(a/b)} \, da\,db$$

or

$$I(A, B) = H(A) - H(A/B) \qquad (4\text{-}26)$$

We see therefore that mutual information for a continuous channel takes on the same form as for the discrete channel. It is also easy to show that $I(A, B)$ is dependent only upon the channel-input probability density function for any given channel. Using Bayes' rule and the initial equation for $I(A, B)$, we have

$$p(a, b) = p(a) \, p(b/a)$$

and

$$\frac{p(a/b)}{p(a)} = \frac{p(b/a)}{p(b)} = \frac{p(b/a)}{\displaystyle\int_{-\infty}^{\infty} p(a, b) \, da}$$

or

$$\frac{p(a/b)}{p(a)} = \frac{p(b/a)}{\displaystyle\int_{-\infty}^{\infty} p(a) \, p(b/a) \, da}$$

and substituting into $I(A, B)$,

$$I(A, B) = \int_{-\infty}^{\infty} \int_{-\infty}^{\infty} p(a) \, p(b/a) \log \left(\frac{p(b/a)}{\displaystyle\int_{-\infty}^{\infty} p(a) \, p(b/a) \, da} \right) da\,db \qquad (4\text{-}27)$$

Thus we see that the only quantities involved are the channel probability $p(b/a)$, which is a constant for any given channel, and the input probability density function $p(a)$. We may also note that

$$\frac{p(a/b)}{p(a)} = \frac{p(b/a)}{p(b)}$$

and hence

$$I(A, B) = \int_{-\infty}^{\infty} \int_{-\infty}^{\infty} p(a, b) \log \left(\frac{p(a/b)}{p(a)}\right) da\,db$$

$$= \int_{-\infty}^{\infty} \int_{-\infty}^{\infty} p(a, b) \log \left(\frac{p(b/a)}{p(b)}\right) da\,db$$

$$= H(A) - H(A/B) = H(B) - H(B/A) \qquad (4\text{-}28)$$

Thus we see from Eq. 4-28 that $I(A, B)$ is symmetrical with respect to a and b. We may also define the channel capacity in the same manner as before and we have

$$C = \max_{p(a)} I(a, b)$$

where $\max\limits_{p(a)}$ denotes the maximumization of $I(A, B)$ with respect to $p(a)$ for a given channel.

Example 4-7

In Example 4-6 we found that a gaussian density function yields the maximum entropy if the mean square value is constrained to a given value. Calculate this entropy, the corresponding mutual entropy and the channel capacity.

The entropy may be calculated in the following manner:

$$H(A) = \int_{-\infty}^{\infty} p(a) \log \frac{1}{p(a)} da$$

$$= \int_{-\infty}^{\infty} \frac{e^{-a^2/2\sigma^2}}{\sqrt{2\pi}\,\sigma} \log \left(\sqrt{2\pi}\,\sigma\, e^{a^2/2\sigma^2}\right) da$$

$$= \int_{-\infty}^{\infty} \frac{e^{-a^2/2\sigma^2}}{\sqrt{2\pi}\,\sigma} \left[\log \left(\sqrt{2\pi}\,\sigma\right) + \log e^{a^2/2\sigma^2}\right] da$$

$$= \int_{-\infty}^{\infty} \frac{e^{-a^2/2\sigma^2}}{\sqrt{2\pi}\,\sigma} \log \left(\sqrt{2\pi}\,\sigma\right) da + \int_{-\infty}^{\infty} \frac{e^{-a^2/2\sigma^2}}{\sqrt{2\pi}\,\sigma} \left(\frac{a^2}{2\sigma^2}\right) \log e\, da$$

$$H(A) = \frac{1}{2} \log (2\pi \, \sigma^2) \int_{-\infty}^{\infty} \frac{e^{-a^2/2\sigma^2}}{\sqrt{2\pi} \, \sigma} \, da + \frac{1}{2\sigma^2} \log e \int_{-\infty}^{\infty} a^2 \frac{e^{-a^2/2\sigma^2}}{\sqrt{2\pi} \, \sigma} \, da$$

$$= \frac{1}{2} \log (2\pi \, \sigma^2) \int_{-\infty}^{\infty} p(a) \, da + \frac{\log e}{2\sigma^2} \int_{-\infty}^{\infty} a^2 \, p(a) \, da$$

$$= \frac{1}{2} \log (2\pi \, \sigma^2) + \left(\frac{\log e}{2\sigma^2} \right) \sigma^2$$

$$= \frac{1}{2} \log (2\pi \, \sigma^2) + \frac{1}{2} \log e = \frac{1}{2} \log (2\pi \, e\sigma^2)$$

$$\therefore H(A) = \frac{1}{2} \log (2\pi \, e\sigma^2) \tag{4-29}$$

The mutual information may be calculated directly if we assume that both the input processes and the output processes are jointly gaussian random variables with variances σ_a^2 and σ_b^2 respectively and correlation coefficient, ρ. The respective density functions are

$$p(a) = \frac{e^{-a^2/2\sigma_a^2}}{\sqrt{2\pi} \, \sigma_a}$$

$$p(b) = \frac{e^{-b^2/2\sigma_b^2}}{\sqrt{2\pi} \, \sigma_b}$$

and the joint density function[†] is

$$p(a,b) = \frac{e^{-\frac{1}{2(1-\rho^2)} \left[\frac{a^2}{\sigma_a^2} - 2\rho \frac{ab}{\sigma_a \sigma_b} + \frac{b^2}{\sigma_b^2} \right]}}{2\pi \, \sigma_a \, \sigma_b \sqrt{1-\rho^2}}$$

Since we may express $I(A, B)$ as (show this)

$$I(A, B) = - \int_{-\infty}^{\infty} \int_{-\infty}^{\infty} p(a,b) \log \frac{p(a) \, p(b)}{p(a,b)} \, da \, db$$

and

$$\log \left(\frac{p(a) \, p(b)}{p(a,b)} \right) = \frac{\ln \left(\frac{p(a) \, p(b)}{p(a,b)} \right)}{\ln 2}$$

$$= \left(\frac{1}{\ln 2} \right) \ln \frac{e^{-a^2/2\sigma_a^2 - b^2/2\sigma_b^2} \, (1 - \rho^2)^{1/2}}{e^{-1/2(1-\rho^2)} \, (a^2/\sigma_a^2 - 2\rho ab/\sigma_a \sigma_b + b^2/\sigma_b^2)}$$

[†]See appendix.

or

$$\log \left(\frac{p(a)\,p(b)}{p(a,b)}\right)$$

$$= \left(\frac{1}{\ln 2}\right) \left[\frac{1}{2}\ln(1-\rho^2) + \left(\frac{\rho^2}{2(1-\rho^2)}\right)\left(\frac{a^2}{\sigma_a^2} - \frac{2ab}{\rho\sigma_a\sigma_b} + \frac{b^2}{\sigma_b^2}\right)\right]$$

Therefore we have

$$I(A,B) = -\frac{\ln(1-\rho^2)}{2\ln 2} \int_{-\infty}^{\infty} \int_{-\infty}^{\infty} p(a,b)\,da\,db$$

$$-\left(\frac{\rho^2}{2(1-\rho^2)}\right) \int_{-\infty}^{\infty} \int_{-\infty}^{\infty} p(a,b)\left(\frac{a^2}{\sigma_a^2} - \frac{2ab}{\rho\sigma_a\sigma_b} + \frac{b^2}{\sigma_b^2}\right) da\,db$$

$$(4\text{-}30)$$

or

$$I(A,B) = \frac{\ln(1-\rho^2)}{2\ln 2} - \left(\frac{\rho^2}{2(1-\rho^2)}\right)(0)$$

or

$$I(A,B) = -\frac{\ln(1-\rho^2)}{2\ln 2} = -\frac{\log(1-\rho^2)}{2} \qquad (4\text{-}31)$$

Thus the mutual information for a gaussian input and gaussian output system with a correlation coefficient ρ between input and output depends only upon the correlation coefficient.

Now suppose we consider the noise entropy of the channel which is $H(B/A)$. This expression may be found from the difference between the entropy of the output and the mutual information. Since the output is assumed gaussian with variance σ_b^2 we may write the entropy directly as

$$H(B) = \tfrac{1}{2}\log(2\pi\,e\sigma_b^2)$$

and

$$H(B/A) = H(B) - I(A,B) = \frac{1}{2}\log(2\pi\,e\sigma_b^2) + \frac{\log(1-\rho^2)}{2}$$

or,

$$H(B/A) = \frac{\log 2\pi\,\sigma_b^2\,e(1-\rho^2)}{2}$$

Now suppose we assume that the input is modified by additive zero mean gaussian noise while traveling through the channel, and as a result the output is

$$b = a + N$$

Then the correlation coefficient is

$$\rho = \frac{E\,[(a)\,(a+N)]}{\sigma_a\,\sigma_b} = \frac{\sigma_a^2}{\sigma_a\,\sigma_b} = \frac{\sigma_a}{\sigma_b}$$

and

$$H(B/A) = \frac{\log\,[2\pi\,\sigma_b^2\,e(1-\rho^2)]}{2} = \frac{\log\,[2\pi\,\sigma_N^2 e]}{2}$$

For this case we see that the mutual information is

$$I(A,B) = \frac{1}{2}\log\left(1 + \frac{\sigma_a^2}{\sigma_N^2}\right)$$

but

$$\frac{\sigma_a^2}{\sigma_N^2} = S/\eta$$

where for zero mean random processes S is the signal power based on one ohm and η is the noise power based on one ohm.

Thus we see for a continuous channel with additive, white, zero mean gaussian noise with variance $\sigma_N^2 = \eta$ the mutual information is a function of the signal power to the noise power.

$$I(A,B) = \frac{1}{2}\log\left(1 + \frac{S}{\eta}\right)$$

and further that the channel capacity is

$$C = \max_{p\,(a)}\,I(A,B) = I(A,B) = \frac{1}{2}\log\left(1 + \frac{S}{\eta}\right) \qquad (4\text{-}32)$$

A remark about the units is in order. The channel capacity C, Eq. 4-32, has units of bits per sample. So far we have not introduced the concept of time or bandwidth in conjunction with the capacity. The systems we have been dealing with are continuous amplitude but time discrete systems and the capacity of Eq. 4-32 represents the maximum rate at which information may be transmitted per sample of the continuously varying amplitude. If we consider each sample that is taken as being statistically independent of the other samples and if we are taking and transmitting $2B$ samples per second, the channel capacity C in bits per second would be

$$C_t = 2BC = B\log\left(1 + \frac{S}{\eta}\right) \qquad (4\text{-}33)$$

It is also worth noting that if the white gaussian noise has power spectral density W watts per cycle, then the noise power is

$$\eta = WB \text{ watts}$$

Lest one jump to the conclusion that increasing the bandwidth to infinity would allow an infinite information rate, it is easy to show that this is not the case, that in fact the channel capacity is bounded.

$$\lim_{B \to \infty} C_t = \lim_{B \to \infty} B \log \left(1 + \frac{S}{\eta}\right)$$

$$= \lim_{B \to \infty} B \log \left(1 + \frac{S}{WB}\right)$$

$$= \lim_{B \to \infty} \frac{S}{\eta} \left[\frac{\eta B}{S} \log \left(1 + \frac{S}{WB}\right)\right] \qquad (4\text{-}34)$$

$$= (\log_2 e) \frac{S}{\eta} \left(\lim_{B \to \infty} \left[\frac{\eta B}{S} \ln \left(1 + \frac{S}{WB}\right)\right]\right)$$

or

$$\lim_{B \to \infty} C_t = 1.44 \left(\frac{S}{W}\right) \qquad (4\text{-}35)$$

Thus we see that after reaching a certain point increasing bandwidth gives limiting returns and the only way to further increase the channel capacity is to increase the signal to noise ratio.

4-6. REMARKS

In this chapter we have dealt with memory type sources and have determined several facts that show the similarity between special types of Markov sources and zero-memory sources. Namely we have shown that for regular Markov sources the source entropy is bounded by the same bound as that for zero-memory sources, log n. In Sec. 4-4 the interrelationship between information theory and coding is illustrated with a simple example.

In Sec. 4-5 we have developed the relationships for source entropy, mutual information, and channel capacity for the continuous channel. The source entropy for the continuous channel was seen to vary as we changed the source through transformations of random variables. Maximizations of the source entropy is more involved for the continuous channel, and we see that although the channel capacity is directly related to the channel bandwidth, we do not obtain infinite channel capacity with infinite channel bandwidth.

In the remainder of the text we shall be concerned with the subject of coding and its advantages.

```
C   EXAMPLE #4-1   HANDBALL PLAYER WITH PSYCHOLOGICAL HANGUP
      DIMENSION P(2,2,20)
      READ(5,1)   ((P(I,J,1),I=1,2),J=1,2)
1     FORMAT(4F10.8)
      K=1
100   K=K+1
      DO 102 J=1,2
      DO 102 I=1,2
      PROB=0.0
      DO 101 N=1,2
```

```
101     PROB=P(I,N,K-1)*P(N,J,1)+PROB
102     P(I,J,K)=PROB
        IF(K.LT.3)GO TO 100
        IFLAG=0
        DO 103 L=1,2
        DO 103 M=1,2
        PCHEK=ABS(P(L,M,K)-P(L,M,K-2))
103     IF(PCHEK.LE.0.0009)IFLAG=IFLAG+1
        IF(IFLAG.EQ.4)GO TO 200
        IF(20-K)200,200,100
200     WRITE(6,201)
201     FORMAT('1')
        KK=K
        K=-1
202     K=K+2
        K1=K+1
        WRITE(6,203)P(1,1,K),P(1,2,K),P(1,1,K1),P(1,2,K1)
203     FORMAT(' ',20X,'(',F5.3,1X,F5.3,1X,')',20X,'(',F5.3,
        11X,F5.3,1X,')')
        WRITE(6,204)K,K1
204     FORMAT(' ',6X,'FOR K=',I2,2X,'P = (',12X,')',6X,'FOR'
        2' K=',I2,2X,'P = (',12X,')')
        WRITE(6,203)P(2,1,K),P(2,2,K),P(2,1,K1),P(2,2,K1)
        WRITE(6,205)
205     FORMAT('0')
        KCHEK=KK-K1
        IF(KCHEK-1)400,302,202
302     K=K+2
        WRITE(6,303)P(1,1,K),P(1,2,K)
303     FORMAT(' ',20X,'(',F5.3,1X,F5.3,1X,')')
        WRITE(6,304)K
304     FORMAT(' ',6X,'FOR K=',I2,2X,'P = (',12X,')')
        WRITE(6,303)P(2,1,K),P(2,2,K)
        WRITE(6,205)
400     IF(KK.LT.20)GO TO 502
        WRITE(6,401)
401     FORMAT('0',,'AFTER 20 ATTEMPTS, A STATIONARY MATRIX '
        3'WAS NOT OBTAINED')
        GO TO 600
502     WRITE(6,303)P(1,1,KK),P(1,2,KK)
        WRITE(6,503)
503     FORMAT(' ',16X,'S = (',12X,')    THE STATIONARY MATRIX')
        WRITE(6,303)P(2,1,KK),P(2,2,KK)
600     STOP
        END
```

```
0.667      0.250      0.333      0.750
                 (  .667   .333  )                    (  .528   .472  )
    FOR K= 1   P = (              )       FOR K= 2   P = (              )
                 (  .250   .750  )                    (  .354   .646  )


                 (  .470   .530  )                    (  .446   .554  )
    FOR K= 3   P = (              )       FOR K= 4   P = (              )
                 (  .398   .602  )                    (  .416   .584  )


                 (  .436   .564  )                    (  .432   .568  )
    FOR K= 5   P = (              )       FOR K= 6   P = (              )
                 (  .423   .577  )                    (  .427   .573  )


                 (  .430   .570  )                    (  .429   .571  )
    FOR K= 7   P = (              )       FOR K= 8   P = (              )
                 (  .428   .572  )                    (  .428   .572  )


                 (  .429   .571  )                    (  .429   .571  )
    FOR K= 9   P = (              )       FOR K=10   P = (              )
                 (  .429   .571  )                    (  .429   .571  )


                 (  .429   .571  )
        S = (              )       THE STATIONARY MATRIX
                 (  .429   .571  )
```

PROBLEMS

4-1.   Consider the three-state discrete-transition Markov process shown below. Determine the three-step transition probabilities $p_{11}(3)$, $p_{12}(3)$, $p_{13}(3)$ both from a sequential sample space and by using Eq. 4-5.

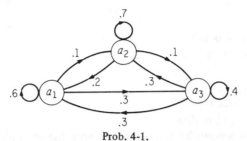

Prob. 4-1.

4-2.   Identify the transient, recurrent, and periodic states of the discrete-state discrete-transition Markov process described by

$$[P]^1 = \begin{bmatrix} 0.5 & 0 & 0 & 0 & 0.5 & 0 & 0 \\ 0.3 & 0.4 & 0 & 0 & 0.2 & 0.1 & 0 \\ 0 & 0 & 0.6 & 0.2 & 0 & 0.2 & 0 \\ 0 & 0 & 0 & 0.5 & 0 & 0 & 0.5 \\ 0.3 & 0.4 & 0 & 0 & 0.3 & 0 & 0 \\ 0 & 0 & 0.4 & 0.6 & 0 & 0 & 0 \\ 0 & 0 & 0 & 0.6 & 0 & 0 & 0.4 \end{bmatrix}$$

4-3.   A first-order Markov source with alphabet $A = \{a_1, a_2\}$ has a transition matrix P as

$$[P]^1 = \begin{bmatrix} 1 - p & p \\ q & 1 - q \end{bmatrix}$$

(a) Prove that the stationary source probabilities are $p(a_1) = q/(p + q)$ and $p(a_2) = p/(p + q)$.

(b) Draw the state diagram and find the source entropy $H(A)$. Plot $H(A)$ versus p for $p = q$.

4-4.   Draw a Markov diagram for a game of tennis. Assume that a player has a probability of .60 for winning each point. Find the probability of winning a game.

4-5.   If a chain has a transition probability matrix as shown determine whether the chain is regular or ergodic. Find the S matrix,

$$[P] = \begin{bmatrix} 0 & 1 \\ 1 & 0 \end{bmatrix}$$

4-6. A first-order Markov source has alphabet $A = \{a_1, a_2, a_3\}$ with initial probabilities $p_1 = 1/3$, $p_2 = 16/27$, $p_3 = 2/27$ and transition matrix

$$[P] = \begin{bmatrix} 0 & 4/5 & 1/5 \\ 1/2 & 1/2 & 0 \\ 1/2 & 2/5 & 1/10 \end{bmatrix}$$

(a) How many possible states are there?
(b) Draw the state diagram.
(c) Write a typical sequence.
(d) Is the source ergodic?
(e) Is the source regular?
(f) Find the $[S]$ matrix.

4-7. Consider a second-order Markov source with the same alphabet and initial probability vector as in Prob. 4-6. The symbol transition probabilities are

	a_1	a_2	a_3
$a_1 a_1$	1/6	1/2	1/3
$a_1 a_2$	1/4	1/4	1/2
$a_1 a_3$	1/5	2/5	2/5
$a_2 a_1$	1/4	1/8	5/8
$a_2 a_2$	2/7	2/7	3/7
$a_2 a_3$	1/2	1/4	1/4
$a_3 a_1$	1/2	1/3	1/6
$a_3 a_2$	1/5	1/5	3/5
$a_3 a_3$	1/3	1/3	1/3

(a) Draw the state diagram.
(b) Show that this source is regular. (See John B. Thomas, *Introduction to Statistical Communication Theory*, Wiley, New York, 1969, p. 509.)

4-8. Prove the relation $|J(A/B)|\, J(B/A) = \pm 1$

4-9. Given the random variables A and B and the transformation

$$b_i = \sum_{j=1}^{n} c_{ij} a_j \qquad i = 1, 2, \ldots, n$$

where $A = \{a_1, a_2, \ldots, a_n\}$
$B = \{b_1, b_2, \ldots, b_n\}$
Find $H(B)$ in terms of $H(A)$ and the coefficients c_{ij}.

4-10. Find the probability density functions $\rho(a)$ that maximizes the entropy of the source $A = \{a\}$ if the source variable has the following constraints:
(a) If the source variable is restricted to a maximum value $|E|$.
(b) If the source variable is restricted to positive values and a maximum value E.

(c) If the source variable is restricted such that it has a constant mean and only positive values.

4-11. Prove Eq. 4-31 by showing that the second integral of Eq. 4-30 is zero and that the logarithms transform as indicated in Eq. 4-31.

4-12. Prove Eq. 4-35 starting with Eq. 4-34.

4-13. Using your digital computer facility write a program to calculate the channel capacity versus bandwidth using Eq. 4-34. Increase the bandwidth in increments until the limiting value of the channel capacity is closely approximated.

CHAPTER 5

Codes—Basic Definitions, Theorems, and Techniques

5-1. INTRODUCTION

In our everyday life we are not much concerned with accurate transmission of information. The main reason is the redundancy in what we usually use for communication—the English language. In conversation, lectures, or in radio, television and telephone communications we may miss several words or even sentences yet still grasp the meaning or intent of the message. Our concern with accuracy increases when we deal with more precise languages such as numbers. In scanning the stock market quotations, the misreading of a few digits in the Dow Jones averages or in the listings for our personal stocks could have a marked effect upon financial status.

As we strive to send more information in a shorter time we are forced to eliminate unnecessary redundancy in our language. However, as our language becomes less redundant, errors in transmission become more serious.

The primary objectives in coding are twofold—increase in the efficiency of the communication system and reduction of errors in transmission.

The large-scale use of digital computers in industry has promoted interest and a need for error control of the binary language which computers use. Each digit is important, and much care is taken to prevent accidental alteration of these digits. Several methods of reducing errors are the increase of channel power and heavy shielding to reduce noise interference, but these methods are costly. With a small reduction in information transfer efficiency, perhaps 10 percent, less expensive channels may be used with high reliability by the use of error-correcting codes.

In the area of military communications the high reliability of information transfer necessary may not always be purchased with higher power levels, but may be achieved with error-correcting coding techniques.

Perhaps the most popular conception of codes and their application are in the area of national security—secret service or espionage operations.

During the Civil War a Union spy dressed as a Confederate captain sent bogus orders from the telegraph office in Richmond to confound the defense strategy during Grant's final siege. From this small beginning, the science of military codes and coding progressed to a level in World War II where U.S. cryptographers were able to break the complicated Japanese code (without the enemy's knowledge) by building a duplicate of the Japanese coding machine without ever having seen one. (See the selected reading list.)

Today there are literally acres of high-speed computer facilities at the National Security Agency used only for military and national security intelligence.

Thus the three facets of coding are interwoven combinations of efficiency, reliability, security.

The original concepts of coding theory were not immediately followed by widespread adoption by the engineering confraternity. There were several reasons for this slow acceptance of coding theory, among them the difficulty of finding methods of decoding that were not too complicated for implementation, and the lack of white gaussian noise channels. Unfortunately most channels of interest were not and are not modeled by white gaussian noise. It was the interest in space missions that gave us the apparently classical white gaussian noise channel.

There are two schools of endeavor in the area of coding, the block-code school and the convolutional-code school. In general terms, block codes are generated by use of the properties and structure of abstract algebra and include such codes as parity check codes, cyclic codes, and group codes. The convolutional codes are not as well understood or developed on a theoretical basis as the block codes but they are usually simpler to construct and perform well.

At this point, very general definitions of block codes and convolutional codes might be clarifying.

DEFINITION. A *block code* is one in which a particular message from a source is always coded into the same fixed sequence of code symbols. Thus if we have sixteen messages and use a four-digit binary code to represent these messages by writing the binary equivalent of the message number for the code word, we have a block code. For this code we always send the code word 1011 for message number eleven.

DEFINITION. A *convolutional code* is one in which there are no distinct blocks.

Typically we construct a convolutional code by preparing checking numbers for each information digit as it arrives at the transmitting point. These checking numbers are computed by using the incoming digit and one or more digits that have preceded or follow the incoming digit. Thus each message is in a sense coded not independently of the preceding or following message but dependently with the preceding or following message. Thus a message will most probably be coded into different code words at different times. The number of information digits used in computing the checking numbers defines the constraint length of the convolutional code.

A typical communication system including coding is illustrated in Fig. 5-1.

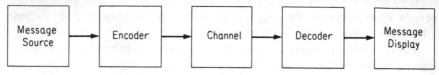

Fig. 5-1. Communication system with coding.

If we assume the output of the message source is an information rate of R bits per second which will pass to an encoder which has a code rate of k/n (i.e., the encoder will add $n - k$ check bits for every k information bits) then the transmitted rate will be nR/k bits per second. (Note that if the encoder adds $n - R$ bits to each R bits of input the output rate will be $n - R + R = n$ bits per second.)

In this chapter the basic definitions and theorems of coding theory will be presented and the following chapters will endeavor to present some of the methods of encoding and decoding.

5-2. BASIC DEFINITIONS AND THEOREMS

Before discussing codes we must define our terminology. In Fig. 5-2 the subgroupings of the general field of codes is illustrated, the definitions of which

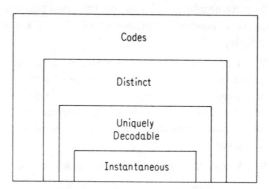

Fig. 5-2. Subgroupings of codes.

follow. The reader can find two or more sets of terminology of codes and sub-grouping of codes in the literature and in current texts. For instance, Reza[14] presents one set of terms such as coding, block codes, separable or uniquely decipherable codes, and irreducible codes (or codes having the prefix property), while Abramson[16] gives a set of roughly analogous terms such as codes, block codes, singular codes, uniquely decodable codes, instantaneous codes. The author has used a set of terms analogous to those of Abramson for various reasons—they are more up to date and there are some advantages to the definitions.

The most general group of Fig. 5-2 is that of codes. We may define a code as:

DEFINITION. A *code* is a mapping (assignment) of words from the source alphabet into the words of the code alphabet. More basically, a code is a mapping of source-symbol sequences into code-symbol sequences. (See also *IRE Standards Dictionary.*)

Let us designate $A = \{a_1, a_2, \ldots, a_q\}$ as the source alphabet and $C = \{c_1, c_2, \ldots, c_r\}$ as the code alphabet. Then a code may be illustrated as in Fig. 5-3.

The above definition is very broad and includes many undesirable properties. For instance, the sequence of symbols from Fig. 5-3, code *A*

$$01000110010 \tag{5-1}$$

may be decoded in several ways.

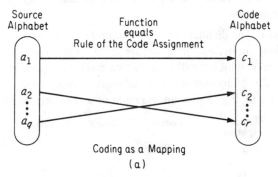

Coding as a Mapping
(a)

Source	Code *A*	Code *B*
a_1	0	0
a_2	01	1
a_3	10	1

A Trinary Source Alphabet and Binary Code Alphabets

(b)

Fig. 5-3. A trinary source alphabet and binary code alphabets.

The sequence of Eq. 5-1 may be either

$$a_1 a_3 a_1 a_2 a_3 a_2 a_1$$

or

$$a_2 a_1 a_1 a_2 a_3 a_1 a_3$$

Recovery of the original message is not guaranteed by the definition for a code. Obviously we need to make some further restrictions so that useful codes are guaranteed, but first let a definition for "word" be offered, since we are using the term a great deal.

DEFINITION. A *word* is a finite sequence of symbols from an alphabet. Thus if the alphabet is $A = \{a_1, a_2, a_3, a_4\}$ then some possible words are:

$$a_1, a_3, a_1 a_3 a_4, a_2 a_3 a_1 a_5, a_1 a_1 a_1, \text{etc.}$$

From Fig. 5-3 we see that Code B, while satisfying the definition of a code, has two members which are not distinct. This would automatically preclude recovery of the original message and hence must be restricted in some manner.

DEFINITION. A code is *distinct* if each word of the code is distinguishable from other code words. Thus code A is distinct but code B is not.

However, we still have the problem of recovering the original message from a sequence of code words such as Eq. 5-1. This difficulty may be overcome with the following restriction.

DEFINITION. A distinct code is *uniquely decodable* if every word is identifiable when immersed in a sequence of code words. Thus any two sequences of source symbols will lead to two distinct sequences of code words, and thus we are able to recover our original message every time.

For example, in Fig. 5-4 is an example of a uniquely decodable code. If

Source Symbols	Code A	Code B	Code C
a_1	00	10	1
a_2	01	100	01
a_3	10	1000	001
a_4	11	1100	0001

Fig. 5-4. Uniquely decodable codes.

two source sequences are sent as shown the corresponding code word sequences would be as shown.

$a_1 a_3 a_4 a_2 a_1$	Source sequence
0010110100	Code A sequence
101000110010010	Code B sequence
$a_1 a_3 a_4 a_1 a_2$	Source sequence
0010110001	Code A sequence
101000110010100	Code B sequence

Since we know the first and last digits of the sequences we are able to recover the original message in each case. However, we are not able to decode the code sequences on a word-by-word basis as the sequences arrive, since we must know the next digit in some instances before we know whether a word has ended or not. Such is the case when receiving the code B sequence for a source sequence of $a_2a_1a_3$, 100101000. The fourth digit must be received before we know whether an a_2 or an a_3 was sent first. The restriction of having to wait for an arriving sequence to be completely received before decoding produces a time lag which is undesirable. This time lag can be eliminated if we restrict ourselves further in the type of codes we use.

DEFINITION. A uniquely decodable code is *instantaneously decodable* if the end of any code word is recognizable without the need of inspection of succeeding code symbols.

In Fig. 5-4 the code C is an instantaneously decodable code. Consider any sequence, upon receipt of the 1 we know immediately that the code word has ended and we may state the corresponding source word immediately rather than waiting for the next code symbol, which we know will be a 0.

The requirement for instantaneous decodability may be stated in another fashion: a code is instantaneously decodable if no code word may be formed by adding code alphabet symbols to another code word. Thus we say no code word is a prefix to another. Instantaneously decodable codes are said to have the *prefix property.*

We know that the prefix property is a necessary condition for instantaneously decodable codes, since a code that does not have the prefix property will have at least two words such that one of them is contained as the front part of the other. Thus we will have to wait at least one digit more than the shorter word length before we can say which word was received. That the prefix property is sufficient follows from the definition of an instantaneously decodable code, which merely states that each code word can be recognized immediately upon its complete receipt without need to refer to the next digit that follows. Since a code with the prefix property has no words that are prefixes of another code word, we will be able to recognize any code word immediately.

Thus the prefix property is a necessary and sufficient condition for a code to be instantaneously decodable.

Our desire is to construct optimal codes where optimal codes are defined as follows.

DEFINITION. A code is said to be *optimal* if it has two properties—if it is instantaneously decodable, and if it has minimum average length L for a given source with a given probability assignment for the source symbols.

It is easily shown that optimal codes have the shorter code words assigned to the higher probability source symbols.

Proof. Assume that the source symbol a_i has a probability of occurrence

$p(a_i)$ and has a code word assigned to it of length l_i and that source symbol a_j with probability $p(a_j)$ has a code word of length l_j. If $p(a_i) > p(a_j)$, then let $l_i < l_j$.

The average length L_1 is

$$L_1 = l_i p(a_i) + l_j p(a_j)$$

If the word assignments are interchanged so that symbol a_i is assigned the code word of length l_j and a_j with l_i, then the average length is

$$L_2 = l_j p(a_i) + l_i p(a_j)$$

Then the difference $L_2 - L_1$ is positive, and hence the assignment of source symbols and code-word lengths corresponding to the average length L_1 is shorter, which is a requirement for optimal codes.

$$L_2 - L_1 = l_j p(a_i) + l_i p(a_j) - l_i p(a_i) - l_j p(a_j)$$
$$= (l_j - l_i) p(a_i) - (l_j - l_i) p(a_j)$$
$$= [p(a_i) - p(a_j)] (l_j - l_i)$$

but $p(a_i) > p(a_j)$ and $l_j > l_i$ by assumption. Therefore $L_2 - L_1 > 0$.

The necessary and sufficient conditions for the existence of an instantaneously decodable code have been shown by Kraft[17]. These conditions are proven in the form of a theorem.

Theorem 1. Given a source with alphabet $A = \{a_1, a_2, \ldots, a_m\}$. Assume that the assigned code-word lengths corresponding to the symbols $a_1, a_2, \ldots, a_m$ are $l_1, l_2, \ldots, l_m$ respectively, and further assume that the code alphabet C has r members, or $C = \{c_1, c_2, \ldots, c_r\}$.

A necessary and sufficient condition for the *existence* of an instantaneous code with word lengths $l_1, l_2, \ldots, l_m$ is

$$\sum_{i=1}^{m} r^{-l_i} \leqslant 1 \qquad (5\text{-}2)$$

Eq. 5-2 is called the *Kraft inequality*.

Proof. Let us arrange the code words in ascending order of word length so that we will have an ordered set of m positive integers $\{l_1, l_2, \ldots, l_m\}$, where each integer $l_1, l_2, \ldots$, etc. correspond to the code-word lengths and $l_1 \leqslant l_2 \leqslant \ldots \leqslant l_m$.

Since our code alphabet has only r symbols, we can have a *most r* instantaneously decodable sequences of length one, otherwise the prefix property would be violated if we used r symbols for $r + 1$ or more one symbol sequences.

Let n_K denote the actual number of encoded messages (code words) of length K. Then we know

$$n_K \leqslant r$$

(If the code alphabet is binary with symbols $c_1 = 0$, $c_2 = 1$ then we have $n_1 = 2$ and the two words of length one are c_1 and c_2 respectively.)

The number of actual instantaneously decodable two symbol words (instantaneously distinguishable from each other and from the n_1 words) must obey the rule

$$n_2 \leqslant (r - n_1) r = r^2 - n_1 r$$

since the first symbol of the two symbol words may be picked in $r - n_1$ ways (the remaining code symbols after assigning n_1 of the code symbols to one symbol words) and the second symbol may be picked from the code alphabet at random and hence in r ways.

The number of actual instantaneously decodable three-symbol words (instantaneously distinguishable from each other and from the n_1 and n_2 words) must obey the rule

$$n_3 \leqslant [(r - n_1) r - n_2] \, r = r^3 - n_1 \, r^2 - n_2 r$$

since the first two symbols may be chosen in $(r - n_1) r - n_2$ ways (the symbols remaining after creating the n_1 and n_2 words) and the third element in r ways. [Note that if the number of two symbol words n_2 created were equal to $(r - n_1)r$ rather than being less than $(r - n_1)r$, then we would not be able to make any three-symbol words since $(r - n_1)r$ would equal n_2 and hence $n_3 \leqslant 0$.]

In general,

$$n_K \leqslant r^K - n_1 r^{K-1} - \cdots - n_{K-1} r$$

or rewriting,

$$n_K r^{-K} \leqslant 1 - n_1 r^{-1} - \cdots - n_{K-1} r^{1-K}$$

or

$$n_K r^{-K} + n_{K-1} r^{-(K-1)} + n_{K-2} r^{-(K-2)} + \cdots + n_1 r^{-1} \leqslant 1$$

or

$$\sum_{j=1}^{K} n_j \, r^{-j} \leqslant 1 \qquad (5\text{-}3)$$

Remembering that n_K is a number (a positive integer in fact) we may rewrite Eq. 5-3 as

$$\overset{\text{1st}\quad\text{2nd}\qquad\qquad\qquad n_1\text{th}\;(n_1+1)\text{th}\qquad\qquad\;(n_1+n_2)\text{th}\qquad\qquad\qquad\qquad n_m\text{th}}{\sum_{j=1}^{K} n_j r^{-j} = \underbrace{r^{-1}+r^{-1}+\cdots+r^{-1}}_{n_1\text{ times}} + \underbrace{r^{-2}+r^{-2}+\cdots+r^{-2}}_{n_2\text{ times}} + \cdots + \underbrace{r^{-K}+r^{-K}+\cdots+r^{-K}}_{n_K\text{ times}}}$$

$$= \sum_{i=1}^{n_1} r^{-1} + \sum_{i=1}^{n_2} r^{-2} + \cdots + \sum_{i=1}^{n_K} r^{-K} \tag{5-4}$$

In Eq. 5-4 we have singled out some of the members so that it may be realized that the superscript of the first term is simply minus the length of the first code word l_1, of the second term is simply minus the length of the second code word l_2, and etc., until we have the last term, which has a superscript of minus the length of the mth code word l_m. Remember that we arranged the order of the code words in ascending order of length, and that n_K stands for the actual number of words of length K code symbols. Therefore (since we have one code word for every source symbol),

$$n_1 + n_2 + \cdots + n_K = \text{total number of code words} = m$$

Since Eq. 5-4 is actually m terms each of the form r^{-l_i}, where i varies from 1 to m, we may write Eq. 5-4 as

$$\sum_{j=1}^{K} n_j r^{-j} = \sum_{i=1}^{m} r^{-l_i} \tag{5-5}$$

From Eq. 5-3 we know that

$$\sum_{i=1}^{m} r^{-l_i} \leqslant 1 \tag{5-6}$$

Equation 5-6 tells us that the set of positive integers l_i must satisfy this inequality and thus proves the necessary part of the theorem. The sufficient part of this theorem is shown when we realize that the inequality was derived by a procedure that produced instantaneously decodable code words.

Although the Kraft inequality assures us of the existence of an instantaneously decodable code with code-word lengths that satisfy the inequality, it does *not* show us how to obtain these code words *nor* does it say that any code that has word lengths that satisfy the inequality is automatically instantaneously decodable.

The following examples illustrate the use of the Kraft inequality and also illustrate the above points.

Example 5-1

Let us consider an information source with symbols $A = \{a_1, a_2, a_3, a_4\}$. Table 5-1 lists four possible codes for encoding the source into a binary alphabet.

TABLE 5-1. Possible Codes of the Four-Symbol Source

Source Symbols	Code A	Code B	Code C	Code D	Code Word
a_1	00	0	0	0	1
a_2	01	100	100	10	2
a_3	10	110	110	110	3
a_4	11	111	11	11	4

By applying the Kraft inequality to the above codes we will see that codes A, B, and C all satisfy the inequality but that only A and B are indeed instantaneously decodable and that C is not. (Note that both codes C and D violate the prefix property.) Code D will not satisfy the inequality.

For code A,

$$\sum_{i=1}^{m} r^{-l_i} = \sum_{i=1}^{4} 2^{-l_i} = 2^{-l_1} + 2^{-l_2} + 2^{-l_3} + 2^{-l_4}$$

But $l_1 = 2, l_2 = 2, l_3 = 2, l_4 = 2$, and hence

$$\sum_{i=1}^{4} 2^{-l_i} = 2^{-2} + 2^{-2} + 2^{-2} + 2^{-2} = 1$$

For code B,

$$\sum_{i=1}^{m} r^{-l_i} = \sum_{i=1}^{4} 2^{-l_i} = 2^{-l_1} + 2^{-l_2} + 2^{-l_3} + 2^{-l_4}$$

but $l_1 = 1, l_2 = 3, l_3 = 3, l_4 = 3$, and hence

$$\sum_{i=1}^{4} 2^{-l_i} = 2^{-1} + 2^{-3} + 2^{-3} + 2^{-3} = 7/8 < 1$$

For code C,

$$\sum_{i=1}^{m} r^{-l_i} = \sum_{i=1}^{4} 2^{-l_i} = 2^{-1} + 2^{-3} + 2^{-3} + 2^{-2} = 1$$

For code D,

$$\sum_{i=1}^{m} r^{-l_i} = \sum_{i=1}^{4} 2^{-l_i} = 2^{-1} + 2^{-2} + 2^{-3} + 2^{-2} = 1\tfrac{1}{8}$$

Example 5-2

Suppose you are a liaison officer to an unfriendly nation. You are supplied with the following messages to send over a Morse code set. You decide to encode these messages into an instantaneously decodable code.

Message	Code
1. Nothing of interest	.
2. Troops are moving North	− .
3. Troops are moving South	− − . . .
4. Troops are moving East	− − − . .
5. Troops are moving West	− − − − .
6. I think I am in trouble	− − − . −
7. Send help immediately	− − . . −
8. Too late to send help	− − . − −

Since Morse code is made up of two symbols, we shall let the dot represent the most frequent message which is number 1. (Believe it or not—read documented cases if you don't.)

Using the procedure we used in proving the Kraft inequality, this means that we may pick $n_2 \leqslant 4 - 2 = 2$ words of length 2. If we pick both of these words as two-symbol words it will not leave any unused prefixes for the remainder of the message. Hence we pick one of the two, − . , for the next most common message number 2. (This country is located in Southern Hemisphere). (Note we could not pick a . − or we would violate prefix property.)

Using the Kraft inequality, we may now derive the length of the remaining six code words if we assume some lengths for them. Let them all be equal in length.

$$\sum_{i=1}^{8} 2^{-l_i} = 2^{-1} + 2^{-2} + (6)\, 2^{-l_i} \leqslant 1$$

or

$$2^{-l_i} \leqslant \frac{1 - 2^{-1} - 2^{-2}}{6} = \tfrac{1}{24}$$

or

$$2^{l_i} \geqslant 24$$

or

$$l_i \geqslant 5$$

Thus an instantaneously decodable code with the code-word lengths of 1 symbol, 2 symbol, and the remaining code words with length 5 symbols exist. Now we must find the remaining code words. The inequality does not tell us how to find these code words, but trial and error will help now and later we shall see a method by which we may derive such a code. The remaining words are shown opposite their message.

The above code is not optimum even though it is instantaneously decodable, since if we assume messages 3 through 6 are equally likely, it is possible to derive a code with shorter average length.

The Kraft inequality shows the necessary and sufficient condition for the existence of an instantaneously decodable code. Since these codes are also uniquely decodable it follows that the Kraft inequality is also a sufficient condition for the existence of uniquely decodable codes. McMillan[18] has shown that the inequality is also a necessary requirement for the existence of uniquely decodable codes.

For any given source alphabet and code alphabet we are able to construct many codes that are instantaneously decodable. However, to achieve an optimal code we need to construct the instantaneously decodable code which has the shortest average length. How do we recognize this code when we have it? In Chapter 4 we stated the existence of a lower bound on average code length for a given source alphabet and code alphabet. We shall now prove that lower bound and show that it may be our test for optimal codes.

DEFINITION. Let a code map the source symbols $A = \{a_1, a_2, \ldots, a_q\}$ into the code *words* $C = \{c_1, c_2, \ldots, c_q\}$. If the probabilities of occurrence of the source symbols are $p(a_1), p(a_2), \ldots, p(a_q)$ and the *lengths* of the code words are $l_1, l_2, \ldots, l_q$, then the average length of the code is defined by:

$$L = \sum_{i=1}^{q} p(a_i)\, l_i \tag{5-7}$$

and remembering that an instantaneously decodable code will be called *optimal* if its average length is less than or equal to the average length of all other instantaneously decodable codes for the same source and the same code alphabet, we see that we have defined our coding problem as one of finding optimal codes. Note that both definitions refer *only* to the code word lengths and not to the code words themselves.

Now we shall prove the statement of the lower bound for L that we mentioned in Chapter 4.

Theorem 2. Consider a source $A = \{a_1, a_2, \ldots, a_q\}$ with message probabilities $p(a_1), p(a_2), \ldots, p(a_q)$. Suppose we encode these symbols into a set of code words $C = \{c_1, c_2, \ldots, c_q\}$ using a code alphabet of r symbols, and let the code-word lengths be $l_1, l_2, \ldots, l_q$.

The lower bound of the average code-word length is given by,

$$L \geqslant \frac{H(A)}{\log r}$$

Proof:

The source entropy may be written as

$$H(A) = - \sum_{i=1}^{q} p_i \log p_i$$

where $p_i \equiv p(a_i)$.

In Lemma 8, Chapter 2, we proved the following inequality:

$$- \sum_{i=1}^{q} p_i \log p_i \leqslant - \sum_{i=1}^{q} p_i \log q_i \qquad (5\text{-}8)$$

Since the q_i's are any set of positive numbers such that $\sum_{i=1}^{q} q_i = 1$, we may define the q_i's as any set of such numbers we desire. Thus let

$$q_i = \frac{r^{-l_i}}{\displaystyle\sum_{j=1}^{q} r^{-l_j}} \qquad (5\text{-}9)$$

Note these are a set of nonnegative numbers which do sum to one over all i. Using the defined value for q_i we may write the source entropy as

$$H(A) \leqslant - \sum_{i=1}^{q} p_i \log q_i = - \sum_{i=1}^{q} p_i \log \frac{r^{-l_i}}{\displaystyle\sum_{j=1}^{q} r^{-l_j}}$$

or

$$H(A) \leqslant (\log r) \sum_{i=1}^{q} p_i l_i + \sum_{i=1}^{q} p_i \log \left(\sum_{j=1}^{q} r^{-l_j} \right)$$

or

$$H(A) \leqslant (\log r) \sum_{i=1}^{q} p_i l_i + \log \sum_{j=1}^{q} r^{-l_j}$$

But $\displaystyle\sum_{j=1}^{q} r^{-l_j}$ must be less than or at most equal to 1 for instantaneously de-codable codes. Therefore the quantity

$$\log \sum_{j=1}^{q} r^{-l_j} \leqslant 0$$

Hence

$$H(A) \leqslant (\log r) \sum_{i=1}^{q} p_i l_i = (\log r) L$$

or,

$$L \geqslant \frac{H(A)}{\log r} \qquad (5\text{-}10)$$

Achievement of the lower bound occurs only for the particular case where

$$p(a_i) = r^{-l_i} \text{ and } \sum_{j=1}^{q} r^{-l_j} = 1 \qquad \text{for all } i$$

since this is the case when $p_i = q_i$, and hence equality of Eq. 5-10 holds. In general this will not be the case since if $p(a_i) = r^{-l_i}$, then

$$l_i = -\log_r p(a_i)$$

and we must choose the word lengths to be $-\log_r p(a_i)$.
For the equality to hold therefore, the quantity

$$-\log_r p(a_i)$$

must be an integer for each i.

Example 5-3

Consider code B of Table 5-1. If we assign the source symbol proba-bilities as follows:

$$p(a_1) = \tfrac{1}{2}, \ \ p(a_2) = \tfrac{1}{4}, \ \ p(a_3) = \tfrac{1}{8}, \ \ p(a_4) = \tfrac{1}{8}$$

then the entropy of the source is:

$$H(A) = -\sum_{i=1}^{4} p(a_i) \log p(a_i)$$

$$= -\tfrac{1}{2} \log \tfrac{1}{2} - \tfrac{1}{4} \log \tfrac{1}{4} - \tfrac{1}{8} \log \tfrac{1}{8} - \tfrac{1}{8} \log \tfrac{1}{8}$$

$$= .500 + .500 + .375 + .375$$

or

$$H(A) = 1.750.$$

Since the code alphabet consists of a 0 and a 1, we have

$$\log r = \log 2 = 1.000$$

Thus

$$\frac{H(A)}{\log r} = \frac{1.750}{1.000} = 1.750$$

The average length may be calculated as

$$L = \sum_{i=1}^{4} p(a_i) \, l_i = \tfrac{1}{2} \, (1) + \tfrac{1}{4} \, (3) + \tfrac{1}{8} \, (3) + \tfrac{1}{8} \, (3)$$

$$= .500 + .750 + .375 + .375$$

$$= 2.000$$

Thus we see the inequality is strict, since

$$L = 2.000 > 1.750 = \frac{H(A)}{\log r}$$

Example 5-4

Consider the following code for the source with the following source probabilities:

Source Symbols	Source Probabilities	Code
a_1	$\frac{1}{2}$	0
a_2	$\frac{1}{4}$	10
a_3	$\frac{1}{8}$	110
a_4	$\frac{1}{8}$	111

The average length is:

$$L = \tfrac{1}{2} \, (1) + \tfrac{1}{4} \, (2) + \tfrac{1}{8} \, (3) + \tfrac{1}{8} \, (3)$$

$$= .500 + .500 + .750$$

$$= 1.750.$$

The source entropy is:

$$H(A) = - \tfrac{1}{2} \log \tfrac{1}{2} - \tfrac{1}{4} \log \tfrac{1}{4} - \tfrac{1}{8} \log \tfrac{1}{8} - \tfrac{1}{8} \log \tfrac{1}{8}$$

$$= 1.750$$

The code alphabet has two symbols, hence,

$$\log r = \log 2 = 1.000$$

Thus we see the equality is strict, since

$$L = 1.750 = \frac{H(A)}{\log r}$$

We have derived the lower bound for the average length of a code and some interesting results are gained by considering the possible values of L which result. The average length of a code may be expressed as a fraction of a code bit per source symbol, but we know that each individual code word will have an integral number of code bits. Thus we are faced with the problem of what to chose for the value of l_i, the number of code bits in code word i corresponding to source symbol a_i, when the quantity

$$l_i = -\log_r p_i$$

is not an integer. Suppose we chose l_i to be the next integer greater than the value $-\log_r p_i$. If this is the case we have

$$-\log_r p_i \leqslant l_i \leqslant -\log_r p_i + 1$$

or,

$$\frac{-\log p_i}{\log r} \leqslant l_i \leqslant \frac{-\log p_i}{\log r} + 1$$

or,

$$-\sum_{i=1}^{q} \frac{p_i \log p_i}{\log r} \leqslant \sum_{i=1}^{q} l_i p_i \leqslant -\sum_{i=1}^{q} \frac{p_i \log p_i}{\log r} + \sum_{i=1}^{q} p_i$$

or,

$$\frac{H(A)}{\log r} \leqslant L \leqslant \frac{H(A)}{\log r} + 1 \tag{5-11}$$

If we now consider the entropy of the nth extension of the source $H(A^n) = nH(A)$ the above relation then becomes

$$\frac{H(A)}{\log r} \leqslant \frac{L(n\text{th})}{n} \leqslant \frac{H(A)}{\log r} + \frac{1}{n} \tag{5-12}$$

where $L(n\text{th})$ is the average length of a code word of the nth extension.

Equation 5-12 is usually termed the *noiseless coding theorem* and is the embodiment of what is referred to as *Shannon's first theorem*. (It is appropriate here to point out to the reader that we have not considered any effects of noise on our codes. We have only considered how to most efficiently encode our source. Later we shall deal with error-detecting and correcting codes which consider errors caused by noise, its effects, and how to detect and correct these errors.)

SHANNON'S FIRST THEOREM (Noiseless Coding Theorem)

Given a code with an alphabet of r symbols and a source with an alphabet of q symbols the average length of the code words per source symbols may be made as arbitrarily close to the lower bound $H(A)/\log r$ as desired by encoding extensions of the source (sequences of source symbols) rather than encoding each source symbol individually. The drawback is the increased complexity of the encoding procedure and in the increased time required for encoding and transmitting the signal.

So far we have dealt only with the word lengths and we have not seen any prescribed method for generating such code words, much less any techniques for obtaining optimal codes. In the next section we shall deal with several code-generating techniques. Shannon's binary encoding method is presented as an introduction and for historical interest. The Shannon-Fano code and Huffman's minimum-reduction coding method are presented because they are methods that may produce optimum codes for discrete message ensembles.

5-3. SOME BASIC CODES AND THEIR CONSTRUCTION

Shannon proposed a method of code construction for binary codes which is based upon Eq. 5-11. The technique is easy to use and produces codes which are fairly efficient. The procedure is as follows:

1. List the source symbols in order of decreasing probabilities (if two or more symbols are equal in probability of occurrence it does not matter which is written first.) Thus

$$p(a_1) \geqslant p(a_2) \geqslant p(a_3) \geqslant \cdots \geqslant p(a_q)$$

2. Compute a set of numbers, α_i's in the following manner:

$$\alpha_1 = 0$$
$$\alpha_2 = p(a_1) + 0 = p(a_1) + \alpha_1$$
$$\alpha_3 = p(a_2) + p(a_1) = p(a_2) + \alpha_2$$
$$\vdots \qquad \vdots \qquad \vdots$$
$$\alpha_{q+1} = p(a_q) + p(a_{q-1}) + \cdots + p(a_1) = p(a_q) + \alpha_q$$

3. Determine a set of integers l_i which are the smallest integers that satisfy the inequality

$$2^{l_i} p(a_i) \geqslant 1 \qquad \text{for } i = 1, 2, 3, \ldots, q$$

Thus if the probabilities $p(a_1) = .5$ and $p(a_2) = .4$, we would have

$$2^{l_1} (.5) \geqslant 1 \longrightarrow l_1 = 1$$
$$2^{l_2} (.4) \geqslant 1 \longrightarrow l_2 = 2$$

where the l_i's are the word lengths of the code words of the corresponding source symbols. Thus the length l_2 of the code word for source symbol a_2 would be two code symbols.

4. Expand the decimal numbers α_i in binary form to l_i places only! Thus if $\alpha_2 = .625$ and $l_2 = 2$ we would express α_2 in binary form as

Integer		Decimal Value		Binary Equivalent
α_2	=	.625	=	.10|1

Note the following equivalents:

Decimal Value	Binary Equivalent
1.00	1.0
2.00	10.0
4.00	100.0
0.50	0.1
0.25	0.01

The code word for the source symbol a_2 would be $W_2 = 10$ using only the first l_2 places of the binary equivalent of the decimal number α_2.

Example 5-5

Consider the source $A = \{a_1, a_2, a_3, a_4\}$ with probabilities $\{p(a_i)\} = \{.5, .3, .1, .1\}$. Determine a binary code for this source using Shannon's method.

a_1	.5	$\alpha_1 = 0$	$2^{l_1}\,(.5) \geqslant 1 \longrightarrow l_1 = 1$
a_2	.3	$\alpha_2 = .5$	$2^{l_2}\,(.3) \geqslant 1 \longrightarrow l_2 = 2$
a_3	.1	$\alpha_3 = .8$	$2^{l_3}\,(.1) \geqslant 1 \longrightarrow l_3 = 4$
a_4	.1	$\alpha_4 = .9$	$2^{l_4}\,(.1) \geqslant 1 \longrightarrow l_4 = 4$
		$\alpha_1 = .0\|000$	$W_1 = 0$
		$\alpha_2 = .10\|00$	$W_2 = 10$
		$\alpha_3 = .1100\|1$	$W_3 = 1100$
		$\alpha_4 = .1110\|0$	$W_4 = 1110$

The average length of this code is

$L = 1(.5) + 2(.3) + 4(.1) + 4(.1) = 1.9$ code bits/source symbols, and $H(A) = -.5 \log .5 - .3 \log .3 - .1 \log .1 - .1 \log .1 = 1.685$ and $\log 2 = 1.0$

Therefore

$$L = 1.9 > \frac{H(A)}{\log r} = 1.685$$

The Shannon-Fano encoding method is useful for constructing fairly efficient codes and if the equality holds

$$p(a_i) = r^{-l_i} \qquad i = 1, 2, \ldots, q \qquad (5\text{-}13)$$

the resulting code is optimum. The procedure is outlined below and the two examples which follow serve to illustrate the optimal result and the nonoptimal result.

1. List the source symbols in order of decreasing probabilities:

$$p(a_1) \geqslant p(a_2) \geqslant \cdots \geqslant p(a_q)$$

2. List the r code symbols in a fixed order:

$$c_1, c_2, \ldots, c_r$$

3. Partition the set of source symbols a_i into r groups with equal probabilities. Thus each group has probability $1/r$. If Eq. 5-13 holds then this partition is always possible. If Eq. 5-13 does not hold for all i, a fairly efficient code may still be constructed by partitioning the source symbols into r most equiprobable groups.
4. Now assign the code symbols to the r groups as c_1 as the first digit for members of group 1, c_2 as the first digit for members of group 2, etc.
5. Each group is now treated in a similar manner using steps 3 and 4 repeatedly, with each application deciding one additional code digit in the sequence.

Example 5-6

Consider a source alphabet $A = \{a_1, a_2, \ldots, a_8\}$ with probabilities $\{p(a_i)\} = \{\frac{1}{4}, \frac{1}{4}, \frac{1}{8}, \frac{1}{8}, \frac{1}{16}, \frac{1}{16}, \frac{1}{16}, \frac{1}{16}\}$.

Source Symbols	Probabilities	Step 1	Step 2	Step 3	Step 4
a_1	$\frac{1}{4}$	0	00	00	00
a_2	$\frac{1}{4}$	0	01	01	01
a_3	$\frac{1}{8}$	1	10	100	100
a_4	$\frac{1}{8}$	1	10	101	101
a_5	$\frac{1}{16}$	1	11	110	1100
a_6	$\frac{1}{16}$	1	11	110	1101
a_7	$\frac{1}{16}$	1	11	111	1110
a_8	$\frac{1}{16}$	1	11	111	1111

Step 4 contains the code words derived by the technique when Eq. 5-13 holds for all i. The result is an optimum code, since

$$L = 2(\tfrac{1}{4}) + 2(\tfrac{1}{4}) + 3(\tfrac{1}{8}) + 3(\tfrac{1}{8}) + 4(\tfrac{1}{16}) + 4(\tfrac{1}{16})$$
$$+ 4(\tfrac{1}{16}) + 4(\tfrac{1}{16}) = 2\tfrac{3}{4},$$

and

$$H(A) = 2\tfrac{3}{4}$$
$$\log r = 1$$

Example 5-7

Consider a source alphabet $A = \{a_1, a_2, \ldots, a_7\}$ with probabilities $\{p(a_i)\} = \{.4, .2, .12, .08, .08, .08, .04\}$.

Source Symbols	Probabilities	Step 1	Step 2	Step 3	Step 4
a_1	.4	0	00	00	00
a_2	.2	0	01	01	01
a_3	.12	1	10	100	100
a_4	.08	1	10	101	101
a_5	.08	1	11	110	110
a_6	.08	1	11	111	1110
a_7	.04	1	11	111	1111

Step 4 contains the code words but the result is not an optimum code, since

$$L = 2(.4) + 2(.2) + 3(.12) + 3(.08) + 3(.08) + 4(.08) + 4(.04) = 2.52$$

and

$$H(A) = 2.42$$

$$\log 2 = 1$$

A code of shorter average length may be constructed by letting the first partition fall between a_1 and a_2 rather than between a_2 and a_3.

The Huffman minimum-redundancy code is a procedure that guarantees an optimal code even if Eq. 5-13 is not satisfied for all i. The procedure is outlined below and consists of a step-by-step source reduction followed by a code construction, starting with the reduced source and working backward to the original source.

1. List the source symbols in order of decreasing probabilities.
2. List the r code symbols in a fixed order.
3. Since we want to reduce the source until we have r symbols left the original source must have a particular number of symbols to start with. The required number of symbols may be determined by realizing that as we make each reduction we will reduce the number of symbols by $r - 1$, since each reduction will consist of adding the r least likely symbol probabilities and reordering the resulting $q - (r - 1)$ probabilities. This is done an integral number of times, α, until we are reduced to r symbols. Thus the required number of starting symbols is

$$M = r + \alpha(r - 1)$$

If the number of source symbols $q \neq M$ then we merely add dummy source symbols with zero probability until we have the required number. After the encoding procedure we may ignore these dummy symbols.

4. Now assign the first code symbol c_1 as the first digit in the code word for all the source symbols associated with the first probability of the reduced source, c_2 as the first digit in the code word for all the second probability symbols, etc.

5. We now work our way back to the original source in this manner.

Example 5-8

Consider a source with alphabet $A = \{a_1, a_2, \ldots, a_{11}\}$ with probabilities as shown. Let the code alphabet be $\{0, 1, 2, 3\}$

Source Symbol	Probability	Code Word	Reduced Source 1	Code Word	Reduced Source 2	Code Word	Reduced Source 3	Code Word
a_1	.25	1	.25	1	.25	1	.37	0
a_2	.15	3	.15	3	.23	2	.25	1
a_3	.12	00	.12	00	.15	3	.23	2
a_4	.10	01	.10	01	.12	00	.15	3
a_5	.08	02	.08	02	.10	01		
a_6	.06	20	.07	03	.08	02		
a_7	.06	21	.06	20	.07	03		
a_8	.06	22	.06	21				
a_9	.05	23	.06	22				
a_{10}	.04	030	.05	23				
a_{11}	.03	031						
dummy $\{$ a_{12}	0	032						
symbols $\{$ a_{13}	0	033						

Note that $11 \neq 4 + \alpha(4 - 1) = 4 + 3\alpha$, where α is any integer.

Thus we added two source symbols since then.

$$13 = 4 + \alpha(4 - 1) = 4 + 3\alpha$$

where $\alpha = 3$ reductions.

A decoding algorithm for the Huffman code is presented at the end of this section for those interested in the decoding problem.[†] It is one thing to encode and a different matter to decode.

5-4. REMARKS

In this chapter we have introduced the basics of noiseless coding. The basic terminology of codes such as distinct, uniquely decodable, instantaneous has been presented and we have seen that coding is in essence a mapping of a word from one alphabet to another.

The requirements for a code to be instantaneously decodable were derived,

[†]Courtesy of Mr. Keith Hall, graduate student of Mississippi State University.

and a lower bound on code-word lengths was found. From this lower bound we were able to produce Eq. 5-12, which is the basis of Shannon's first (noiseless coding) theorem, and some basic codes were presented: Shannon's binary code construction, the Shannon-Fano encoding method, and the Huffman minimum redundancy code.

At this point we are ready to consider what the effects of noise on our codes might be and how we can overcome these effects. Shannon's first theorem is followed by his second theorem in Chapter 6, which deals with noisy coding techniques.

```
C   THIS PROGRAM DECODES A HUFFMAN CODE USING A GIVEN TABLE
C   AND THE TREE SEARCH METHOD
C   ****************************************************
C   PROB. *LETTER*HUFF. CODE    *   PROB. *LETTER*HUFF. CODE
C   ****************************************************
C   0.1589* SPACE* 000          *   0.0574*  N  * 1001
C   0.0642*  A  * 0100          *   0.0632*  O  * 0110
C   0.0127*  B  * 011111        *   0.0152*  P  * 011110
C   0.0218*  C  * 11111         *   0.0008*  Q  * 0111001101
C   0.0317*  D  * 01011         *   0.0484*  R  * 1101
C   0.1031*  E  * 101           *   0.0514*  S  * 1100
C   0.0208*  F  * 001100        *   0.0796*  T  * 0010
C   0.0152*  G  * 011101        *   0.0228*  U  * 11110
C   0.0467*  H  * 1110          *   0.0083*  V  * 0111000
C   0.0575*  I  * 1000          *   0.0175*  W  * 001110
C   0.0008*  J  * 0111001110    *   0.0013*  X  * 0111001100
C   0.0049*  K  * 01110010      *   0.0164*  Y  * 001111
C   0.0321*  L  * 01010         *   0.0005*  Z  * 0111001111
C   0.0198*  M  * 001101        *   AVERAGE LENGTH = 4.1195
C   ****************************************************
C
C   THE ABOVE TABLE WAS TAKEN FROM THE FOLLOWING REFERENCE
C   REFERENCE:  REZA, 'AN INTRODUCTION TO INFORMATION THEORY'
C
C   M(I) IS THE BINARY BIT (0 OR 1) BEING OBSERVED    I=1,2,--L
C   Y(J) IS THE ALPHABET LETTER (OR SPACE) BEING FORMED FROM
C   THE CODE.
C
        DIMENSION M(320),Y(100)
        READ(5,99980)L
99980 FORMAT(I3)
99981 READ(5,99982) (M(I),I=1,L)
99982 FORMAT(60I1)
        WRITE(6,99983)
99983 FORMAT('1','THE MESSAGE TO BE DECODED IS:'/)
        WRITE(6,99984) (M(I),I=1,L)
99984 FORMAT(' ',60I1)
        WRITE(6,99985)
99985 FORMAT('0',23X,'I',5X,'J',5X,'Y(J)')
        N=L+1
        I=0
        J=0
        GO TO 99003
99001 WRITE(6,99002)I,J,Y(J)
99002 FORMAT(' ',21X,I3,5X,I3,5X,A1)
        IF(I.EQ.L)GO TO 99991
        IF(I.GT.L)GO TO 99989
99003 I=I+1
        J=J+1
1       IF(M(I).EQ.1)GO TO 12
11      I=I+1
        IF(I.EQ.N)GO TO 99989
        IF(M(I).EQ.1)GO TO 22
21      I=I+1
        IF(I.EQ.N)GO TO 99989
        IF(M(I).EQ.1)GO TO 32
```

```
 31     Y(J)=' '
        GO TO 99001
 12     I=I+1
        IF(I.EQ.N)GO TO 99989
        IF(M(I).EQ.1)GO TO 24
 23     I=I+1
        IF(I.EQ.N)GO TO 99989
        IF(M(I).EQ.1)GO TO 36
 35     I=I+1
        IF(I.EQ.N)GO TO 99989
        IF(M(I).EQ.1)GO TO 410
409     Y(J)='I'
        GO TO 99001
 36     Y(J)='E'
        GO TO 99001
410     Y(J)='N'
        GO TO 99001
 24     I=I+1
        IF(I.EQ.N)GO TO 99989
        IF(M(I).EQ.1)GO TO 38
 37     I=I+1
        IF(I.EQ.N)GO TO 99989
        IF(M(I).EQ.1)GO TO 414
413     Y(J)='S'
        GO TO 99001
414     Y(J)='R'
        GO TO 99001
 38     I=I+1
        IF(I.EQ.N)GO TO 99989
        IF(M(I).EQ.1)GO TO 416
415     Y(J)='H'
        GO TO 99001
416     I=I+1
        IF(I.EQ.N)GO TO 99989
        IF(M(I).EQ.1)GO TO 532
531     Y(J)='U'
        GO TO 99001
532     Y(J)='C'
        GO TO 99001
 22     I=I+1
        IF(I.EQ.N)GO TO 99989
        IF(M(I).EQ.1)GO TO 34
 33     I=I+1
        IF(I.EQ.N)GO TO 99989
        IF(M(I).EQ.1)GO TO 406
405     Y(J)='A'
        GO TO 99001
406     I=I+1
        IF(I.EQ.N)GO TO 99989
        IF(M(I).EQ.1)GO TO 512
511     Y(J)='L'
        GO TO 99001
512     Y(J)='D'
        GO TO 99001
 34     I=I+1
        IF(I.EQ.N)GO TO 99989
        IF(M(I).EQ.1)GO TO 408
407     Y(J)='O'
        GO TO 99001
408     I=I+1
        IF(I.EQ.N)GO TO 99989
        IF(M(I).EQ.1)GO TO 516
515     I=I+1
        IF(I.EQ.N)GO TO 99989
        IF(M(I).EQ.1)GO TO 630
629     I=I+1
        IF(I.EQ.N)GO TO 99989
        IF(M(I).EQ.1)GO TO 758
757     Y(J)='V'
        GO TO 99001
630     Y(J)='G'
        GO TO 99001
```

```
758     I=I+1
        IF(I.EQ.N)GO TO 99989
        IF(M(I).EQ.1)GO TO 8116
8115    Y(J)='K'
        GO TO 99001
8116    I=I+1
        IF(I.EQ.N)GO TO 99989
        IF(M(I).EQ.1)GO TO 9232
9231    I=I+1
        IF(I.EQ.N)GO TO 99989
        IF(M(I).EQ.1)GO TO 10462
10461   Y(J)='X'
        GO TO 99001
10462   Y(J)='Q'
        GO TO 99001
9232    I=I+1
        IF(I.EQ.N)GO TO 99989
        IF(M(I).EQ.1)GO TO 10464
10463   Y(J)='J'
        GO TO 99001
10464   Y(J)='Z'
        GO TO 99001
516     I=I+1
        IF(I.EQ.N)GO TO 99989
        IF(M(I).EQ.1)GO TO 632
631     Y(J)='P'
        GO TO 99001
632     Y(J)='B'
        GO TO 99001
32      I=I+1
        IF(I.EQ.N)GO TO 99989
        IF(M(I).EQ.1)GO TO 404
403     Y(J)='T'
        GO TO 99001
404     I=I+1
        IF(I.EQ.N)GO TO 99989
        IF(M(I).EQ.1)GO TO 508
507     I=I+1
        IF(I.EQ.N)GO TO 99989
        IF(M(I).EQ.1)GO TO 614
613     Y(J)='F'
        GO TO 99001
614     Y(J)='M'
        GO TO 99001
508     I=I+1
        IF(I.EQ.N)GO TO 99989
        IF(M(I).EQ.1)GO TO 616
615     Y(J)='W'
        GO TO 99001
616     Y(J)='Y'
        GO TO 99001
99989   WRITE(6,99990)
99990   FORMAT('0','THIS IS NOT A VALID ENCODING OF A MESSAGE')
        GO TO 99999
99991   WRITE(6,99992)
99992   FORMAT('0'///)
        WRITE(6,99993)
99993   FORMAT('0','THE DECODED MESSAGE IS:'/)
        K=J
        WRITE(6,99994) (Y(J),J=1,K)
99994   FORMAT(' ',60A1)
99999   STOP
        END


306
0100011111111111000010111010011000000111011110100000001110011
1001110010010100000011011001011000011110011100110111101000011
0000101111000001110000011100111001100000001111011100111100000
0001110011110011110000111001100001110011100000011110000101100
0001101011100110101111000001101001001101000010100111001001110
001110
```

THE MESSAGE TO BE DECODED IS:

```
010001111111111000010111010011000000111011110100000001110011
100111001001010000001101100101100000111100111001101110100011
000010111100000111000001110011100110000000111101110011110000
000111001111001111000011100110000011100111000000011110001011100
000110101110011010101110000011010010011010000010100111001001111
001110
```

I	J	Y(J)
4	1	A
10	2	B
15	3	C
18	4	
23	5	D
26	6	E
32	7	F
35	8	
41	9	G
45	10	H
49	11	I
52	12	
62	13	J
70	14	K
75	15	L
78	16	
84	17	M
88	18	N
92	19	O
95	20	
101	21	P
111	22	Q
115	23	R
118	24	
122	25	S
126	26	T
131	27	U
134	28	
141	29	V
147	30	W
157	31	X
160	32	
166	33	Y
176	34	Z
179	35	
182	36	
192	37	Z
198	38	Y
201	39	
211	40	X
217	41	W
224	42	V
227	43	
232	44	U
236	45	T
240	46	S
243	47	
247	48	R
257	49	Q
263	50	P
266	51	
270	52	O
274	53	N
280	54	M
283	55	
288	56	L
296	57	K
306	58	J

THE DECODED MESSAGE IS:

ABC DEF GHI JKL MNO PQR STU VWX YZ ZY XWV UTS RQP ONM LKJ

PROBLEMS

5-1. Listed below are several possible code outputs of a source with indicated probabilities.
(a) Which codes are uniquely decodable?
(b) Which are instantaneously decodable?
(c) Calculate the average length of each of the codes of part (a).

Source Symbol	$P(a_i)$	B	C	D	E	F
a_1	$\frac{1}{2}$	000	0	1	0	0
a_2	$\frac{1}{4}$	001	10	10	100	10
a_3	$\frac{1}{8}$	010	110	100	101	110
a_4	$\frac{1}{16}$	011	1110	1000	110	1110
a_5	$\frac{1}{16}$	100	11110	10000	111	1011

5-2. For the codes that are not uniquely decodable or instaneously decodable in Prob. 5-1, write a sequence of symbols that illustrates the problem.

5-3. Which of the following sets of word lengths are acceptable for the existence of an instantaneous code? The code alphabet is $A = \{0, 1, 2\}$.

	Number of Words of Length l_i		Word Length, l_i
Code B	Code C	Code D	
2	2	1	1
1	2	4	2
2	2	6	3
4	3	0	4
1	1	0	5

5-4. Derive a shorter average length code for Example 5-2.

5-5. Prove that q_i of Eq. 5-9 sums to unity over all i.

5-6. Using Shannon's encoding method, determine a binary code for the source $A = \{a_1, a_2, a_3, a_4\}$ with probabilities $\{p_i\} = \{0.4, 0.3, 0.1, 0.2\}$.

5-7. Calculate the average length of the code derived for Prob. 5-6.

5-8. For the following source alphabet A, find the Shannon, Shannon-Fano, and Huffman binary codes.

Symbol	Probability
a_1	.22
a_2	.16
a_3	.15
a_4	.13
a_5	.12
a_6	.09
a_7	.08
a_8	.05

5-9. Calculate the average length and efficiency of the codes derived in Prob. 5-8.

5-10. Find an optimum binary code for the source $A = \{a_1, a_2, a_3\}$ with probabilities $\{p_i\} = \{.5, .2, .3\}$.

CHAPTER 6

Advanced Codes and Their Schemes

6-1. INTRODUCTION

In this chapter we are going to treat the problem of encoding for noisy channels; that is, what do we do when our receiver emits a symbol? That is a question that has been handled by a class of codes usually termed *error-detection and correcting codes*.

We introduce the chapter with a discussion of the probability of error in receiving a symbol and assigning to it a source symbol, the decision rule, a relationship between this probability of error and the channel capacity (Fano bound), and a discussion of Shannon's second, or noisy coding, theorem. The remainder of the chapter will discuss different methods of constructing error-detection and correction codes.

6-2. BASIC THEOREMS FOR NOISY CODING

For the sake of illustration let us consider an AM type of pulse-modulating system such that we have four possible signals to transmit—a zero-volt pulse, a 5-volt pulse, a 10-volt pulse, and a 15-volt pulse. To these various levels we may assign various symbols as shown in Fig. 6-1a. In Fig. 6-1b we see that the received signal may vary in amplitude by an amount ρ equal to $d/2$ before we are unable to tell which symbol was transmitted. If we are sending these signals over an atmospheric path for which statistical information of the amplitude of the noise is known we may compute the probability of noise distorting our signal by the amount ρ. From this information we may derive a channel matrix with which to model our transmission of information.

The reception of an output symbol is used to determine an input symbol. The method of determination is called the decision rule. If we denote the as-

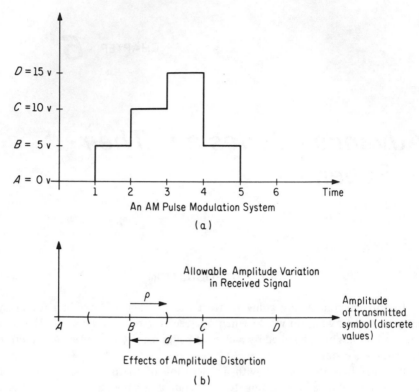

Fig. 6-1. Effects of amplitude distortion.

sumed source symbol to be a^*, then we may choose a^* by the rule

$$p(a^*/b_j) \geqslant p(a_i/b_j) \qquad \text{for all } i \qquad (6\text{-}1)$$

It can be shown that this decision rule minimizes the probability of error of the channel. The channel error may be expressed as

$$p(E) = \sum_j p(E/b_j)p(b_j)$$

where $p(E/b_j)$ is the probability of making an error when a b_j is received. Now it is true that

$$p(a^*/b_j) + \sum_{\substack{\text{over} \\ \text{remaining} \\ i}} p(a_i/b_j) = 1$$

since we must have transmitted one of the source symbols. Hence the term $p(E/b_j)$ is

$$p(E/b_j) = \sum_{\substack{\text{over} \\ \text{remaining} \\ i}} p(a_i/b_j) = 1 - p(a^*/b_j) \qquad (6\text{-}2)$$

Thus the error for a specific decision rule is

$$p(E/b_j)_{a^*} = 1 - p(a^*/b_j) \leqslant 1 - p(a_i/b_j) = p(E/b_j)_{a_i}$$

Now using Bayes' theorem we may write Eq. 6-1 as

$$p(a^*/b_j) = \frac{p(a^*)p(b_j/a^*)}{p(b_j)} \geqslant \frac{p(a_i)p(b_j/a_i)}{p(b_j)}$$

or for equally likely input source symbols,

$$p(a_i) = 1/q$$

and

$$p(a^*/b_j) = \frac{p(b_j/a^*)}{q\,p(b_j)}$$

and Eq. 6-2 becomes

$$p(E/b_j)_{a^*} = 1 - \frac{p(b_j/a^*)}{q\,p(b_j)}$$

and the probability of error is

$$p(E) = \sum_j p(b_j)\left[1 - \frac{p(b_j/a^*)}{q\,p(b_j)}\right]$$

or

$$p(E) = 1 - \frac{1}{q}\sum_j p(b_j/a^*) \qquad (6\text{-}3)$$

Equation 6-3 is the probability of error for a channel with q equally likely source symbols and the decision rule of Eq. 6-1. The decision rule of Eq. 6-1 is termed the *ideal observer decision rule*.†

Example 6-1
Consider the amplitude modulation system of Fig. 6-1. If the transmission noise is distributed such that p (noise < 0) $= 0, p$ (noise < 2.5 v) $= \frac{3}{4}$, p (2.5 v $\leqslant$ noise < 7.5 v) $= \frac{3}{16}$, and p (7.5 v $\leqslant$ noise < 12.5 v) $= \frac{1}{16}$, and p (noise $\geqslant 12.5$ v) $= 0$ then we could model the channel with the fol-

†The decision rule $p(b_j/a^*) \geqslant p(b_j/a_i)$ for all i is termed the maximum likelihood decision rule and is commonly encountered.

lowing channel matrix:

Output

$$
\begin{array}{c} & \begin{array}{cccc} b_1 & b_2 & b_3 & b_4 \end{array} \\ \text{Input} \begin{array}{c} a_1 \\ a_2 \\ a_3 \\ a_4 \end{array} & \left[\begin{array}{cccc} 3/4 & 3/16 & 1/16 & 0 \\ 0 & 3/4 & 3/16 & 1/16 \\ 0 & 0 & 3/4 & 1/4 \\ 0 & 0 & 0 & 1 \end{array} \right] \end{array}
$$

If we have equally likely source symbols then the probability of making an error when using the maximum likelihood decision rule would be,

$$
p(E) = 1 - \tfrac{1}{4} \sum_{j=1}^{4} p(b_j/a^*)
$$

where the decision rule is as follows

$$
p(b_1/a_1) > p(b_1/a_2) = p(b_1/a_3) = p(b_1/a_4)
$$

Then for reception of b_1 we assign $a^* = a_1$. Likewise for reception of the remaining symbols we make the following assignments:

b_j	a^*
b_1	a_1
b_2	a_2
b_3	a_3
b_4	a_4

The probability of error then becomes

$$
p(E) = 1 - \tfrac{1}{4} \left[p(b_1/a_1) + p(b_2/a_2) + p(b_3/a_3) + p(b_4/a_4) \right]
$$
$$
= 1 - \tfrac{1}{4} \left[3/4 + 3/4 + 3/4 + 1 \right] = 1 - 13/16 = 3/16
$$

If we have as a channel matrix

Output

$$
\begin{array}{c} & \begin{array}{cccc} b_1 & b_2 & b_3 & b_4 \end{array} \\ \text{Input} \begin{array}{c} a_1 \\ a_2 \\ a_3 \\ a_4 \end{array} & \left[\begin{array}{cccc} 3/4 & 3/16 & 1/16 & 0 \\ 0 & 1/4 & 3/4 & 0 \\ 0 & 3/4 & 0 & 1/4 \\ 0 & 0 & 1/4 & 3/4 \end{array} \right] \end{array}
$$

the decision rules would be

b_j	a^*
b_1	a_1
b_2	a_3
b_3	a_2
b_4	a_4

and the probability of error would be

$$p(E) = 1 - \frac{1}{4}\left[\frac{3}{4} + \frac{3}{4} + \frac{3}{4} + \frac{3}{4}\right]$$

$$= 1 - \frac{12}{16} = \frac{4}{16}$$

The relationship between the probability of making an error in the channel and the rate at which information is sent over the channel has been shown by Fano and the mathematical expression is known as the *Fano bound*. This bound is related to Shannon's second theorem and will be illustrated next in anticipation of Shannon's second theorem.

The expression for the conditional probability of making an error when assigning one of m possible input symbols as corresponding to an output symbol (decoding) may be expressed as[†]

$$p(E/b_j) = 1 - p(a_j/b_j) = \sum_{i \neq j} p(a_i/b_j)$$

The conditional entropy $H(A/B)$ is by definition

$$H(A/B) = \sum_j H(A/b_j)\, p(b_j)$$

where

$$H(A/b_j) = - \sum_i p(a_i/b_j) \log p(a_i/b_j)$$

Now let us rewrite the above equation utilizing the above expression for $p(E/b_j)$:

$$H(A/b_j) = - p(a_j/b_j) \log p(a_j/b_j) - \sum_{i \neq j} p(a_i/b_j) \log p(a_i/b_j)$$

$$= - [1 - p(E/b_j)]\, \log [1 - p(E/b_j)] - \sum_{i \neq j} p(a_i/b_j) \log p(a_i/b_j)$$

If we add and subtract the term

$$p(E/b_j) \log p(E/b_j)$$

[†] The derivation has been drawn from Fano.[19]

we have

$$H(A/b_j) = - [1 - p(E/b_j)] \log [1 - p(E/b_j)] - p(E/b_j) \log p(E/b_j)$$

$$- p(E/b_j) \sum_{i \neq j} \frac{p(a_i/b_j)}{p(E/b_j)} \log \frac{p(a_i/b_j)}{p(E/b_j)} \qquad (6\text{-}4)$$

The summation on the right-hand side of Eq. 6-4 is the entropy of $m - 1$ terms (the mth term $i = j$ is not allowed). The maximum entropy of $m - 1$ symbols is $\log (m - 1)$. Hence,

$$H(A/b_j) \leqslant - [1 - p(E/b_j)] \log [1 - p(E/b_j)] - p(E/b_j) \log p(E/b_j)$$

$$+ p(E/b_j) \log (m - 1)$$

Now inserting the above equation into the equation for $H(A/B)$ and averaging with respect to the output symbols b_j we have

$$H(A/B) \leqslant - \sum_j ([1 - p(E/b_j)] \log [1 - p(E/b_j)] - p(E/b_j) \log p(E/b_j)) p(b_j)$$

$$+ \sum_j p(E/b_j) \log (m - 1) p(b_j)$$

But we may consider the first summation as the entropy of a binary decision. The decision is one of error versus no error. Hence if we denote this as $H[p(E/B)]$ we have

$$H(A/B) \leqslant H[p(E/B)] + p(E) \log (m - 1)$$

We know from Sec. 2-5, Remark 4, that $H(p(E)/B) \leqslant H[p(E)]$. Hence we have the final result

$$H(A/B) \leqslant H[p(E)] + p(E) \log (m - 1) \qquad (6\text{-}5)$$

Equation 6-5 is known as the *Fano bound*.

The meaning of Eq. 6-5 may be explained as follows. The quantity $H(A/B)$ is the equivocation or the average uncertainty about the transmitted symbol, averaged over all the received signals. Thus this quantity yields a measure of information lost in the transmission of a symbol through the channel, or equivalently it is the average additional information needed at the decoder to determine which symbol was sent.

The Fano bound is the upper limit on this average amount of additional information required. It is composed of two parts, $H[p(E)]$ and $p(E) \log (m - 1)$. $H[p(E)]$ is the average amount of information required just to determine whether or not an error was made in transmission. The remaining term on the right is the additional amount of information required to determine which of the remaining $m - 1$ symbols was sent in the case when an error was made.

Since the channel capacity is related to the mutual information $I(A/B)$, which in turn is related to the equivocation, $H(A/B)$, the Fano bound relates the probability of making an error with the channel's capacity.

The noisy-coding theorem, Shannon's second theorem, proves that channel capacity is a fundamental property of an information channel. In fact the theorem states that it is *possible* to transmit information through the channel with as small a probability of error as we desire if we transmit at any rate less than the channel capacity. While this statement at first seems to offer a cure for all the problems of sending information over noisy channels in an error-free manner, we must realize that it does not. The theorem merely states that we are guaranteed the *existence* of a code that may be transmitted at any rate close to but less than that of channel capacity and still be received and decoded with arbitrarily small probability of error—it does *not* give us a method of finding this code scheme.

The proof of this theorem for the general channel is quite involved and lengthy. Rather than working through the general proof we shall discuss in detail the simple but very useful BSC and then present a formal statement of the theorem.

Let a source consist of a finite set of m messages $S = \{s_1, s_2, s_3, \ldots, s_m\}$. It will be assumed that the occurrence of these messages is independent and equally likely. This last assumption may be satisfied by encoding an original source alphabet A into long sequences. For instance, each message s_r may consist of a sequence of a_k's so that

$$s_r = a_1 a_2 a_3 \cdots a_p$$

where the length p of the message s_r may be large. Then the source entropy is given by

$$H(S) = \log m$$

since all the messages are equally likely.

Each of the messages will be encoded into a code word by what is commonly referred to as *Shannon's random encoding method*. Each word is encoded into a sequence of n binary digits for transmission over the BSC channel. The number of possible code words of length n is 2^n and the number of messages is m, so the number of binary digits required is found from choosing n such that the number of possible code words is greater than or equal to the number of messages:

$$2^n \geq m$$

or,

$$n \geq \log m$$

Shannon's random encoding method is simply the assumption that the code words will be assigned at random, that is, the probability that a particular n-place code word, out of the 2^n-possible code words, will be chosen to represent a specific message s_r out of the m possible messages is equal to $m/2^n$.

Note that Shannon's random encoding method is no surefire formula for finding our code, since we must allow each code word of the 2^n possible code words to be available for assignment to each of the m messages. Thus it is possible, though very unlikely, that we might assign the same code word to each of the m messages! (What would the probability of this unusual event be?) If the same code word is assigned to more than one message we would then have a nondistinct code, which of course is very undesirable. (What is the probability that one of the 2^n code words would be assigned to two messages? What relation between m and 2^n is highly desirable for this type of coding?)

As previously stated the channel to be used is a BSC type with the probability of a correct output for an input equal to p and of an incorrect output for an input equal to $q = 1 - p$,

$$[p\{y_i/x_j\}] = \begin{bmatrix} p & 1-p \\ 1-p & p \end{bmatrix}$$

The criterion for decision of which message was sent given a received message is based upon finding the source message which differs from the received message in the least number of binary digits.

Thus the calculation of the probability of an erroneous decision is essentially a calculation of the probability of receiving exactly r digits that have been altered in transmission and $n - r$ digits that have not been altered—that is, the probability of receiving an n-digit code word with exactly r errors in the n digits. This is a familiar problem in statistics and the probability in question is easily calculated by the use of the binomial distribution and considering our sequence of n 1's and 0's as a sequence of independent Bernoulli trials in which error free transmission of each of the binary digits occurs with probability p and erroneous transmission of each of the binary digits occurs with probability $q = 1 - p$. Thus the probability of exactly r errors occurring in a received message is:

$$P\{r \text{ errors}\} = \binom{n}{n-r} p^{n-r} q^r, \quad r = 0, 1, 2, \ldots, n$$

where

$$\binom{n}{n-r} = \frac{n!}{(n-r)!\,r!}$$

The average number of errors in a received transmission of a message of n binary digits is now found by calculating the expected value of the above expression. Thus,

$$E(r) = \overline{r} = \sum_{r=0}^{n} rP\{r \text{ errors}\}$$

$$= \sum_{r=0}^{n} r \binom{n}{n-r} p^{n-r} q^r = \sum_{r=1}^{n} r \binom{n}{n-r} p^{n-r} q^r$$

or

$$E(r) = nq = n(1-p) \tag{6-6}$$

Thus the average number of errors per received message is nq.

Due to the random nature of our code construction the number of code words that differs from a received sequence by *exactly r* digits is $\binom{n}{r}$ and hence the total number M of code words that differ from a received sequence by nq digits or less is

$$M = \binom{n}{0} + \binom{n}{1} + \ldots + \binom{n}{nq} = \sum_{i=0}^{nq} \binom{n}{i} \tag{6-7}$$

For $q < \frac{1}{2}$ each succeeding term for the above series is larger than the preceding term, so that we have

$$M \leqslant (nq+1) \binom{n}{nq} = (nq+1) \frac{n!}{(nq)!(n-nq)!}$$

When n is large, the factorial in the above equation is approximated by Stirling's formula.

$$n! \approx \sqrt{2\pi} \, e^{-n} \, n^{n+1/2}$$

Using the above approximation for the factorial, M may be written as

$$M \leqslant \sqrt{\frac{(nq+1)^2}{2\pi \, npq}} \; q^{-nq} \, p^{-np}$$

Now of the M sequences that, on the average, can be considered the possible message that was transmitted only one is correct and $M-1$ are possible mistakes. Since we have m possible messages and 2^n possible code words the probability that an n-digit sequence; selected at random, corresponds to one of the m messages is $m/2^n$. Since we have M total possible received sequences, each of which has a probability of correspondence to one of the randomly picked n-digit sequences, we have as the expected number of messages that could be changed by transmission errors into the original message and hence be confused with the original message

$$N = \frac{Mm}{2^n} \leq \sqrt{\frac{(nq + 1)^2}{2\pi npq}} \; m2^{-n} \, q^{-nq} \, p^{-np}$$

But since,

$$x^y = 2^{y \, \log x}$$

we may rewrite q^{-nq} as $2^{-nq \, \log q}$ and p^{-np} as $2^{-np \, \log p}$. Hence

$$2^{-n} \, q^{-nq} \, p^{-np} = 2^{-n(1 + p \, \log p + q \, \log q)}$$

but the capacity of a BSC is

$$C = 1 + p \, \log p + q \, \log q$$

Thus we have

$$N \leq m \; \sqrt{\frac{(nq + 1)^2}{2\pi npq}} \; 2^{-nC} \tag{6-8}$$

The entropy of the input to the channel when we let the number of messages be $2^{nC}/n$ is

$$\underset{\text{input}}{H(X)} = \frac{\log m}{n} \quad \text{bits/digit}$$

$$= \frac{\log 2^{nc} - \log n}{n} \approx C - \frac{\log n}{n} \tag{6-9}$$

If we take the limit as $n \longrightarrow \infty$ of Eqs. (6-8) and (6-9) we have

$$\lim_{n \to \infty} N = 0$$

and

$$\lim_{n \to \infty} \underset{\text{input}}{H(X)} = C$$

Thus for very long message sequences we see that the average number of messages that could be erroneously decoded approaches zero, hence the probability of making an error approaches zero, while simultaneously the information is conveyed at a rate approaching the channel capacity C.

A more formal statement of the noisy-coding theorem is given below:

Consider a channel, memoryless, with a capacity C and a discrete source with entropy H and any number $\epsilon > 0$. If we have $0 < H < C$ it is possible to encode sequences of the m-source message symbols in code words of length n digits for transmission over the channel so that the probability is less than ϵ that such a sequence will be incorrectly decoded. The positive integer n is chosen so that $m \geq 2^{nH}$ and then we are able to select the m transmitted sequences

$u_1, u_2, \ldots, u_m$ such that at the receiver end we can associate them with m distinct sequences of receiver outputs $v_1, v_2, \ldots, v_m$:

$$p\,[u_j{}^*/u_j] \geqslant 1 - \epsilon$$

where $u_j{}^*$ is our assumed input. Thus the assumed input is picked with probability arbitrarily close to one.

The converse to the theorem states that if we try to send information through the channel at a rate greater than C, then it is not possible to encode the message alphabet so that detection may be accomplished with arbitrarily small probability of error. This does not mean that transmission at a rate greater than channel capacity is not possible or effective. In fact one can sometimes communicate at a rate greater than channel capacity with a probability of error that is acceptable for systems that do not require an extremely high reliability.

6-3. ERROR DETECTION

Although the noisy-coding theorem does not give us a deterministic method for deriving a code with which we may have an arbitrarily small probability of error at rates close to but less than channel capacity we are not completely left in the dark for a method of deriving a code scheme that will reduce the probability of making an error. There are two approaches to this problem—error detection, and correction of the detected error.

In 1950 Hamming[20] gave us the first complete error-detecting and error-correcting encoding procedure. In this section we shall discuss the error-detecting capability of the parity check code.

An n-digit parity check code consists of m digits which are used to convey information and the remaining $r = n - m$ digits which are used to detect and possibly correct errors. The r digits are called parity checks and are chosen so that the total number of ones in an n-digit word is even, termed *even parity*. Correspondingly one may use odd parity as a check. For instance, consider a seven digit information sequence with an eighth digit used for parity check:

message	8th digit as even parity	8th digit as odd parity
0101110	0	1

The message digits plus parity check digit would make up an eight-digit sequence as follows:

Message plus parity check digit		Transmitted sequence
Even parity	0101110 + 0 ⟶	01011100
Odd parity	0101110 + 1 ⟶	01011101

Where we use a single-parity check digit we are able to detect all single-digit errors in a code sequence, but we are unable to either detect more than one error or to correct the single error.

Obviously two errors may cancel each other for parity purposes while yielding a different code word, since a code sequence 01011101 may be received as 01101101 with two errors, and may still be considered as valid by the parity check. Even if only a single error is made we are not able to determine which position has the erroneous digit. Thus a code of 01011101 may be received as either 01111101 or 00011101 and we are able to detect the existence of an error but not the position of the erroneous digit.

One might wonder about the increased probability of error when we add extra digits to the basic message sequence, but it is easy to see that this is not a serious problem. The probability of exactly one error occurring in a sequence of n digits has been shown to be an independent Bernoulli trial problem with probability of correct transmission of each digit equal to p and the probability of erroneous transmission of each digit equal to $q = 1 - p$. Thus the probability of receiving exactly $n - 1$ digits correctly and 1 digit erroneously is

$$P(\text{exactly 1 error in } n \text{ digits}) = \frac{n!}{(n-1)!1!} p^{n-1} q^1$$

and the probability of receiving exactly two errors in a sequence of $n + 1$ digits (remember we are now capable of detecting that first error) is

$$P(\text{exactly 2 errors in } n + 1 \text{ digits}) = \frac{(n+1)!}{(n+1-2)!2!} p^{n+1-2} q^2$$

Hence we see that

$$\frac{P(2/n+1)}{P(1/n)} = \frac{P(\text{exactly 2 errors in } n+1 \text{ digits})}{P(\text{exactly 1 error in } n \text{ digits})} = \frac{(n+1)! p^{n+1-2} q^2 (n-1)!1!}{(n+1-2)!2!n! p^{n-1} q^1}$$

$$= \frac{(n+1)(n)! p^{n-1} q^2 (n-1)!}{(n-1)! 2! n! p^{n-1} q^1} = \frac{(n+1)q}{2}$$

or

$$\frac{P(2/n+1)}{P(1/n)} = \frac{(n+1)}{2} q$$

For a message sequence of seven digits and a probability of correct transmission of .99 we would have

$$\frac{P(2/n+1)}{P(1/n)} = \frac{8}{2} (.01) = .04$$

Thus we see that the probability of making two errors in $n + 1$ digits is .04 times the probability of making one error in n digits, and we have gained the ability of detecting one-digit errors. However, detection of an error does not buy us much, since we still have no way of determining what message sequence was sent, the best we can do at the present is have the word sent again—which is very wasteful and sometimes not possible.

6-4. ERROR CORRECTION

A very simple error-detecting and error-correcting encoding method has been devised by Hamming as we have noted in Sec. 6-3. (From now on we shall mention only error correcting and assume that one realizes we must have detected an error before correcting it.) This method is based upon the concept of "distance" between code words, and this "distance" property has been termed the Hamming Distance, $d(u,v)$.

The quantity $d(u,v)$ refers to the number of binary digits in which the two n-digit sequences u and v disagree. If the distance is zero then there are no differences between u and v and hence they must be identical. In Fig. 6-2 are shown

u	v	$d(u,v)$
000	000	0
111	111	0
110	111	1
110	101	2
010	101	3

Fig. 6-2. Hamming distance between two code sequences.

several sequences and their distance is noted. Another way of defining the distance is to state that it is the number of binary digits one must change in sequence u to make it identical to sequence v. Mathematically we may calculate the distance between two sequences u and v if we are willing to introduce a slightly more involved notation. Let u_j represent the jth digit in the u sequence. Then we may write

$$d(u,v) = \sum_{j=1}^{n} (u_j \oplus v_j)$$

where $\oplus$ is a binary addition operation which is defined as

$$0 \oplus 0 = 0$$
$$0 \oplus 1 = 1$$

$$1 \oplus 0 = 1$$
$$1 \oplus 1 = 0$$

The properties of the Hamming distance are:
1. $d(u, v) = 0$ if u is identical to v
2. $d(u, v) = d(v, u) > 0$ if u is not identical to v
3. $d(u, w) + d(v, w) \geqslant d(u, v)$

Example 6-2

Consider the following sequences:

$$u = 10010$$
$$v = 11001$$
$$w = 01101$$

Then we have

$$d(u, v) = 3$$
$$d(u, w) = 5$$
$$d(v, w) = 2$$

and note $d(u, w) + d(v, w) = 5 + 2 > 3 = d(u, v)$.

Now let us see how we may construct a very simple error-correcting code using the Hamming distance criterion. If we construct a set of code words with a distance of at least 3 between words we will be able to determine which word was originally sent if only one error is made in transmission. Thus we will have a single-error-correcting code, although in this case we are not actually correcting the erroneous digit. Thus we might have

Message $A \longrightarrow$ 000

$$\left.\begin{array}{l} 001 \\ 010 \\ 100 \end{array}\right\}$$
Correctable single error sequences, if one of these is received we assume message A

$$\left.\begin{array}{l} 011 \\ 101 \\ 110 \end{array}\right\}$$
Correctable single error sequences, if one of these is received we assume message B

Message $B \longrightarrow$ 111

Now let us generalize this simple method to higher orders of distance.

Distance Between Words	Type of Coding Possible
1	No detection or correction
2	Single-error detection
3	Single-error correction
4	Single-error correction; double-error detection
5	Double-error correction
6	Double-error correction; triple-error detection

In general we can correct q errors if the minimum distance between code words is

$$d(u, v) \geqslant 2q + 1 \qquad (6\text{-}10)$$

Our next item for concern should be a question. How many words can be selected from a set of 2^n possible binary sequences of length n to construct a code capable of correcting q errors? If we are to correct q errors or less, then all the sequences which differ from u_j by q digits or less must be assigned to the message sequence u_j. We have seen that the total number of code words M of length n that differ from a specific sequence by q digits or less is (see Eq. 6-7)

$$M = \sum_{i=0}^{q} \binom{n}{i}$$

For every code word then we must reserve M sequences and hence if there are r code words to consider we must reserve a total number of sequences equal to

$$rM = r \sum_{i=0}^{q} \binom{n}{i}$$

The number of possible sequences of length n is 2^n and hence we must have

$$r \sum_{i=0}^{q} \binom{n}{i} \leqslant 2^n \qquad (6\text{-}11)$$

or the maximum number of code words must be

$$r \leqslant \frac{2^n}{\displaystyle\sum_{i=0}^{q} \binom{n}{i}} \qquad (6\text{-}12)$$

Equation 6-12 is not a sufficient condition for an upper bound on the number of code words that may be used out of 2^n possible words and still be able to correct q errors. However, it is a necessary condition. The insufficiency is easily shown by considering the case of four-digit sequences. Applying Eq. 6-12 we see that the maximum number of words available for messages for single-error correcting would seem to be

$$r \leqslant \frac{2}{\binom{4}{0}+\binom{4}{1}} = \frac{16}{\dfrac{4!}{4!}+\dfrac{4!}{3!}} = \frac{16}{1+4} = 3.2$$

or it would seem possible that we could use three words for messages. However then we find from Eq. 6-10 that the minimum distance required to correct single errors is 3. It is easily shown that one can only find two words in four-digit sequences with distance equal to three. It is not possible to pick three words with minimum distance 3 between all three words. (*Hint*: write out all 16 possible four-digit sequences and show this!)

So far we have not been able to detect the position of the erroneous digit. This is a very desirable outcome and we have at our disposal a method for detecting the position of the erroneous digit. This method is Hamming's single-error correcting code and is discussed below. (See also Ref. 20 or 21).

In Fig. 6-3 a code-word sequence has been depicted to illustrate several of the terms we shall use.

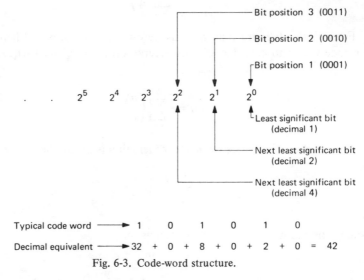

Fig. 6-3. Code-word structure.

Hamming's single-error correcting code is constructed in the following manner:

1. A K-bit checking number is derived such that its value indicates the erroneous bit's position number. The K-bit checking number must have enough possible states to identify any one of the erroneous-bit position

numbers possible or tell us that no error was made. Hence if we have m message bits required in the total number of bits per code word n, then we must have $n = m + K$. Since a K-bit number can represent 2^K different states (or numbers) we must then have

$$2^K \geqslant m + K + 1 \qquad (6\text{-}13)$$

In Table 6-1 a set of K values required for specific message lengths is shown.

TABLE 6-1. Required Values of K for Various Message Lengths

Message Length	Minimum K Required
1	2
2–4	3
5–11	4
12–26	5

2. The n different bit positions in the code are numbered from 1 to n starting with the least significant bit (Fig. 6-3). The K bits used for checking are labeled $P_0, P_1, P_2, \ldots, P_{K-1}$ and are placed in the bit positions numbered $1, 2, 4, 8, \ldots, 2^{K-1}$ respectively. We see that the (P_i)th checking bit is inserted in the (2^i)th bit position of the code sequence. The message bits, m in all, may be placed in the remaining bit positions as desired, but a good bookkeeping method is to place them in order of increasing significance starting with bit position 3, skipping those bit positions assigned to checking bits of course.

3. If we use even parity then each checking bit is chosen so the number of ones in the bit positions it is responsible for is even. In general if we were to represent the bit position number in binary form (Fig. 6-3) we would assign P_i as a checking bit for all the bit positions whose binary position number contains a one in the (2^i)th position (Table 6-2). Thus P_0 checks parity on bit positions $1, 3, 5, 7, 9, 11, 13, 15, \ldots$ in each code word, P_1 checks parity on bit positions $2, 3, 6, 7, 10, 11, 14, 15, \ldots$ in each code word, and so on.

4. The error detection and correction takes place as the K-bit binary checking number given by

$$\ldots . P_3 P_2 P_1 P_0$$

is calculated. P_0 is the least significant bit, P_1 the next least significant bit, etc. If the K-bit checking number is zero it is assumed that no errors occurred during transmission, otherwise the equivalent decimal value of the K-bit checking number indicates the erroneous digit's bit position number, assuming a single error was made.

TABLE 6-2. P_i checks Parity on the Bit Positions Whose Binary Position Numbers Have a One in the (2^i)th position

Bit Position	Binary Equivalent	P_0 Checks	P_1 Checks	P_2 Checks
1	0001	✓		
2	0010		✓	
3	0011	✓	✓	
4	0100			✓
5	0101	✓		✓
6	0110		✓	✓
7	0111	✓	✓	✓
8	1000			
9	1001	✓		
10	1010		✓	
11	1011	✓	✓	
12	1100			✓
13	1101	✓		✓
14	1110		✓	✓
15	1111	✓	✓	✓
.	.			
.	.			
.	.			

Example 6-3

Consider the following sixteen messages each of four binary digits in length. The number of checking bits required may be found from Eq. 6-13 as 3 bits (each message has length $m = 4$ digits). Hence bit positions numbered 1, 2, and 4 are reserved for the checking bits P_0, P_1, and P_2 as shown. The message code bits are shown as A, B, C, and D.

TABLE 6-3. A Hamming Code Example

Bit Position

Message Number	7	6	5	4	3	2	1 ← Bit-position number
	D	C	B	P_2	A	P_1	P_0 ← Bit assignment
0	0	0	0	0	0	0	0
1	0	0	0	0	1	1	1
2	0	0	1	1	0	0	1
3	0	0	1	1	1	1	0
4	0	1	0	1	0	1	0
5	0	1	0	1	1	0	1
6	0	1	1	0	0	1	1
7	0	1	1	0	1	0	0
8	1	0	0	1	0	1	1
9	1	0	0	1	1	0	0
10	1	0	1	0	0	1	0
11	1	0	1	0	1	0	1
12	1	1	0	0	0	0	1
13	1	1	0	0	1	1	0
14	1	1	1	1	0	0	0
15	1	1	1	1	1	1	1

Now suppose a message was received as 0110111. Then we would calculate the checking number as

$$K = P_2 P_1 P_0$$

where $P_2 = (4, 5, 6, 7) = 0 \oplus 1 \oplus 1 \oplus 0 = 0$
$\quad\;\; P_1 = (2, 3, 6, 7) = 1 \oplus 1 \oplus 1 \oplus 0 = 1$
$\quad\;\; P_0 = (1, 3, 5, 7) = 1 \oplus 1 \oplus 1 \oplus 0 = 1$

and hence $K = 011$, indicating an error.

We see that the checking number has a decimal equivalent of 3, indicating that the bit in the third position is erroneous. Changing the bit in the third position from a one to a zero we then have the code 0110011, which corresponds to message six. Note that the K-bit checking number is now

$$K = P_2 P_1 P_0$$

where $P_2 = (4, 5, 6, 7) = 0 \oplus 1 \oplus 1 \oplus 0 = 0$
$\quad\;\; P_1 = (2, 3, 6, 7) = 1 \oplus 0 \oplus 1 \oplus 0 = 0$
$\quad\;\; P_0 = (1, 3, 5, 7) = 1 \oplus 0 \oplus 1 \oplus 0 = 0$

and hence $K = 000$, indicating no errors.

There are several variations of parity check codes such as applying them to blocks checking not only rows but columns of digits. We shall defer discussion of these variations to Sec. 6-6 so that we may gain some knowledge of another general area in coding—group codes—before we consider specific techniques.

6-5. GROUP CODES

A study of error-correcting codes is generalized by mathematical group theory which allows us a concise notation with which we may discuss codes in general. The following material closely parallels the developments by W. W. Peterson[22] in his book *Error Correcting Codes*. The reader who finds himself deeply interested in the area of codes is referred to this basic text on the subject of error-correcting codes. This subject warrants a course of its own and in the present text we cannot hope to cover every topic in depth. Rather our aim here is to give the reader sufficient background that he may decide in what area his interests lie.

The discussion of general codes must be accomplished with a mathematical model—one that is accurate enough to describe our system yet allow us some insight. There are various mathematical systems and some of them bear such importance that special names are attached to them—group, ring, field, integral domain, linear algebra, geometry, and topology. We are interested in the basic properties of the first three systems mentioned.

The group is a system which has only one operation and its inverse. The operation may be as desired so long as the results of the operation satisfy the four laws governing a group. These laws (called *postulates*) are

1. Closure. If $a, b \in G$, then $a \odot b \in G$, where $\odot$ is read "operation" or "product," and ϵ means "is an element of."
2. Associative law. If $a, g, c \in G$, then $(a \odot b) \odot c = a \odot (b \odot c)$.
3. Identity (unity) element. There exists an element, written as u, in G such that for each $b \in G$, $u \odot b = b \odot u = b$. If our operation is addition then $u \equiv 0$ and we have $a + 0 = 0 + a = a$; if our operation is multiplication then $u \equiv 1$ and we have $a \odot 1 = 1 \odot a = a$.
4. Every element of a group has an inverse element: For each $b \in G$, there exists an element $b^* \in G$ such that $b \odot b^* = u$, where u is the identity element. If our operation is addition then $b^* = -b$ and we have $b + (-b) = 0 =$ the identity element; if our operation is multiplication then $b^* = 1/b = b^{-1}$ and we have $b \cdot b^{-1} = 1 =$ the identity element.

Example 6-4

The positive, negative, and zero integers form a group under the operation of addition. Postulate one is satisfied since the sum of two integers is a third integer. The second postulate is satisfied since the sum of integers is associative; i.e., $5 + (3 + 1) = (5 + 3) + 1 = 9$. The identity element is 0 since for any integer $b + 0 = 0 + b = b$. The inverse of any integer b is $(-b)$ and hence we have for any integer (say 6) $6 + (-6) = 0 =$ identity element.

Example 6-5

The integers do *not* form a group under multiplication since no integer would have an inverse (except ± 1). For instance 5 would not have an inverse under multiplication since the identity element would be 1 for multiplication and only $1/5 = 5^{-1}$ is an inverse for 5 in that case, but 5^{-1} does not belong to the group of *integers*.

Example 6-6

The rational numbers, with zero excluded, form a group under the operation of multiplication.

Note that the inverse of a product is the product of inverses *in reverse order* since $1 = a \cdot a^{-1} = a \cdot 1 \cdot a^{-1} = a \cdot b \cdot b^{-1} \cdot a^{-1} = (ab)(b^{-1}a^{-1})$, and hence multiplying both sides by $(ab)^{-1}$ we have $(ab)^{-1} = (b^{-1} a^{-1})$.

Note there is a group with only two elements. One element must be the identity element (why?) and the other element is called a. Then we know that under addition $a + 0 = a \neq 0$, $a^* \neq 0$ since a must have an inverse, hence a^* must be the only other element which is a. Thus we see the addition table for the two element group must be:

$$a + 0 = 0 + a = a, \quad a + a^* = a^* + a = 0, \quad 0 + 0 = 0$$

(Do you see the Boolean algebra rules in the two element group? $0, 1 \in G$ and $0 + 0 = 0, 1 + 1 = 0, 1 + 0 = 0 + 1 = 1$.)

   DEFINITION. A group having only a finite number of elements is called a *finite group*. The number of elements in a finite group is the *order* of the group.

   DEFINITION. A *subgroup* of a group G is a set of elements of G which, by themselves, satisfy the rules for a group. (Obviously the identity element must be a member of any subgroup.)

Example 6-7

   The set of all positive, negative, and zero integers form a group G under addition. The set S of all multiples of any integer m, say 7, is a subgroup of G. Thus,

$$S(\ldots, -14, -7, 0, 7, 14, 21, 28, \ldots) \in G(\ldots, -3, -2,$$
$$-1, 0, 1, 2, 3, 4, \ldots).$$

   Now let us construct an array which is formed using a subgroup S of a finite group G. The first row is the subgroup with the first entry from the left being the identity element (we will assume the group operation to be multiplication) and the other elements of the subgroup appearing only once. The first element of the second row is any one of the elements of G which is not an element of S. The rest of the elements of that row are formed by the operation of the first element of this row with the rest of the elements of the subgroup S. (Note the first entry on the left of row 2 has been formed by the operation of itself with the first element on the left of row 1, which is the identity element.) We continue building each row by using an unused element of G as the first entry on the left for that row, until finally all the elements of G appear somewhere in the array. The constructed array is called a *coset array*, Fig. 6-4.

$s_1 = 1$	s_2	s_3	s_4	$\cdot\ \ \cdot\ \ \cdot$	s_n
$g_1 s_1 = g_1$	$g_1 s_2$	$g_1 s_3$	$g_1 s_4$	$\cdot\ \ \cdot$	$g_1 s_n$
$g_2 s_1 = g_2$	$g_2 s_2$	$g_2 s_3$	$g_2 s_4$	$\cdot\ \ \cdot$	$g_2 s_n$
$\cdot$	$\cdot$	$\cdot$	$\cdot$		$\cdot$
$\cdot$	$\cdot$	$\cdot$	$\cdot$		$\cdot$
$\cdot$	$\cdot$	$\cdot$	$\cdot$		$\cdot$
$g_m s_1 = g_m$	$g_m s_2$	$g_m s_3$	$g_m s_4$		$g_m s_n$

$S = \text{subgroup of } G = \{s_1, s_2, \ldots, s_n\}$

$G = \text{group with } m + n \text{ elements} =$
$\{g_1, g_2, \ldots, g_m, s_1, s_2, \ldots, s_n\}$

Fig. 6-4. Coset array.

Each row of this array is called a *left coset* and the first element on the left is the *coset leader*. Thus the element $g_2 s_1 = g_2$ is the coset leader for the left coset whose elements are $g_2 s_1, g_2 s_2, g_2 s_3, \ldots, g_2 s_n$. (Note that we could have built the array from the right with elements of the form $s_3 g_2$ etc.; this would have been a *right coset* array and the two coset arrays would be equal only if the group operation is commutative.)

Two very useful properties of cosets are the following:

1. Two elements g and g' of a group G are in the same left coset of a subgroup S if and only if $g^{-1} g'$ is an element of S. Thus if g and g' belong to the same coset with leader g_i, then $g = g_i s_j$ for some $j, g' = g_i s_k$ for some k, and $g^{-1} g' = (g_i s_j)^{-1} (g_i s_k) = s_j^{-1} s_k$ which is in the subgroup S.

2. Every element of the group G is in *one* and *only* one coset of a subgroup S.

Example 6-8.

Consider the group G consisting of the set of all possible binary words with five digits. Thus the group has $2^5 = 32$ members. A subgroup S may be formed by constructing a Hamming single-error-correcting parity check code which has two binary digits per message; thus it must have a minimum of $K = 3$ checking digits from Eq. 6-13 and the words are (see Example 6-3)

$$s_1 = 00000 = \text{identity element}$$

$$s_2 = 00111$$

$$s_3 = 11001$$

$$s_4 = 11110$$

We may now form the left coset array for the subgroup S as follows. [Note the binary group operation is $\oplus$ so that $(00110) \oplus (11110)$ would be equal to (11000).]

s_1	s_2	s_3	s_4
00000	00111	11001	11110
10000	10111	01001	01110
01000	01111	10001	10110
00100	00011	11101	11010
00010	00101	11011	11100
00001	00110	11000	11111
01100	01011	10101	10010
01010	01101	10011	10100

The Hamming weight of a code group is defined as the number of nonzero digits. Thus the code word 01001 has a Hamming weight of 2. We see that the coset leaders in the above array (the first column) have weight less than or at most equal to that of the other elements in that coset. The above array is termed a *standard array*, since its coset leaders are minimal weight for their coset.

Before we continue our discussion of group codes (or binary linear codes) we will need to become familiar with some commonly used terms of *fields*, *vectors*, and *matrices*. Indeed the typical engineering student knows most of the operations involved but lacks schooling in the formal terminology. The serious student of advanced codes should study modern higher algebra to gain a broad well-grounded understanding of the subject. Our intent here is to familiarize the student with these areas so that he knows of their existence and some of the basic results; the material presented is hoped to be sufficient for understanding of what follows. For a more detailed viewpoint of what follows one should consult a mathematics text such as Ref. 23.

It is the laws (postulates) of a *field* that are most often implied by the phrase, "the rules of ordinary algebra." In particular a field is a set of elements $a, b, c, \ldots$ for which two operations $+$ and $\cdot$ are defined. The Field Postulates are for all elements $a, b, c \in D$.

Under $+$	Under $\cdot$
1. closure: $a + b \in D$	1. Closure: $a \cdot b = ab \in D$
2. Associativity: $(a + b) + c = a + (b + c)$	2. Associativity: $(ab)c = a(bc)$
3. Additive identity: There exists an identity element, 0, such that $b + 0 = 0 + b = b$	3. Multiplicative identity: There exists an identity element, 1, such that $b \cdot 1 = 1 \cdot b = b$
4. Additive inverse: For each element, say a, there exists a corresponding $-a$ such that $a + (-a) = (-a) + a = 0$	4. Multiplicative inverse: For each $b \neq 0$, there exists a corresponding $1/b = b^{-1}$ such that $bb^{-1} = b^{-1} b = 1$
5. Commutativity: $a + b = b + a$	5. Commutativity: $ab = ba$

DISTRIBUTIVE LAWS:

$$a(b + c) = ab + ac$$
$$(b + c)a = ba + ca$$

The set of all real numbers form a field. The minimum number of elements a field could have is two, 0 and 1. The addition and multiplication rules for the two element field are:

$$
\begin{array}{ll}
0 + 0 = 0 & 0 \cdot 0 = 0 \\
0 + 1 = 1 & 0 \cdot 1 = 0 \\
1 + 0 = 1 & 1 \cdot 0 = 0 \\
1 + 1 = 0 & 1 \cdot 1 = 1
\end{array}
$$

These are the rules for Boolean algebra and we will (and have been) use them often in our study of binary codes!

A quick summary of vector spaces and matrices is in order before we consider group-coding theory. The postulates of vector algebra are familiar to engineers and are set forth below:

1. The vector space over a field is a commutative group under addition.
2. If v is any vector and k any field element (number or scalar,) the product is a vector.
3. The distributive laws and associative laws hold for vectors and scalars. Thus $k(v_1 + v_2) = kv_1 + kv_2$ and $k_1(k_2 v_1) = (k_1 k_2)v_1$.
4. In addition to vector addition and scalar multiplication we define a third operation called *inner* (dot) *multiplication*. Thus if $v_1 = (x_1, x_2, x_3)$ and $v_2 = (x_4, x_5, x_6)$ then $v_1 \cdot v_2 = x_1 x_4 + x_2 x_5 + x_3 x_6$ = a scalar.
5. If the inner product of two vectors vanishes (is zero) then we say the vectors are *orthogonal*.
6. Vectors have a dual personality, one geometric and one algebraic. We are interested in vectors from the algebraic point of view and hence we say a vector of order n is an *n-tuple* over a field and we have $V = (x_1, x_2, \ldots, x_n)$. (*Note:* A vector of order 1 is one-dimensional geometrically, a vector of order 2 is two-dimensional geometrically, a vector of order 3 is three-dimensional geometrically, etc.)

We have the following definitions and theorems, the proofs of which are simple and may be found in Ref. 23.

On vectors:

1. A set of vectors over the real field that is closed under addition and scalar multiplication is called a *vector space over the real field*.
2. The set of all linear combinations of a given set of vectors forms a vector space.
3. The space of all linear combinations of a given set of vectors is called the *space generated by* (or spanned by) *the given set of vectors*.
4. A set of vectors $v_1, v_2, \ldots, v_n$ is linearly dependent if and only if there are scalars $c_1, c_2, \ldots, c_n$ not all zero such that $c_1 v_1 + c_2 v_2 + \cdots + c_n v_n = 0$.
5. If a set of n vectors spans a vector space that contains a set of m linearly independent vectors, then $n \geqslant m$.
6. If two sets of linearly independent vectors span the same space, there are the same number of vectors in each set.
7. The *dimension* of a vector space is equal to the maximum number of linearly independent vectors contained in the vector space.
8. If $v_1, v_2, \ldots, v_m$ are vectors of a space such that *every* vector of the space can be written as a linear combination of the above m vectors, then the m vectors is called a *generating system* of the vector space.
9. A linearly independent generating system of a vector space is called a *basis* of that vector space.

On matrices:

1. An $n \times m$ array of elements of the form

$$\begin{bmatrix} a_{11} & a_{12} & \cdots & a_{1m} \\ a_{21} & a_{22} & \cdots & a_{2m} \\ \vdots & & & \vdots \\ a_{n1} & a_{n2} & \cdots & a_{nm} \end{bmatrix}$$

is called a *matrix*. The rows of a matrix may be thought of as *row vectors*.

2. The vector space consisting of all linear combinations of the row vectors of a matrix is called the *row space* of the matrix. Similarly we have the *column vectors* and *column space* of a matrix.

3. The *row rank* of a matrix is the dimension of its row space. Thus the row rank is the maximum number of linearly independent row vectors of the matrix.

4. The set of elementary row operations defined for matrices are
   (a) Interchange of any two rows.
   (b) Multiplication of any row by a nonzero field element (number).
   (c) Addition of any multiple of one row to another.

5. The row rank and the row space of a matrix are invariant under elementary operations.

6. Elementary row operations can be used to simplify a matrix to a standard form known as its *echelon canonical form* in which every leading term of a nonzero row is 1, every column containing such a leading term has all its other entries zero, and the leading term of any row is to the right of the leading term in every preceding row. All zero rows are below all nonzero rows. (See appendix for an example.)

7. A second matrix called the transpose of a matrix A, A^T, is formed by reflecting the elements of A in the main diagonal; that is by writing the rows of A as columns. Then we have, for A and A^T,

$$\text{If } [A] = \begin{bmatrix} a_{11} & a_{12} & a_{13} \\ a_{21} & a_{22} & a_{23} \\ a_{31} & a_{32} & a_{33} \end{bmatrix}, \text{ then } [A]^T = \begin{bmatrix} a_{11} & a_{21} & a_{31} \\ a_{12} & a_{22} & a_{32} \\ a_{13} & a_{23} & a_{33} \end{bmatrix}$$

8. The set of all n vectors (n-tuples) orthogonal to a subspace V_1 of n-tuples forms a subspace V_2 of n-tuples. The subspace V_2 is called the *null space* of V_1. Thus if a vector is orthogonal to every vector of a set which spans V_1 it is in the null space of V_1.

9. If the dimension of a subspace of n-tuples is k, the dimension of the null space is $n - k$.

10. If A_1 and A_2 are two matrices that have n columns and if $A_1 A_2^T$ is a

matrix that has all zero elements, then the row space of A_2 is contained in the null space of A_1 and vice versa. If the row rank of A_1 and the row rank of A_2 add to n, then the row space of A_2 is the null space of A_1 and vice versa. (See Ref. 22, p. 35.)

Now let us apply the preceding discussion to code theory and in particular to the subject of Hamming's codes, where our familiarity should help us understand the application of the linear algebra concepts to coding theory.

A linear code is a collection of n-tuples (vectors of order n). A group code is a binary linear code. We know that a linearly independent generating system of a vector space is a basis of that space. Correspondingly, we have a basis for our linear code V and this basis may be written as a matrix called the *generating matrix* of V, and the row space of the generating matrix is the linear code V. Hence each code word is a vector that is a result of a linear combination of the row vectors of the generating matrix.

Example 6-9

Consider the set V of all possible binary code words three digits in length. Thus V is a binary linear code or a group code. The code vectors total eight (2^3) in number and are:

$$
\begin{array}{ll}
V_1 = 000 & V_5 = 100 \\
V_2 = 001 & V_6 = 101 \\
V_3 = 010 & V_7 = 110 \\
V_4 = 011 & V_8 = 111
\end{array}
$$

A possible generating matrix for the above group is

$$
[G] = \begin{bmatrix} 100 \\ 010 \\ 001 \end{bmatrix}
$$

We see that the row vectors of G are linearly independent since there exist no constants, c_i's, for which $\sum_{i=1}^{3} c_i v_i = 0$ except $c_i = 0$ for each i.

That is,

$$
c_1 V_5 + c_2 V_3 + c_3 V_2 = 0 \qquad \text{(for what } c\text{'s?)}
$$

where $V_5 = 100$
$V_3 = 010$
$V_2 = 001$

Thus $c_1 (1, 0, 0) + c_2 (0, 1, 0) + c_3 (0, 0, 1)$ or remembering that the V's are vectors and hence may be written as

$$V_5 = 1a_1 + 0a_2 + 0a_3$$
$$V_3 = 0a_1 + 1a_2 + 0a_3$$
$$V_2 = 0a_1 + 0a_2 + 1a_3$$
$$c_1 a_1 + c_2 a_2 + c_3 a_3 = 0 \quad \text{(for what c's?)}$$

But in solving for vectors we must equate components so that we have,

$$c_1 a_1 = 0 \quad \therefore c_1 = 0$$
$$c_2 a_2 = 0 \quad \therefore c_2 = 0$$
$$c_3 a_3 = 0 \quad \therefore c_3 = 0$$

Thus we see that the three vectors V_5, V_2, V_3 are linearly independent. (Note that in this example a_1, a_2, a_3 are merely vector direction indicators or vector component indicators such as i_x, i_y, i_z for rectangular coordinates.)

It is easily shown that the eight possible code vectors are simply linear combinations of the three row vectors of G and hence we have the relationship that the row space of G equals the group code V.

$$V_1 = V_5 + V_5 = (1, 0, 0) + (1, 0, 0)$$
$$= (1 + 1, 0 + 0, 0 + 0)$$
$$V_1 = (0, 0, 0)$$
$$V_4 = V_3 + V_2 = (0 + 0, 1 + 0, 0 + 1) = (0, 1, 1) \quad \text{etc.}$$

Now consider a code space (vector space) A_1 as:

$$[A_1] = \begin{bmatrix} 0 & 0 & 0 \\ 1 & 1 & 0 \\ 1 & 0 & 1 \\ 0 & 1 & 1 \end{bmatrix}$$

Then

$$[G_1] = \begin{bmatrix} 1 & 1 & 0 \\ 0 & 1 & 1 \end{bmatrix}$$

and

$$[A_2] = \begin{bmatrix} 0 & 0 & 0 \\ 1 & 1 & 1 \end{bmatrix} \quad \text{the null space of the vector space } A_1$$

Thus A_1 is a subspace of V and we have the dimension of A_1 (number of linearly independent vectors of A_1) as $k = 2$, and A_1 is an $n = 4$ vector space (number of vectors equals 4). Then since A_1 is a subspace of dimension $k = 2$ and consists of $n = 4$ vectors, its null space A_2 is a vector space of dimension $n - k = 4 - 2 = 2$. Now a matrix H of rank $n - k = 2$ whose row space is A_2 can be made with a basis for A_2 being used as the rows of H. Then A_1 is the null space of H and a vector a_i is in A_1 if and only if it is orthogonal to every row of H, that is, if

$$a_i \, [H]^T = 0$$

Thus the code vectors of a group code must satisfy a set of $n - k$ independent equations, called a *set of generalized parity checks*. H is called the *parity check matrix* of the group code A_1.

For our A_1 and H, note that $a_4 = 011$ and

$$a_4 \, [H]^T = [011] \begin{bmatrix} 1 & 0 \\ 1 & 0 \\ 1 & 0 \end{bmatrix} = (0 + 1 + 1, 0 + 0 + 0) = (0, 0) = 0$$

Hence a_4 is a member of A_1, whereas the vector 010 is not in A_1, since

$$[0 \quad 1 \quad 0] \begin{bmatrix} 1 & 0 \\ 1 & 0 \\ 1 & 0 \end{bmatrix} = (0 + 1 + 0, 0 + 0 + 0) = (1, 0) \neq 0$$

Thus any vector in the group code space say a_i (expressed as $a_i = (x_1, x_2, x_3)$ where x_1, x_2, x_3 are the values of the code point; for instance, the code vector 011 has $x_1 = 0, x_2 = 1, x_3 = 1$) must satisfy these equations of H as

$$1x_1 + 1x_2 + 1x_3 = 0$$

and

$$0x_1 + 0x_2 + 0x_3 = 0$$

An important result of the group algebra analysis of codes may be stated as follows:

Let a code vector $a = (x_1, x_2, \ldots, x_k, \; b_1, b_2, \ldots, b_{n-k})$ be an arbitrary n-tuple where the k digits, x_j, are the arbitrarily specified information digits and the $n - k$ digits b_i are the parity check digits. Then the parity check digits may be found from

$$b_i = \sum_{j=1}^{k} h_{ij} x_j \qquad i = 1, 2, \ldots, n - k$$

where the h_{ij}'s are the elements of the parity check matrix H. This is expressible in matrix form as

$$[B] = [H] [X]$$

where the $[B]$, $[H]$, and $[X]$ matrices have the following form:

$$[B] = \begin{bmatrix} b_1 \\ b_2 \\ \vdots \\ b_{n-k} \end{bmatrix}, \quad [H] = \begin{bmatrix} h_{11} & h_{12} & \cdots & h_{1k} \\ h_{21} & h_{22} & \cdots & h_{2k} \\ \vdots & & & \end{bmatrix}, \quad [X] = \begin{bmatrix} x_1 \\ x_2 \\ \vdots \\ x_k \end{bmatrix}$$

The problem of devising a Hamming code (a class of systematic codes) reduces to finding a suitable parity check matrix, whose row space is the null space of the code vector space. This problem has been discussed in the literature (see Ref. 24).

Now suppose we form a standard array of the vector space V using the vector subspace A_1 as the building block:

$$\begin{array}{cccc} 000 & 110 & 101 & 011 \\ 001 & 111 & 100 & 010 \end{array}$$

A useful property of standard arrays is the fact that any element of a standard array is at least as close to the element on the top of its column as it is to any other element in the array. (Note that this is true for standard arrays, not for any coset array.) This leads us to a method for determining which code vector was sent. Suppose we receive the code vector 100. We note that it was not one of the original code vectors of our transmitter alphabet A_1, but it is in the column headed by the code vector 101, hence we would assume the original message sent was 101 with no greater risk of making an error than if we chose any other original code vector. For this simple example we don't see the benefits as clearly as we will in a later example.

Peterson has shown that the probability of correct decoding, using a standard array table as the decoding table, for a BSC channel with probability of correct transmission p is

$$P \text{ (correct decoding)} = \gamma_0 p^n + \gamma_1 q p^{n-1} + \gamma_2 q^2 p^{n-2} \cdots \qquad (6\text{-}14)$$

where the *number* of coset leaders of weight i is denoted by the symbol γ_i. Peterson also proves that for the BSC if we assume code vectors are equally likely to be transmitted, then the average probability of correct decoding is as large as possible for this code if the standard array table is used for the decoding table.

Example 6-10

Suppose we have sixteen messages we wish to send using a single-error-correcting, double-error-detecting code. Devise this code space and calculate the probability of correct decoding and the probability of error in decoding. Assume a BSC is to be used for transmission with probability of correct transmission p equal to 0.99.

We will require four binary information digits to encode sixteen messages. From Eq. 6-13 we find the minimum number of checking bits required, b, to be three checking bits. A suitable parity check matrix is given as†

$$[H] = \begin{bmatrix} 1 & 0 & 1 & 1 \\ 1 & 1 & 0 & 1 \\ 1 & 1 & 1 & 0 \end{bmatrix}$$

and a code vector matrix

$$[X] = \begin{bmatrix} x_1 \\ x_2 \\ x_3 \\ x_4 \end{bmatrix}$$

Note that we have an (n, b) code where $n = 7$ is the total number of digits per transmitted vector m, and $b = 3$ is the number of binary check digits required. The matrix $[H]$, is an $(n - k, k)$ matrix as promised and the code vector matrix is a $(k, 1)$ matrix.

We derive the parity check equations in the following manner:

$$[B] = [H] \, [X]$$

or for each code vector to be transmitted we find the required parity checks to be

$$\begin{bmatrix} b_1 \\ b_2 \\ b_3 \end{bmatrix} = \begin{bmatrix} 1 & 0 & 1 & 1 \\ 1 & 1 & 0 & 1 \\ 1 & 1 & 1 & 0 \end{bmatrix} \begin{bmatrix} x_1 \\ x_2 \\ x_3 \\ x_4 \end{bmatrix}$$

or

$$b_1 = x_1 + x_3 + x_4$$
$$b_2 = x_1 + x_2 + x_4$$
$$b_3 = x_1 + x_2 + x_3$$

†D. Slepian has published a table of suggested parity check matrices for a BSC. See Ref. 25 and the Appendix Table T-4.

At this point we must assign the message digits for each word so that we may calculate the check digits required and thus construct the vectors to be transmitted. The assignment of the message digits may be made at random as we noted previously. Let us pick the sixteen required message codes from the $2^4 = 16$ possible code vectors by letting the code word for message 1 be the four-digit binary code for one, 0001; the code word for message 2 be the four-digit binary code for two, 0010, etc. Thus we have the following message code vectors:

$x_1 x_2 x_3 x_4$		$x_1 x_2 x_3 x_4$		$x_1 x_2 x_3 x_4$	
$a_1 =$	0001	$a_7 =$	0111	$a_{13} =$	1101
$a_2 =$	0010	$a_8 =$	1000	$a_{14} =$	1110
$a_3 =$	0011	$a_9 =$	1001	$a_{15} =$	1111
$a_4 =$	0100	$a_{10} =$	1010	$a_{16} =$	0000
$a_5 =$	0101	$a_{11} =$	1011		
$a_6 =$	0110	$a_{12} =$	1100		

For each message code vector we must calculate the required binary check digits b_1, b_2, b_3 so that each transmitted code vector of the form u may be constructed, where we have u to be

$$u = x_1, x_2, x_3, x_4, b_1, b_2, b_3$$

The procedure for calculating b_1, b_2, b_3 is illustrated for the message code vectors a_3 and a_{12} below.

For a_3,

$$b_1 = x_1 + x_3 + x_4 = 0 + 1 + 1 = 0$$
$$b_2 = x_1 + x_2 + x_4 = 0 + 0 + 1 = 1$$
$$b_3 = x_1 + x_2 + x_3 = 0 + 0 + 1 = 1$$

thus the transmitted code vector u, corresponding to the message code vector a_3 is

$$u_3 = 0011011$$

For a_{12},

$$b_1 = x_1 + x_3 + x_4 = 1 + 0 + 0 = 1$$
$$b_2 = x_1 + x_2 + x_4 = 1 + 1 + 0 = 0$$
$$b_3 = x_1 + x_2 + x_3 = 1 + 1 + 0 = 0$$

Thus the transmitted code vector u_{12} corresponding to the message code vector a_{12} is

$$u_{12} = 1100100$$

The complete set of transmitted code vectors is listed below: (The student should verify several of these)

$$u_1 = 0001110 \qquad u_9 = 1001001$$
$$u_2 = 0010101 \qquad u_{10} = 1010010$$
$$u_3 = 0011011 \qquad u_{11} = 1011100$$
$$u_4 = 0100011 \qquad u_{12} = 1100100$$
$$u_5 = 0101101 \qquad u_{13} = 1101010$$
$$u_6 = 0110110 \qquad u_{14} = 1110001$$
$$u_7 = 0111000 \qquad u_{15} = 1111000$$
$$u_8 = 1000111 \qquad u_{16} = 0000000$$

If the standard array were to be constructed using the above sixteen vectors as a coset to build with, we could count the coset leaders with weight 1, 2, etc. However, we may also calculate γ_i, the number of coset leaders of weight i, since γ_i must satisfy the following relations

$$\gamma_i \leqslant \binom{n}{i} \qquad \text{and} \qquad \sum_{i=0}^{n} \gamma_i = 2^{n-k}$$

In Ref. 25 and in the appendix the values of γ_i for specified n and k are given. For this example the γ_i's are as follows: $\gamma_0 = 1$, $\gamma_1 = 7$. Since we will have eight cosets (eight rows, sixteen vectors in each row of the standard array) we see that the identity element (0000000) is the only coset leader of weight 0 and there are of course only seven coset leaders of weight 1 possible. These are of course the following vectors:

$$\begin{array}{cc} 0000001 & 0010000 \\ 0000010 & 0100000 \\ 0000100 & 1000000 \\ 0001000 & \end{array}$$

The probability of correct decoding using Eq. 6-14 is

$$P(\text{correct decoding}) = (1)p^7 + (7)qp^6 = p^6(p + 7q)$$

If $p = 0.99$ we have

$$P(\text{correct decoding}) = .9973$$

The probability of making an error when decoding is

$$P(\text{erroneous decoding}) = [1 - P(\text{correct decoding})] = .0027$$

We have seen before that the probability of making an error when sending sixteen messages by using a four-binary-digit code with no error correction can be calculated by using the equation for Bernoulli trials as

$$P \text{ (erroneous decoding with no error correction)} = nq = 4(.01) = .04$$

Thus we have decreased our error probability by a factor of almost 15. The price we pay is a longer time required to send the message (or a greater bandwidth if we up the bit rate). The high-reliability bit rate is .571 times the low-reliability bit rate.

6-6. SPECIAL TECHNIQUES

The encoding technique to be discussed next is a geometric type code which is based upon the parity-check concept. It is an iterative method suggested by Peter Elias[26] for binary erasure channels, BEC.

The construction of the code may be explained as follows.

1. Consider a set of m messages, each message being a length $n - 1$ binary digits of information plus one parity digit.
2. We will select the nth binary digit so that each message contains an even number of ones (even parity).
3. The m messages are now arranged in a matrix form where each row is one of the messages. Thus we have m rows and n columns.
4. An extra row, the $(m + 1)$st row, is now added by choosing each bit so that the total number of ones in its column is even. Thus we have a vertical parity check on columns as well as horizontal parity check on rows. We now have an $(m + 1) \times n$ matrix, Fig. 6-5.

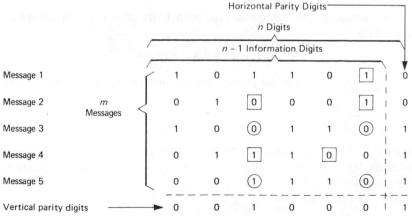

The error pattern indicated by the squares would be detected and corrected while the error pattern indicated by the circles would not. For a BEC channel the errors are received as blanks.

Fig. 6-5. Iterative block code.

For a BEC channel the error digits are received as a blank (erasure) and must be filled in by parity check if possible. In the code block shown in Fig. 6-5 the errors indicated by squares could be corrected by first correcting all single erasures in rows. Thus the upper right-hand error could be corrected by a row parity count. This correction would then allow the error in the sixth column to be corrected by a column parity count. Then the sole remaining error in row 2 may be corrected by a row parity count. This leaves two remaining errors each in separate columns each of which may be corrected by column parity count.

Now let us compare the average number of erasures per block before and after the various coding stages versus the sacrifice in information rate.

We have seen before that the average number of errors in a string of N digits is Nq, where q is the probability of erroneous transmission of a digit. The average number of erasures for a BEC channel is equal to the average number of errors in a sequence of N digits.

Now we can devise the relation between sending corrected and uncorrected messages versus the information rate. If we send a message sequence of N digits with no correction we may expect the average number of erasures to be Nq, with an information rate of N information digits versus N total digits.

With the row-correction scheme we have a correction of all single errors, and hence the average number of erasures is equal to the total average number of erasures less the average number of single erasures which are corrected. Hence we have the average number of erasures after row correction, $\overline{\text{Erasures (r.c.)}}$, as

$$\overline{\text{Erasures (r.c.)}} = Nq - Np^{N-1}q$$
$$= Nq(1 - p^{N-1}) < Nq(1 - p^N) < Nq(1 - 1 + Nq)$$
$$< Nq(Nq) = (Nq)^2$$

If we designate the average erasure probability after row correction as q_1 then we have,

$$\overline{\text{Erasures (r.c.)}} = Nq_1 < (Nq)^2$$

Now let us determine the average erasure probability after column correction, $\overline{\text{Erasures (c.c.)}}$, as

$$\overline{\text{Erasures (c.c.)}} = Mq_2 = Mq_1 - Mq_1 p_1^{N-1} < (Mq_1)^2$$

where q_2 is the average erasure probability after column correction and M the number of digits per column equal to the number of messages sent including the parity check row. Thus $M = m + 1$.

Thus we have the relation

$$Mq_2 < (Mq_1)^2 \quad \text{and hence} \quad q_2 < Mq_1^2$$

and

$$Nq_1 < (Nq)^2 \quad \text{and hence} \quad q_1 < Nq^2$$

For an error probability $q = .01$ and $N = 10 = M$ we have

$$\overline{\text{Erasure (b.c.)}} = Nq = .1$$

$$\overline{\text{Erasure (r.c.)}} = Nq_1 < (Nq)^2 = .01 = 10^{-2}$$

$$\overline{\text{Erasure (c.c.)}} = Mq_2 < (Mq_1)^2 < M^2 N^2 q^4 = 10^{-4}$$

The information rate R is

$$R \text{ (b.c.)} = \text{information digits/total digits} = 1$$

$$R \text{ (r.c.)} = \frac{9}{10} = 0.9$$

$$R \text{ (c.c.)} = \frac{81}{100} = 0.81$$

Thus a thousand times smaller error probability is gained for an information rate decrease of approximately 20 percent.

6-7. A RECENT CODING TECHNIQUE

In a paper by Chung-Yen Ong[27] a combination of block and tree codes, termed a *hybrid tree-block code*, is presented. The hybrid tree-block code (HTB) has several features of interest:

1. The property of a block code that the decoding of each code vector is independent of all preceding and following code vectors. This means there is no error propagation from code vector to code vector as in sequential decoding of tree codes.
2. Decoding may proceed at a faster rate than for a tree code since we may decode a complete block at a time rather than a single digit at a time.
3. Because of the tree structure of the HTB code the concept of sequential decoding may be used to discard nonretained sequences of the tree-code portion and compare the received vector against only the retained sequences instead of every code vector as we would need to do for a block code.

Before we discuss the construction of a HTB code we need to become familiar with *binary convolutional tree codes*. Convolutional codes are specified by their code rate and constraint length. The code rate R is the ratio of information bits to total bits at the encoder output. The constraint length K is equal to the number of bits in the encoding shift register.

Convolutional codes are a subclass of parity check codes but the parity check equations are usually selected by trial and error to match the requirements of the system and channel. These codes may be generated by encoding devices such as that shown in Fig. 6-6.

The connection diagram of the encoder is specified by a set of coefficients $\{g_{lj}\}$, where $l = 1, 2, \ldots, K$ and $j = 1, 2, \ldots, \nu$. If $g_{lj} = 1$ then the lth stage of the K-bit register is connected to the jth modulo-2 adder, denoted by $\oplus$, and if

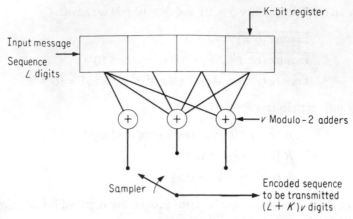

Fig. 6-6. Convolutional encoder for $K = 4$, $\nu = 3$.

$g_{1j} = 0$ then there is no connection. Thus for the encoder of Fig. 6-6 we have the set of g vectors as

$$[g] = \begin{bmatrix} 1 & 1 & 1 \\ 0 & 1 & 0 \\ 0 & 1 & 1 \\ 0 & 1 & 1 \end{bmatrix}$$

The jth column of the g matrix, termed the *generating matrix*, denotes the connections to the jth adder.

The output sequence is derived from the values of the modulo-2 adders each time a digit is shifted into the register. For instance, if we have all zeros in the register of Fig. 6-6, then the output of each adder is zero and the transmitted output would be three zeros. If we then shift a 1 in from the left the output of the adders, sampling from left to right, would be 111. If we then shift a second 1 in from the left, the output of the adders would be 101. If the message input is a five-digit sequence such as 11010, the output would be a series of digits, $(L + K)\nu$ to be exact, as

Output sequence = (111, 101, 001, 111, 001, 011, 011, 000, 000)

where the last series of all zeros has occurred from the requirement that we return the register to its original state of all zeros by shifting in K zeros after the last message digit.

We see the transmission rate is

$$R = \frac{L}{(L + K)\nu} \approx \frac{1}{\nu} \quad L \gg K$$

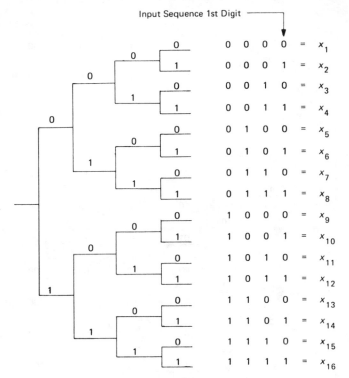

A Tree structure for $2^L = 2^4 = 16$ input messages

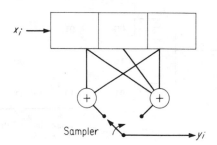

Fig. 6-7. Encoder for $K = 3, L = 4$, and $v = 2$.

The structure of the code may be diagrammed in a code tree by writing the output sequence for each input digit along a tree which has been constructed by moving along the upper path if an input is zero, and moving along the lower path if an input is one. In Fig. 6-7 we have a tree structure shown for the case of $K = 3, L = 4, v = 2$, where the encoder connections are as shown.

In Fig. 6-8 the code tree representing the output of the encoder after each input digit is inserted has been drawn. We see that for an input sequence corresponding to x_6 the output sequence would correspond to $y_6 = (00, 11, 01, 00,$

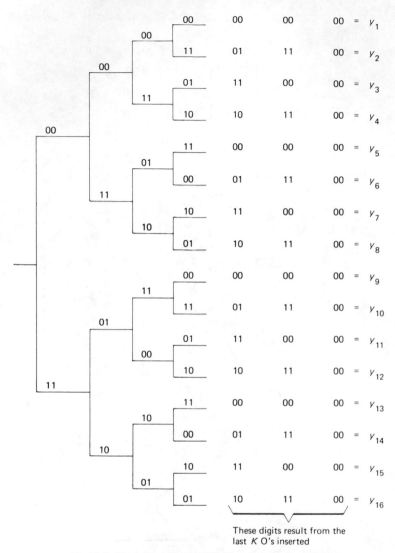

These digits result from the
last K O's inserted

Fig. 6-8. Encoder code tree for $K = 3, L = 4, v = 2$.

01, 11, 00), where the comma represents the insertion of an input digit. The generating matrix for the encoder of Fig. 6-7 is

$$[g] = \begin{bmatrix} 1 & 1 \\ 0 & 1 \\ 1 & 1 \end{bmatrix}$$

A hybrid tree-block code is defined to be a combination of a tree code and a special block code which is put on the tail of the tree code. The block code is constructed by a procedure that insures the minimum distance between any two code words of the HTB code is equal to the minimum distance of the tree-code portion of the HTB code.

The minimum distance of a tree code is defined to be the minimum distance between any code words u_i in the upper half of the tree and u_j in the lower half of the tree. Note that the distance between two code words in the same half of the code tree is in general less than the minimum distance of the tree code as a whole. In fact, two code words in the same half of the tree may have a distance of half or less of that of the tree code as a whole. Thus if we are to add a block code to the tail of the tree code, the minimum distance of the first-order pairs of the block code required will be equal to the minimum distance between any two paths of the tree-code portion. If a tree code has a minimum distance of 7, then the minimum distance between any two segments of the tree code is 3, and the block code to be added must have a minimum distance between first-order pairs of 4, thus insuring the minimum distance between any two code words of the HTB code to be 7.

The block code with its required distance may be constructed through use of a special generating matrix derived from a tree code with minimum distance equal to the required distance of the block code. This has been stated as a theorem by Chung-Yen Ong.

Theorem

Suppose a single-generator binary initial truncated tree code of length L segments is generated by the matrix

$$[G] = \begin{bmatrix} g_L \\ g_{L-1} \\ \cdot \\ \cdot \\ \cdot \\ g_1 \end{bmatrix}$$

where $g_1, g_2, \ldots, g_L$ are row vectors and g_i is the 2^{i-1} path of the tree code which has paths numbered from 0 to $2^L - 1$. Then a block code generated by a generator matrix

$$[H] = \begin{bmatrix} h_1 \\ h_2 \\ \cdot \\ \cdot \\ \cdot \\ h_L \end{bmatrix}$$

where $h_j = g_1 \oplus g_2 \oplus \ldots \oplus g_{L-j+1}$, will have the distance property between first-order pairs of $D_1 \geqslant d(L)$, where $d(L)$ is the minimum distance of a tree code of L segments.

Thus we need only to know the required distance of our block code in order to derive its generating matrix and hence the block code itself. The required distance may be found from the minimum distance of the tree code to which the block code is to be appended.

Example 6-11

Derive the block code for the tree code shown in Fig. 6-9.

The minimum distance of the above tree code is 6. The minimum distance between any two code vectors is 3 and hence a block would need to have a minimum distance between first-order pairs of 3. The following

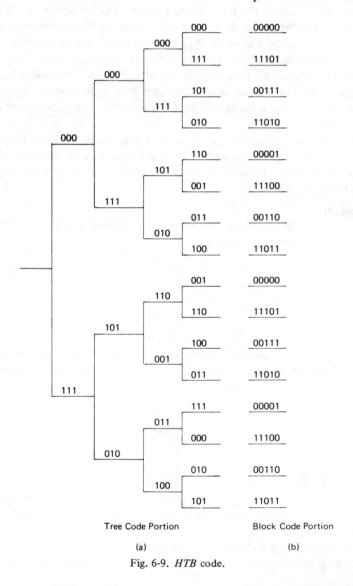

	Tree Code Portion		Block Code Portion
	(a)		(b)

Fig. 6-9. *HTB* code.

tree code has a minimum distance of 3 and hence is suitable for use in constructing the block code.

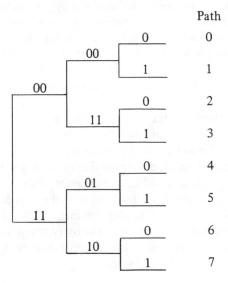

The generating matrix of the above tree code is

$$[G] = \begin{bmatrix} g_1 \\ g_2 \\ g_3 \end{bmatrix} = \begin{bmatrix} 00 & 00 & 1 \\ 00 & 11 & 0 \\ 11 & 01 & 0 \end{bmatrix}$$

and the generating matrix of the block code is

$$[H] = \begin{bmatrix} g_1 \oplus g_2 \oplus g_3 \\ g_1 \oplus g_2 \\ g_1 \end{bmatrix} = \begin{bmatrix} 1 & 1 & 1 & 0 & 1 \\ 0 & 0 & 1 & 1 & 1 \\ 0 & 0 & 0 & 0 & 1 \end{bmatrix}$$

The block code portion of the resulting HTB code is shown in Fig. 6-9.

6-8. REMARKS

In this chapter we have discussed the problem of noisy channels and the coding theorems which have been developed for them. We have seen that it is possible to generate codes which may be transmitted at a rate less than channel capacity with probability of error arbitrarily close to zero, Shannon's second theorem.

The noise contributed by the channel led to the development of error detecting and error-correcting codes. Using the Fano Bound, which is related to Shannon's second (noisy coding) theorem, we were able to calculate the average uncertainty about the transmitted symbol given a received symbol. This gives us a means of comparing various channels.

Hamming's parity check codes give us the ability to detect errors and if we use the Hamming distance criteria we are able to derive codes which allow us to correct errors in transmission in the sense that we may deduce the correct word even though we do not know which bits are in error. From this we progressed to the subject of group codes, a set of codes which are highly structured algebraically and for which we have some methods of generating codes with desired properties.

The method of Elias for iterative codes gave us a way of correcting some types of individual bit errors and the hybrid-tree block codes combine the advantages of block codes and convolutional codes.

The remaining main area of concern is that of dealing with bursts of errors. Up to this point we have assumed that each error made was independent of previous errors but at this point we must realize that errors do not always occur independently of each other. Natural phenomena such as atmospheric disturbances or man made phenomena such as a noisy typewriter (electric) or heavy machinery often generate noise bursts which then give us error bursts. This type of error occurrence is dealt with in Chapter 7.

PROBLEMS

6-1. For the following channel matrix and source symbol probabilities find the ideal observer decision scheme and calculate the probability of error for the scheme. (The ideal observer scheme decodes each b_i as the a posteriori most likely a_i in accord with Eq. 6-1.)

$$P[B/A] = \begin{bmatrix} 1/2 & 3/8 & 1/8 \\ 1/8 & 1/2 & 3/8 \\ 3/8 & 1/8 & 1/2 \end{bmatrix}$$

and $p_1 = 2/3, p_2 = p_3 = 1/6$.

6-2. For the following channel matrix and equally likely source symbols specify the maximum likelihood decision rule and calculate the probability of error.

$$P[B/A] = \begin{bmatrix} 0.5 & 0.3 & 0.2 \\ 0.2 & 0.3 & 0.5 \\ 0.3 & 0.3 & 0.4 \end{bmatrix}$$

6-3. Using the following channel matrix and source symbol probabilities specify the ideal observer decision scheme and the maximum-likelihood decision scheme. Calculate the probability of error for both schemes and point out two major disadvantages of the ideal observer scheme in general.

$$p[b_i/a_j] = \begin{bmatrix} 2/3 & 1/3 \\ 1/10 & 9/10 \end{bmatrix}; \quad p(a_1) = 3/4, \quad p(a_2) = 1/4$$

6-4. Prove the final results of the derivation of the average number of errors per received message, $E(r) = nq = n(1 - p)$, Eq. 6-6.

6-5. For what conditions would the equality of the Fano bound, Eq. 6-5, hold?

6-6. Show that for $n = 3$ and $n = 4$ it is not possible to construct a single-error-correcting code with more than two words. Thus Eq. 6-12 is a necessary but not sufficient condition.

6-7. Use Hamming's single-error-correcting technique to derive a code for the following cases:

Message Bits	Checking Bits
2	3
4	3
5	4

For each case calculate the probability of incorrectly decoding a word sent without error correcting and compare to the probability of incorrectly decoding a word sent with error correcting.

6-8. Prove Example 6-6.

6-9. Write the standard array and calculate the set of γ_i's for Example 6-10.

6-10. Calculate the determinant of the following matrix. Put the matrix in echelon canonical form and show that the rank is 3. Assume the field of three elements.

$$\begin{bmatrix} 1 & 2 & 0 \\ 2 & 2 & 1 \\ 1 & 1 & 1 \end{bmatrix}$$

6-11. Find the set of code vectors that make up the row space of both of the following matrices.

$$x = \begin{bmatrix} 1 & 0 & 0 & 1 & 1 \\ 0 & 1 & 0 & 1 & 0 \\ 0 & 0 & 1 & 0 & 1 \end{bmatrix} \quad y = \begin{bmatrix} 1 & 0 & 0 & 1 & 1 \\ 1 & 1 & 0 & 0 & 1 \\ 1 & 1 & 1 & 0 & 0 \end{bmatrix}$$

6-12. You have eight messages to send using a single-error-correcting, double-error-detecting code.

(a) Devise the code space and calculate the probability of correct decoding and the probability of an error in decoding. Assume a BSC channel with $p = 0.99$.

(b) Write the standard array for the receiver and determine the set of γ_i's. What is the minimum number of checking bits required?

A suitable parity check matrix is available from Table T-4 in the appendix which lists some of the parity-check matrices versus (n, k) where n is the total number of digits per code word and k the number of information digits.

6-13. Devise a single-error-correcting group code for an $(n, k) = (7, 3)$ code. Compute the probability of an erroneous decoding.

6-14. You have just received a code message 11101. The system your company uses is an $(n, k) = (5, 2)$. By referring to your standard array table, determine which message was originally sent.

6-15. Devise a Hamming single-error-correcting code for an eight-message, three-binary-digit source. Arrange the code words (message digits plus check digits) in a column form with each code word being one of the rows. Construct a last row in which each digit is a parity check on the column above it. Calculate the average erasure probability after row correction and after column correction.

CHAPTER **7**

Cyclic Codes

7-1. INTRODUCTION

The subject of cyclic codes is one that requires a fairly comprehensive knowledge of modern algebra concepts for a thorough understanding of these codes. However, it is possible to gain a good insight into the properties of these codes and how they are implemented by considering them from a simpler viewpoint mathematically. The following presentation follows a paper on the subject of cyclic codes that was published in the *Proceedings of the IRE* in 1961, by W. W. Peterson and D. T. Brown.[28] This paper presents the theory of cyclic codes from the viewpoint of polynomials. The developments are easily understood and the mathematics are elementary, but the subject is very important since the cyclic codes are the basis of error-correction schemes for correcting not only a certain number of errors but also bursts of errors. From the introduction of cyclic codes, by E. Prange,[29] many useful codes have been developed, including error-burst correcting codes, Bose-Chaudhuri codes, Zierler codes, and others.

7-2. CODE GENERATION AND PROPERTIES

A few properties of polynomials in general as applies to this subject are presented next. The modulo-2 addition that we have used in the past work with group codes will also be the rule here, since we are concerned with binary systems. Because cyclic codes involve a code word of n bits of which k bits are the message and the remaining $n - k$ bits are check digits we will consider the k highest-order bits which will be sent first as the message bits and the following $n - k$ bits as the check digits. The terminology highest-order will also refer to the coefficients of a polynomial which we use to represent the code.

DEFINITION. A message such as 1101101 will be *represented* by a polynomial in terms of an arbitrary variable x as $1 + x + x^3 + x^4 + x^6$. The digit farthest to the right in the message will carry the highest weight, in this case it is in the 2^6 place, and the polynomial will be written from left to right in ascending order which corresponds to feeding the message into a shift register from left to right, the standard English-language procedure.

All algebraic manipulations may be performed using addition and multiplication under modulo-2 addition rules. Thus if we have two polynomials, $1 + x^3 + x^5$ and $1 + x + x^3 + x^4 + x^6$ then their addition is

$$
\begin{array}{l}
1 + x + x^3 + x^4 + x^6 \\
\underline{1 \quad\ + x^3 \quad + x^5} \\
0 + x + 0 + x^4 + x^5 + x^6 = x + x^4 + x^5 + x^6
\end{array}
$$

and their multiplication is

$$
\begin{array}{l}
1 + x + x^3 + x^4 + x^6 \\
\underline{1 + x^3 + x^5} \\
1 + x + x^3 + x^4 + x^6 \\
\quad\quad\ \ x^3 + x^4 + x^6 + x^7 + x^9 \\
\underline{\quad\quad\quad\quad\ x^5 + x^6 + x^8 + x^9 + x^{11}} \\
1 + x + 0 + 0 + x^5 + x^6 + x^7 + x^8 + 0 + x^{11} \\
= 1 + x + x^5 + x^6 + x^7 + x^8 + x^{11}
\end{array}
$$

These polynomials may be factorized and have unique factors as do ordinary polynomials under the rules of ordinary algebra.

DEFINITION. A *cyclic code* is defined in terms of a generator polynomial $P(x)$ of degree $n - k$. A polynomial of degree less than n is a code word or code polynomial if it is divisible by the generator polynomial $P(x)$.

It will become evident later why this definition has so much merit. For now notice that if the assumed code polynomial is not divisible by $P(x)$, the generator polynomial, then the assumed polynomial is not a valid code word. Also note that similar to group codes the sum of any two code words (polynomials) will result in a valid code word. This follows, since if $C_1(x)$ and $C_2(x)$ are both less than n in degree then their sum is less than n in degree, and if $C_1(x)$ is divisible by $P(x)$ and if $C_2(x)$ is divisible by $P(x)$ then certainly their sum is divisible by $P(x)$. It turns out that cyclic codes are a class of group codes with the additional requirement that if the a word, say, 101010 is a code word then the word obtained by a cyclic shift, 010101, is also a valid code word. In terms of polynomials we have, if $C_1(x) = 1 + x^2 + x^4$ is a code word, then $C(x) = C_1(x)$ after one cycle shift to the right $= x + x^3 + x^5$, a valid code word. Now if we are using a 6-digit word, and if $C_1(x) = x + x^3 + x^5$, then the word $C_2(x) = C_1(x)$ after one cyclic shift to the right $= 1 + x^2 + x^4$ is also a valid code word.

Now given a message word we write its equivalent polynomial form, say, $G(x)$. The following method, while not the only way to derive the code word polynomial, results in a code word that transmits the k message bits first and the $n - k$ check bits last. Thus the higher-order coefficients of the code word polynomial are the message bits while the lower order coefficients are the check bits.

ENCODING METHOD.
1. To encode a message polynomial, $G(x)$, multiply $G(x)$ by the letter x^{n-k} and divide by $P(x)$ obtaining a remainder $R(x)$ and a quotient $Q(x)$.
2. Add the remainder, $R(x)$, to the quantity $x^{n-k}G(x)$ to obtain the code polynomial $F(x)$. Thus we have

$$\frac{x^{n-k}G(x)}{P(x)} = Q(x) + \frac{R(x)}{P(x)} \tag{7-1}$$

or

$$x^{n-k}G(x) = Q(x)P(x) + R(x) \tag{7-2}$$

Now we form $F(x)$ from $x^{n-k}G(x)$ by subtracting from $x^{n-k}G(x)$ the remainder term $R(x)$, remembering that for modulo-2 rules, addition and subtraction are equivalent operations. Therefore,

$$F(x) = x^{n-k}G(x) + R(x) = Q(x)P(x) \tag{7-3}$$

Now since $Q(x)P(x)$ has degree less than n and is certainly a multiple of $P(x)$ it is apparent that $F(x)$ is a code polynomial, and further that since $R(x)$ must be of degree less than $n-k$ and $x^{n-k}G(x)$ necessarily has zero coefficients in the $n-k$ terms, then $F(x)$ has as its k highest order bits those of $G(x)$, the message polynomial, and as its $n-k$ lowest order bits those of $R(x)$ which are the check symbols.

Example 7-1
Given an (n, k) code of $(12, 8)$ and a generator polynomial $P(x) = 1 + x + x^4$, encode the message 10100111.
1.

$$G(x) = 1 + x^2 + x^5 + x^6 + x^7$$
$$\therefore x^{n-k}G(x) = x^{12-8}G(x) = x^4(1 + x^2 + x^5 + x^6 + x^7)$$
$$= x^4 + x^6 + x^9 + x^{10} + x^{11}$$

Dividing, we have,

$$
\begin{array}{r}
x^7 + x^6 + x^5 + x^4 + x^2 = Q(x) \\
P(x)\overline{\smash{\big)}\,x^{n-k}G(x)} = x^4 + x + 1\overline{\smash{\big)}\,x^{11} + x^{10} + x^9 + x^6 + x^4} \\
\underline{x^{11} \qquad\qquad\qquad x^8 + x^7} \\
x^{10} + x^9 + x^8 + x^7 + x^6 + x^4 \\
\underline{x^{10} \qquad\qquad\quad + x^7 + x^6} \\
x^9 + x^8 \qquad\quad + x^4 \\
\underline{x^9 + \qquad x^6 + x^5} \\
x^8 + x^6 + x^5 + x^4 \\
\underline{x^8 + \qquad\quad x^5 + x^4} \\
x^6 \\
\underline{x^6 + x^3 + x^2} \\
x^3 + x^2 = R(x)
\end{array}
$$

2.

$$F(x) = x^4\, G(x) + R(x) = (x^4 + x^6 + x^9 + x^{10} + x^{11}) + (x^2 + x^3)$$

or

$$F(x) = x^2 + x^3 + x^4 + x^6 + x^9 + x^{10} + x^{11} \qquad (7\text{-}4)$$

Thus the code word to be transmitted is

$$C(x) = \underbrace{0011}_{\text{check bits}} \qquad \underbrace{10100111}_{\text{message bits}}$$

Now since the code polynomial is formed in the manner above it is apparent that the received polynomial $Y(x)$ in any system must be divisible by the generating polynomial $P(x)$ for $Y(x)$ to be a valid code polynomial. If $Y(x)$ is not divisible by $P(x)$, then $Y(x)$ must consist of $F(x) + E(x)$ where $F(x)$ is the transmitted polynomial and $E(x)$ is a polynomial which has nonzero terms in the erroneous positions. If $Y(x)$ is divisible by $P(x)$ one has no choice but to accept it as a valid code word even if errors have occurred in transmission, as there is no way of knowing whether there have been errors or not.

Detection of errors is a simple process, for all we must do is test the received polynomial to see if it is divisible by $P(x)$ with no remainder. Thus if we transmit the code word 001110100111 and receive the code word 001111100111 which has the equivalent polynomial

$$Y(x) = x^2 + x^3 + x^4 + x^5 + x^6 + x^9 + x^{10} + x^{11}$$

all we must do is perform the operation of division of $Y(x)$ by $P(x)$ as

$$
\begin{array}{r}
x^7 + x^6 + x^5 + x^4 + x^2 + x \\[2pt]
x^4 + x + 1\ \overline{\big)\ x^{11} + x^{10} + x^9 \qquad\qquad + x^6 + x^5 + x^4 + x^3 + x^2} \\
x^{11} \qquad\quad + x^8 + x^7 \\ \hline
x^{10} + x^9 + x^8 + x^7 + x^6 + x^5 + x^4 + x^3 + x^2 \\
x^{10} \quad + \quad x^7 + x^6 \\ \hline
x^9 + x^8 \qquad\quad + x^5 + x^4 + x^3 + x^2 \\
x^9 \qquad + x^6 + x^5 \\ \hline
x^8 \quad + x^6 \qquad + x^4 + x^3 + x^2 \\
x^8 \qquad\qquad + x^5 + x^4 \\ \hline
x^6 + x^5 \qquad + x^3 + x^2 \\
x^6 \qquad\qquad + x^3 + x^2 \\ \hline
x^5 \\
x^5 + x^2 + x \\ \hline
x^2 + x = E(x)
\end{array}
$$

Since we have a remainder which is nonzero we know the received message is erroneous. Now that we have seen the mechanism involved, the following properties are worth noting.

1. A cyclic code generated by any polynomial $P(x)$ that has more than one term will detect all single errors.
2. Every polynomial divisible by $1 + x$ has an even number of terms.
3. A code generated by the polynomial $P(x)$ will detect all single and double errors if the length n of the code is no greater than the exponent e to which $P(x)$ belongs, where e is defined as the smallest positive integer for which $P(x)$ will divide $x^e - 1 = x^e + 1$ evenly.
4. It is sufficient and necessary for detection of single, double, and triple errors for the code length n to be no greater than the exponent e to which the polynomial $P_1(x)$ belongs, where $P_1(x)$ is obtained from $P(x) = (1 + x)P_1(x)$.

These properties are justified as follows:

1. If a single error occurs in the code polynomial then the error polynomial $E(x) = x^i$, where i is the position of the error in the code polynomial. However if $P(x)$ is restricted to a polynomial that does not have x as a factor, then $P(x)$ must have at least two terms and will not divide x^i evenly for any i. We can justify the restriction of $P(x)$ to a polynomial that does not have x as a factor since if $P(x)$ has a factor x then all code polynomials must also have a factor x, and this would require all code polynomials to have a zero in the zero-order coefficient (the leftmost position). However, if a bit is always a zero then it does not carry any information and may be dropped. Hence $P(x)$ is restricted to polynomials that do not have x as a factor.
2. Proof of this is left to the student as a problem. Since every code generated by a polynomial with $1 + x$ will have an even number of terms it follows that there must be an even number of ones in every code word, and hence odd numbers of errors which produce odd numbers of ones in the code word will be detected. Hence a code generated by a $P(x)$ with $1 + x$ as a factor will detect all single errors and all odd errors and is a parity check code. (Note that a single error is an odd error.)
3. If we are to detect all double and single errors then we must require that $P(x)$ not divide $x^i + x^j$ for any $i, j < n$. Now it is always possible to factor the error polynomial with two errors into a $x^i + x^j$. For example an error polynomial $1 + x$ has $i = 0$, $j = 1$, and $n > 2$; and an error polynomial of $x^3 + x^4$ has $i = 3, j = 4$, and $n > 4$. (Why must n necessarily be > 4?)

   Factoring $x^i + x^j$, we have $x^i(1 + x^{j-i})$, assuming $i < j$, and since $P(x)$ is restricted to not having x as a factor then it will not divide into x evenly, and further, since $P(x)$ belongs to e and $j - i < n \leq e$, we see that $P(x)$ cannot divide into $(1 + x^{j-i})$ evenly either. Hence the code is double-error detecting. Note also that since $P(x)$ has been restricted to more than one term the code is single-error detecting by property 1.
4. By property 2 we have already that the code is triple and single error detecting due to the $(1 + x)$ factor of $P(x)$. Since $P_1(x)$ belongs to the

exponent $e \geqslant n$ we have by property three that the code is double error correcting.

A theorem which is proven in Peterson's[22] text states that every irreducible polynomial $P(x)$ of degree m is a factor of $x^{q^m} + x$ and hence $P(x)$ divides $x^{q^{m-1}} + 1$. From this it follows that for any m there exists an irreducible polynomial of degree m that belongs to $e = 2^m - 1$. These polynomials are called *primitive*. From this we find that for any m there is a double-error-detecting code of length $n = 2^m - 1$ generated by a polynomial $P(x)$ with degree m. The number of check bits is then m and the number of information bits is $2^m - 1 - m$. These codes are equivalent to the Hamming single-error-correcting codes of the last chapter.

At this point we may consider the error-burst-detecting properties of these codes. Before we discuss the error-burst properties it would be appropriate to point out that any double-error-detecting code is capable of correcting single errors, for if a single error occurs we may find it by changing each bit in the word one at a time until the single error is found. If we change a bit that is correct we merely cause two errors, which of course results in an error polynomial that is nonzero again. The basic error-burst properties may be listed in four statements, each of which may be justified.

5. An error-burst of length b is defined as any pattern of errors that encompasses b number of symbols from the start of the errors to the last of the errors. Thus for an error-burst length of 6 the error word and polynomials might be 001011010 and $E(x) = x^2 + x^4 + x^5 + x^7$ respectively. Any cyclic code generated by a polynomial with degree $n - k$ will detect any error-burst of length $n - k$ or less.

6. If the error-bursts have length $b > n - k$ we may make some definitive statements about what percentage of the error-bursts will be detected. For instance, any burst which has an odd number of errors will be detected if $P(x)$ has as a factor $1 + x$ (see Property 2).

7. If the code-generating polynomial $P(x)$ has form $(1 + x) P_1(x)$ where $P_1(x)$ belongs to the exponent e, then the code generated will detect any combinations of two error-bursts of length two or less if the length of the code n is $\leqslant e$.

8. Subject to some constraints on length any combination of two error-burst groups may be detected by a code generated from $P(x) = (x^c + 1) \times P_1(x)$, where $P_1(x)$ must be irreducible and have degree equal to or greater than the length of the shorter burst and where the length of the code n must be $\leqslant$ the least common multiple of $c \times e$, where e is the exponent of $P_1(x)$. The other constraint is placed on $c + 1$ which must be equal to or greater than the sums of the lengths of the bursts.

Property 5 is easily seen since we can express the error polynomial $E(x)$ as $E(x) = x^1 E_1(x)$, where $E_1(x)$ has degree $b - 1$. For instance for the error polynomial $E(x) = x^2 + x^4 + x^5 + x^7 = x^2(1 + x^2 + x^3 + x^5)$, where the burst was of length $b = 6$. Now since $P(x)$ has no factor x it will not divide $E(x)$ evenly unless it divides $E_1(x)$ evenly. But $b \leqslant n - k$ by hypothesis, and $P(x)$ has length $n - k$ which is certainly greater than the degree of $E_1(x)$, $b - 1$. Hence $P(x)$ cannot divide $E(x)$ evenly and thus will detect the error-burst of length $b \leqslant n - k$. As previously stated, because $P(x)$ has no factor of x it will detect all odd errors, and hence all bursts of errors, no matter what length, will be detected if the total number of errors is odd.

Property 6 allows us to make more definite statements about what percentage of error-bursts will be detected if the error-burst length b is greater than $n - k$. Suppose $b = n - k + 1$, then the error polynomial $E(x) = x^1 E_1(x)$, where $E_1(x)$ has degree $b - 1$ and has terms x^0 and x^{b-1}, will have $b - 2$ terms, x^j, where the j values are such that $0 < j < b - 1$. Since each term has either a 1 or a zero coefficient, and since errors are assumed statistically independent, we have 2^{b-2} distinct possible polynomials for $E_1(x)$. Of these 2^{b-2} possible error polynomials for $E_1(x)$ only one will go undetected, and that is the case for which $E_1(x) = P(x)$ [remember $b = n - k + 1$ or $b - 1 = n - k$] and hence $E_1(x)$ and $P(x)$ have the same degree. Thus only one of the 2^{b-2} possible error patterns will go undetected if $b = n - k + 1$ and hence we may state

Percentage of undetected error bursts

$$= (100)2^{-(b-2)} = (100)2^{-(n-k-1)} \qquad b = n - k + 1$$

If $b > n - k + 1$ then the quotient polynomial obtained by dividing $E_1(x)$ by $P(x)$ has terms from x^0 to $x^{(b-1)-(n-k)}$ and has $(b - 2) - (n - k)$ arbitrary coefficients if there is to be no remainder. Therefore, out of the 2^{b-2} possible error polynomials $2^{(b-2)-(n-k)}$ are undetectable and we may state

Percentage of undetected error bursts

$$= (100)[2^{+(b-2)-(n-k)}/2^{+(b-2)}] = (100)\,2^{-(n-k)} \qquad b > n - k + 1.$$

For Property 7 there are four possible types of error patterns:
  1. $E(x) = x^i + x^j$
  2. $E(x) = (x^i + x^{i+1}) + x^j$
  3. $E(x) = x^i + (x^j + x^{j+1})$
  4. $E(x) = (x^i + x^{i+1}) + (x^j + x^{j+1}) = (1 + x)(x^i + x^j)$

For the first case we have shown by Property 3 that $P(x)$ will not divide $x^i + x^j$ evenly. For the second and third cases we note that they both have an odd number of errors and hence are detected due to Property 2. For the fourth case we note that $(1 + x)$ will cancel with the $(1 + x)$ factor of $P(x)$, but that $P_1(x)$ will not divide $(x^i + x^j)$ evenly from Property 3.

The proof of the last property, Property 8, is somewhat longer but still a straightforward argument. The student is encouraged to refer to the article of reference for the proof.

Implementation of the codes both for encoding and for decoding is fairly simple and is discussed in the next section.

7-3. IMPLEMENTATION

The theory of these codes is easily understood in the terms presented above and the implementation is straightforward, utilizing the standard digital circuits available today.

Reviewing the procedure for generating a cyclic code we have the following steps:

1. The message polynomial $G(x)$ is multiplied by x^{n-k} and the result is the same as if we take the message bits and shift them to the right $n-k$ places in a shift register. Remember that we have entered the message digits from left to right starting with the highest-order, most significant bit first.

2. The resulting polynomial $x^{n-k} G(x)$ is divided by the generator polynomial $P(x)$, of degree $n-k$, to obtain a remainder $R(x)$, of degree less than $n-k$. This division process is easily accomplished by a series of modulo-2 addition steps as we shall see later on.

3. The remainder $R(x)$ is then inserted into the last $n-k$ places of the $x^{n-k} G(x)$ polynomial and the result is the code word to be transmitted. Notice that the quotient is not required.

This division process is easily implemented with a shift register as shown in Fig. 7-1, using the generator polynomial and the code polynomial of Example 7-1.

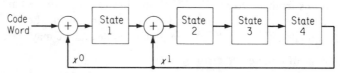

Fig. 7-1. Division by $P[x] = 1 + x + x^4$, using a shift register.

To understand the operation of the shift register, the series of operations performed by the register where the code word is shifted in has been tabulated in Fig. 7-2. Notice that when the code word is inserted it is shifted $n - k = 12 - 8 = 4$ places to the right with no effect caused by the feedback paths, as the output is zero in every case. In fact until the first one is shifted out the right-hand end, no feedback is actuated, since the feedback of a zero does not change any states in the register.

As the first one in the code word is shifted *out* the right-hand stage of the shift register (stage 4 in this case), it is modulo-2 added to the bit *from* stage 1 and the result entered into stage 2, and simultaneously the one shifted out the right-hand stage of the shift register is modulo-2 added to the bit *entering* the register and the result entered into the first stage of the register. This mode of operation is continued until all the code-word bits plus the $n - k$ zeros are shifted into the register. The contents of the register at this time is the remainder $R(x)$ which are the check bits to be added to the code word before transmission. For the division process of Figs. 7-1 and 7-2 we see that the remainder polynomial, $R(x) = x^3 + x^2$ as it did in Example 7-1.

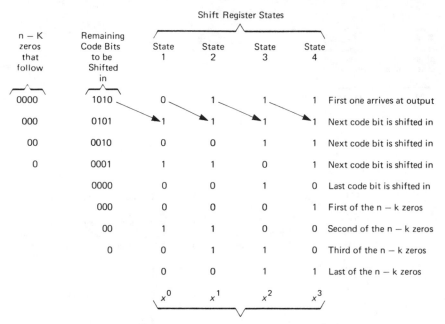

Fig. 7-2. Shifting sequence of encoding register.

A hardware problem that arises when the register of Fig. 7-1 is used to implement the code is the necessity of shifting in the $n - k$ zeros before the remainder $R(x)$ is obtained. This requires us to delay in transmitting the code word for $n - k$ bit times. There are various ways of getting around this condition, but we will not take up the detailed consideration of hardware problems.

Once we have encoded the message and it is ready for transmission we must turn to the problem of decoding the received message. Again the process of decoding may be summarized in the following steps:

1. Divide the received message $Y(x) = F(x) + E(x)$ by the generator polynomial $P(x)$. This is easily done by the same shift register that was used for encoding.

2. After the division of the received message, which includes the $n - k$ remainder digits, the remainder of the register must contain either all zeros, corresponding to no errors, or a nonzero set of terms. If we have a nonzero set of terms we must proceed to step 3.

3. Using the nonzero set of terms we look up the corresponding error polynomial from a storage device such as a table or a set of memory elements.

4. Obtain the original message by adding, modulo-2, the error polynomial to the received message. Again, we may implement the first two steps with the same shift register used for encoding. In Fig. 7-3 a tabulation of the series of operations which are performed when a message polynomial $Y(x) = x^2 + x^3 + x^4 + x^5 + x^6 + x^9 + x^{10} + x^{11}$ is received. The result-

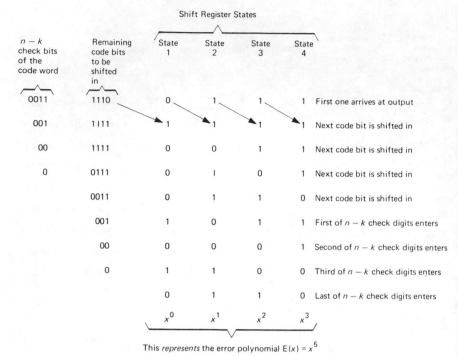

Fig. 7-3. Shifting sequence of decoding register.

ing remaining remainder, $x^2 + x$, is the same as we have seen previously. By using a table of error polynomials and resulting error remainders we may discover that the error polynomial is $E(x) = x^5$, and by adding this to our received message we will have our original message.

In our discussion of cyclic codes we have made use of a primitive polynomial $P(x) = 1 + x + x^4$ for generation of our code. Table 7-1 presents a short listing of primitive polynomials. Example 7-2 illustrates a typical coding problem.

Example 7-2

Derive a code for 16 messages that:
    a. detects all single and double errors
    b. detects all bursts of 5 or less
    c. detects 93 percent of bursts of length 6
    d. detects 96 percent of burst of more than length 6.

By searching through the properties for cyclic codes mentioned above we see that properties 1, 3, 5, and 6 must be met. Further, due to property 3 we see that $P(x)$ must belong to e where $e \geqslant n$, and from property 5 we see that to detect *all* bursts of 5 we must have $n - k = 5 = $ degree of $P(x)$.

We know that k (the number of message bits before coding) must be $k = 4$; therefore, $n - 4 = 5$ or $n = 9 = $ number of bits in code word. Thus we have that $P(x)$ must have degree 5, $n = 9$, and $k = 4$.

TABLE 7-1. Short Listing of Primitive Polynomials*

Polynomial	e
$1 + x$	1
$1 + x + x^2$	3
$1 + x + x^3$	7
$1 + x + x^4$	15
$1 + x^2 + x^5$	31
$1 + x + x^6$	63
$1 + x^3 + x^7$	127
$1 + x^2 + x^3 + x^4 + x^8$	255
$1 + x^4 + x^9$	511

*See also reference 28.

We see that $G(x)$ has degree $k - 1 = 3$, and notice that $1 - 100(2^{-4}) = 93.75$ percent and that $1 - 100(2^{-5}) = 96.875$ percent.

Going to the table of primitive polynomials on this page we see that for $P(x)$ we can use $P(x) = 1 + x^2 + x^5$ and that $P(x)$ belongs to $e = 31$. Now we must design the register and write the code book.

Consider the 10th message, $G(x) = 0101 = x + x^3$, then

$$x^{n-k} G(x) = x^5 G(x) = x^6 + x^8$$

and the division process looks like

$$
\begin{array}{r}
x^3 + x + 1 \\
x^5 + x^2 + 1 \overline{\smash{\big)}\ x^8 + x^6 } \\
\underline{x^8 + x^5 + x^3} \\
x^6 + x^5 + x^3 \\
\underline{x^6 + x^3 + x} \\
x^5 + x \\
\underline{x^5 + x^2 + 1} \\
x^2 + x + 1 = R(x).
\end{array}
$$

Now since we don't need the quotient then division is really equivalent to simply aligning the highest pairs of the divisor and the dividend and adding modulo-2, then aligning the highest pairs of the sum and the divisor and adding, repeating until the difference has degree less than the divisor. This difference is the remainder. Thus writing the above polynomials in terms of their binary equivalents we see that division looks like

$$
\begin{array}{l}
\ x^5 x^4 x^3 x^2 x^1 x^0 \ \ x^8 x^7 x^6 x^5 x^4 x^3 x^2 x^1 x^0 \ = G(x) x^{n-k} \\
P(x) = 1\ 0\ 0\ 1\ 0\ 1 \overline{\smash{\big)}\ 1\ 0\ 1\ 0\ 0\ 0\ 0\ 0\ 0} \\
\ \ \underline{1\ 0\ 0\ 1\ 0\ 1} \\
\ 1\ 1\ 0\ 1\ 0\ 0\ 0 \\
\ \underline{1\ 0\ 0\ 1\ 0\ 1} \\
\ 1\ 0\ 0\ 0\ 1\ 0 \\
\ \underline{1\ 0\ 0\ 1\ 0\ 1} \\
\ 1\ 1\ 1\ = R(x) = x^2 + x + 1.
\end{array}
$$

We can implement this by a shift register and modulo-2 adders. The number of shift register positions (bits) is equal to the degree of $P(x) = n - k = 5$ and the dividend is shifted through high order first and left to right. Multiplication by x^{n-k} is accomplished by shifting in x^{n-k} zeroes behind $G(x)$. As the first one is shifted out the divisor is added by the following procedure:

1. In the addition the highest order terms always cancel so as we shift the one out of the shift register this cancellation is done automatically.

2. Modulo-2 adders are placed so that when a one comes off the end of the register the divisor is then added to the contents of the register (in the right places of course!). The register then contains a difference that is shifted (with no feedback action) until another one comes off the end and then the process is repeated until the entire dividend is shifted into the register (k shifts) and the $(n - k)$ zeroes are shifted in ($n - k$ shifts) for a total of n shifts. At this point the remainder is in the register, highest order bit in the right hand position.

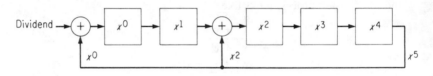

If we clock in $G(x) = 0101$ followed by 5 zeroes we have

$$x^0 \ x^1 \ x^2 \ x^3 \ x^4$$

00000 010	1 0 0 0 0	1st shift
0000 001	0 1 0 0 0	2nd
000 000	1 0 1 0 0	3rd
00 000	0 1 0 1 0	4th
0 000	0 0 1 0 1	5th
000	1 0 1 1 0	6th
00	0 1 0 1 1	7th
0	1 0 0 0 1	8th
	1 1 1 0 0	9th

$$R(x) = x^0 + x^1 + x^2 = 1 + x + x^2$$

$$F(x) = \underbrace{11100}_{R(x)} \ \underbrace{0101}_{G(x)}$$

7-4. RELATED CODES

There are many types of codes and many ways to implement them. Naturally we have barely touched the surface in our study, and this section discusses the various common codes, their properties, and the type of channels they are best suited for.

Geometric codes have been discussed in Chapter 6. They are parity-type codes utilizing both word and block-parity checks for detection and correction of errors. These codes have the advantage of simplicity of implementation, (they are used in most computers to check data transfer) and the ease of adaptation to various code formats such as the American Standard Code for Information Interchange. While the geometric code is not able to offer the guarantee of error rates which may be achieved with other codes, group, cyclic, etc., they are able to offer a good reliability, and in systems with the ability to send information more than once, the reliability of information transfer may be as high as desired.

Several types of cyclic codes are commonly used and among these are the Bose-Chaudhuri (BCH) codes. These codes offer the ability of detecting any combination of $2t$ errors or correcting any combination of t errors. The code length is restricted to $2^m - 1$ and the generator polynomial is of degree no greater than mt. The block length may be varied to match the channel performance.

Zierler codes, which are similar to BCH codes, replace each bit in the BCH code with an x-bit symbol. Thus there are $2^x - 1$ symbols in each Zierler code block and c of these symbols are arbitrarily chosen as check symbols. The code may then be used to correct up to $e = c/2$ symbol errors. This technique has the ability of correcting clusters of errors within a code and still provide a degree of random-error correction.

Time-spread coding is a useful technique that converts block codes into forms that allow a decoder to handle long bursts of errors in an economical manner. This is basically a two-step process that is initiated by constructing code blocks with BCH or other types of block codes. The bits in the coded blocks are then interchanged so that a burst of errors will affect one or two bits in each code block rather than destroy a complete block. In Fig. 7-4 a four-bit code has been time-spread.

A four-bit error burst as shown would prevent correction of the nontime-spread words and cause the loss of two words, whereas a single-error-correcting code would allow all the words to be received if the words have been time-spread.

This technique has both advantages and disadvantages. The codes are simple to implement and have good rates, but they require memory or storage which may or may not be costly depending upon the situation.

Convolutional codes are specified by code rate and constraint length and do not have a specified block structure. In these codes the information message is a single sequence of binary digits with parity check digits interlaced between the information digits. For all practical purposes one may assume that the individual messages are "self-contained," although in theory one would have to consider

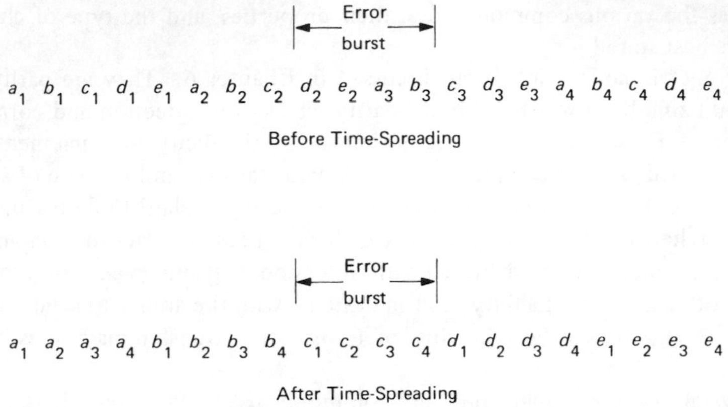

$$a_1 \; b_1 \; c_1 \; d_1 \; e_1 \; a_2 \; b_2 \; c_2 \; d_2 \; e_2 \; a_3 \; b_3 \; c_3 \; d_3 \; e_3 \; a_4 \; b_4 \; c_4 \; d_4 \; e_4$$

Error burst

Before Time-Spreading

Error burst

$$a_1 \; a_2 \; a_3 \; a_4 \; b_1 \; b_2 \; b_3 \; b_4 \; c_1 \; c_2 \; c_3 \; c_4 \; d_1 \; d_2 \; d_3 \; d_4 \; e_1 \; e_2 \; e_3 \; e_4$$

After Time-Spreading

Fig. 7-4. Time-spread coding.

their complete past history. These codes may be used with systems that have varied noise backgrounds. The code length and rate may be varied as needed to provide optimum matching to the channel characteristics. For this reason these codes are used with military-type scatter systems.

TABLE 7-2

Channel Type	Codes Most Commonly Used
1. Hardware, cables	Convolutional, time-spread
2. Line-of-sight microwave links	Convolutional
3. Satellite links or gaussian channels	BCH, time-spread
4. High-frequency channels (burst noise)	BCH, time-spread
5. Tropospheric-scatter channels	Convolutional

A tabulation of the commonly encountered channels and the codes suited for those channels is presented in Table 7-2.

7-5. SYSTEM OPERATING LIMITATIONS

In an article published in the *IEEE Spectrum*[30], G. D. Forney has discussed the application of coding in the power-limited and band-limited operations of communication and has also compared the relative merits of algebraic versus convolutional codes. This section and the next section deal with these topics.

If we reexamine the channel capacity expressed as a function of the signal to noise ratio (Eq. 4-33) we may determine the effects of power-limited or band-limited operations. We have

$$C = B \log \left(1 + \frac{S}{\eta}\right)$$

where $\eta = WB$

W = noise power spectral density, watts per cycle

B = nominal bandwidth, cycles

S = signal power, watts

If we rewrite this expression as

$$\frac{C}{B} = \log \left[1 + \left(\frac{S}{WC}\right)\left(\frac{C}{B}\right)\right] \tag{7-5}$$

and plot the quantity $\frac{C}{B}$ versus $\frac{S}{WC}$ as in Fig. 7-5,[†] we see that for fixed signal to

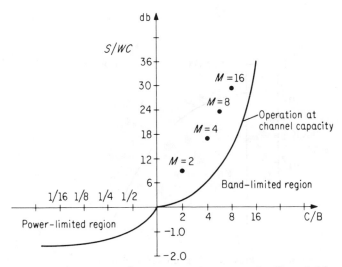

Fig. 7-5. *S/WC* versus *C/B* with operation at capacity illustrated by the solid line. The points labeled *M* illustrate operation with *M*-level amplitudes with $P[E] = 10^{-5}$.

[†] Figures 7-5, 7-6, 7-7, and 7-8 are drawn from Forney, ref. 30.

noise ratio $\dfrac{S}{W}$ we have a more efficient communication system as the bandwidth

B is increased. That is, as the bandwidth is increased we see that C/B decreases and that a smaller and smaller value of S/WC (or S/W, since C is a constant for any given channel) is required to operate close to the channel capacity line. In the limit we see that for infinite bandwidth we have a limiting value for S/WC, the Shannon limit, of -1.6 db.

The space-communication systems used to date have by practical necessity been operated in a power-limited mode and in general have had more than sufficient bandwidth. Even though we reach the Shannon limit only for infinite bandwidth we may state that we are approximately there for a C/W ratio of about $1/2$; for *PSK* this amounts to an approximate code rate of $1/4$.

Another way of illustrating the above results is in the more standard presentation of Fig. 7-6, which gives a plot of the probable error rate $P[\epsilon]$ versus the signal-to-noise ratio used. From the graph we see that if we have the power available we may achieve low error rates, but if we are able to operate at

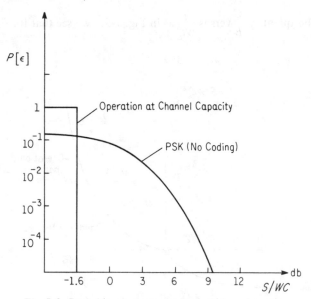

Fig. 7-6. Probable error rate versus signal-to-noise ratio.

channel capacity we only need enough power to have a signal-to-noise ratio of -1.6 db. For an error rate of 10^{-4}, 99.99 percent, we would save approximately 10 db by operating at capacity versus using *PSK*.

When our system is band-limited rather than power-limited, such as hardwire systems like the telephone or telegraph, we have a much different situation. If we increase the power such that the quantity $S/WC \gg 1$ then, since we are taking the log to the base 2 in Eq. 7-5, for each additional increase in power by a factor of 4 we have C increasing by 1. Then if we increase the power by a factor of k fours or 4^k times, we will increase C by a factor of k.

Now we have seen that to increase the channel capacity by coding we may increase the number of levels with which to modulate while keeping the spacing of the levels constant to maintain the same probability of error. But each time we double the number of levels this requires an increase of four in power. (Double the levels means doubling the dynamic voltage range of the transmitter.) Thus an increase in power by k factors of four yields an increase of capacity by a factor k for coding (by allowing a doubling of levels k times) just as it yielded an increase in capacity of k for the noncoded system. Hence in the limit we have

$$\lim_{k \to \infty} \frac{C \text{ noncoded}}{C \text{ coded}} \to 1$$

From Fig. 7-4 we see that for various M level systems the C noncoded and C coded approach each other fairly rapidly as the power is increased and we go deeper into the band-limited region.

It should be kept in mind that increases in power by factors of four with present-day technology is expensive. In addition to the actual transmitters, the added weight for cooling and for power supplies are also large problems.

7-6. ALGEBRAIC CODES VERSUS CONVOLUTIONAL CODES

It seems fitting to show some curves that compare the performance of algebraic codes versus convolutional codes.

In Fig. 7-7 a comparison of various block codes is illustrated. Although the correlation detection would seem superior to the same system using the algebraic error detection, one must remember that the algebraic decoding method remains feasible for much longer code lengths and numbers of information bits than for the correlation-detection method, which becomes too cumbersome computationally.

For a correlation-detection method the 32 received binary digits would be treated as the 32 components of a received signal vector. Thus the received signal vector would be correlated with the 64 possible signals, assuming a (32, 6) code, and the possible signal vector with the largest correlation would be selected as the original signal. If we use algebraic code detection each incoming

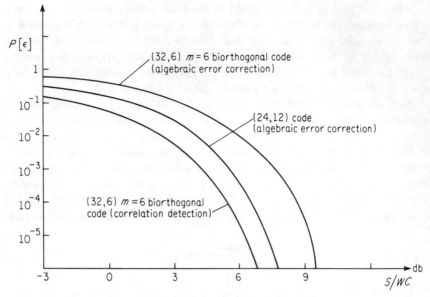

Fig. 7-7. Performance of various block codes.

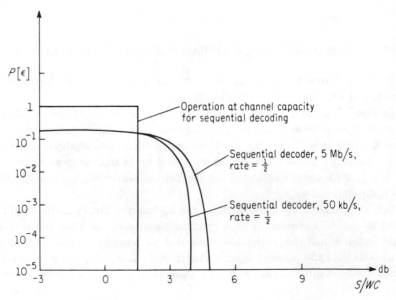

Fig. 7-8. Performance of some convolutional decoders.

bit would be decided upon as a zero or a one as they arrive. Then the 32-bit word is in the algebraic domain again and the hamming distance of the received code word is compared to the possible code words and the original (hopefully) code word is determined. The decision of whether an incoming bit is a zero or a one is called a *hard decision*.

In Fig. 7-8 we see the performance of some sequential decoders[31] which are a class of convolutional codes. These codes in fact perform better than the block codes illustrated, however it is also true that the block codes do well in error-burst correction which is intolerable for sequential decoding.

The performance of sequential decoding depends upon the modulation and detection schemes used and upon the data rate relative to the internal computational rate. The internal computation rate of the decoders of Fig. 7-8 is 13.3 Mb/s. The curves shown are for the Codex decoder produced by the Codex Corporation, Watertown, Mass., where Dr. G. D. Forney is Director of Research.

7-7. REMARKS

We have started with the most basic assumptions about one idea of information—developed a measure of information, applied this measure to developing tools with which to analyze systems, devised various means and methods for overcoming noise and imperfections in our systems and as a result we are able to perform some types of communications with some prediction of reliability.

In this chapter we have discussed a type of code—cyclic—that allows one to produce codes with known error-correcting capabilities, and with predictable error rates and information rates. The overall state of the art, however, is still short of the Shannon prediction.

In all of the codes for error detection and error correction the occurrence of errors was assumed to be statistically independent with the exception of the error-burst correction schemes. It is true that much of the work to which coding is applied does satisfy this basic assumption, but in many cases the occurrence of an error is dependent upon the previous occurrence of errors. Several schemes for detection and correction of errors have been proposed and utilized. In particular, the error-burst codes have been investigated by N. Abramson, P. Fire, and D. Hagelbarger. These codes are now seen to be specific cases of the more general cyclic codes, but as is often the case the specialized cases came first and gave insight to the generalized theory.

The text has stressed the digital aspects of the subject throughout due to the past, present, and future importance of digital systems in modern technology, and because the mathematical techniques are quite simple. The analog concept of communication is quite dependent upon statistical estimation theory rather than on the statistical decision theory used in digital analysis. The difference lies in the fact that for digital systems discrete decisions must be made (in the case of binary was it a "zero" or a "one"?), whereas in the analog systems one is faced with estimating as "best" as possible the value or range of values of continuous random parameters.

There is a great deal of information available to the interested reader in almost any aspect of the subjects we have discussed, and the interested reader is encouraged to seek out and assimilate all that he desires—and more.

PROBLEMS

7-1. Prove Property 2 for cyclic codes. (The proof is very short and is easily done by reasoning.)

7-2. Prove Property 8 for cyclic codes. (The student is referred to the articles of reference.)

7-3. Consider a code for which $n = 15$ and $k = 10$. If the generator polynomial is $P(x) = 1 + x^2 + x^4 + x^5$ encode the message 1010010001 and write the code word to be transmitted.

7-4. For the generator polynomial of Prob. 7-3, draw the schematic (block diagram) of the encoder. Show that your encoder works by constructing the table of operation sequences similar to Fig. 7-2 and derive the remainder polynomial for the check digits $R(x)$.

7-5. Is the received message 110101100010001 a valid message? Prove your answer. Refer to 7-3.

7-6. If your school has a digital logic trainer, program the encoder of Prob. 7-4 and test by feeding it the message polynomial of Prob. 7-3.

7-7. Write a computer program for the general polynomial division used in this chapter and check your program with Prob. 7-3.

Appendix A

PROBABILITY THEORY

A very useful method for computing the number of ways that an event can take place is by use of binomial coefficients. This method may be stated as the number of ways in which n things can be grouped r at a time, irrespective of their order or sequence, and is given by

$$C(n, r) = \binom{n}{r} = \frac{n!}{(n-r)\,!\,r!} \qquad \text{(A-1)}$$

where the numbers $\binom{n}{r}$ are known as *binomial coefficients* because they are the coefficients of $(x + 1)^n$ when written in expanded form. An example will illustrate the use of Eq. A-1.

Example A-1
Two cards are drawn at random from an ordinary deck of 52 cards. Find the likelihood (probability) that both are spades.

The total number of ways we may draw 2 cards from 52 cards is the total number of ways 52 things may be grouped two at a time and is given by

$$\binom{52}{2} = \frac{52!}{(52-2)\,!\,2!} = \frac{1{,}326 \text{ ways to draw}}{2 \text{ cards from } 52}$$

Of these 1,326 possibilities only those combinations consisting of 2 spades are desired. There are 13 spades, so the number of ways 2 of these can be drawn is

$$\binom{13}{2} = \frac{13}{(13-2)\,!\,2!} = \frac{78 \text{ ways to draw}}{2 \text{ spades from } 13}$$

Thus the likelihood of drawing 2 cards and those 2 cards being spades is

$$p = {}^{78}\!/_{1326} = {}^1\!/_{17}$$

Note that we have introduced one way of defining probability. This is the concept that most people have of probability—that of relative frequency of occurrence of some event.

If an event can happen N ways each of which is equally likely, and if among these N ways m are favorable to the occurrence of a particular situation A, then the probability of occurrence of A in a single trial is

$$P(A) = \frac{m}{N}$$

For example, we know that if we throw a die any one of the six faces is equally likely to come up (assuming the die is not loaded). Thus we say that the probability of a four is one sixth:

$$P(4) = {}^1\!/_6$$

If we then throw the die 60 times we would expect to have a four turn up six times. However we know that on a small number of throws, say 6 throws, the number four may not turn up at all. Thus we must say that on the average over a large number of trials the probability of an event A may be written as

$$P(A) = \begin{array}{c} \text{limit as the} \\ \text{number of trials} \\ {\scriptstyle N \to \infty} \end{array} \left(\frac{\text{number of times } A \text{ occurs}}{\text{total number of trials, } N} \right)$$

We may also model probability systems as geometric or continuous spaces. The set S of all possible outcomes of some given experiment is called the sample space. A particular outcome, i.e., an element in S, is called a *sample point* or *sample*. An event A is a set of outcomes or a subset of the sample space S.

Two events A and B may be combined to form new events in the following manner (refer to Fig. A-1).

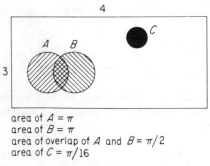

area of $A = \pi$
area of $B = \pi$
area of overlap of A and $B = \pi/2$
area of $C = \pi/16$

Fig. A-1.

The event $A \cup B$ is the event that occurs if a sample point is in A or B or both. Thus any of the shaded area of Fig. A-1 would be in the subset of points $A \cup B$ and the probability of the event $A \cup B$ is

$$P(A \cup B) = \frac{\pi + \pi - \pi/2}{12} = \frac{3\pi}{24}$$

where we have taken the ratio of the area of A and B to the total area of the sample space S (being careful to include the overlap area only once).

The event $A \cap B = AB$ is the event that occurs if a sample point is in both A and B. Thus the double hatched area in Fig. A-1 includes all the points of AB and the probability of AB is

$$P(AB) = \frac{\pi/2}{12} = \frac{\pi}{24}$$

Two events are said to be *mutually exclusive* if they are disjoint, i.e., if the occurrence of one of the events prevents or excludes the others from occurring. Thus the event AC in Fig. A-1 has probability of occurrence zero and we see that A and C are mutually exclusive. If a sample point occurs in C it certainly cannot be in A as well.

Now we may see that the probability of $A \cup B$ may be written as $P(A \cup B) = P(A) + P(B) - P(AB)$ and if A and B are mutually exclusive we have $P(A \cup B) = P(A) + P(B)$.

Two events are said to be *independent* if the occurrence of one does not influence the occurrence of the other. Thus the probability of two independent events occurring is the product of their individual probabilities,

$$P(AB) = P(A)P(B) \qquad \text{if } A \text{ and } B \text{ are independent}$$

There is no geometrical way to show this, but consider the toss of a coin. We say that the probability of throwing two heads is the probability of throwing a heads the first time ($1/2$) times the probability of throwing a heads the second time ($1/2$) and is ($1/2$) ($1/2$) = ($1/4$).

The probability that a sample point is in event A may be expressed as $P(A)$ and for Fig. A-1 we have $P(A) = \pi/12$.

The probability that a sample point is in event A if we *know* that it is in event B may be written as $P(A/B)$ and is *not* equal to $P(A)$ in general. We may see from Fig. A-1 that if we know that the sample point which has occurred *is* in B, then the probability that it is in A *also* is different from the probability that a sample point is in A without knowing whether it is in B. We say that the *conditional* probability of A given B is

$$P(A/B) = \frac{P(AB)}{P(B)}$$

From Fig. A-1 we have $P(A/B) = \dfrac{\pi/2}{\pi} = \frac{1}{2}$, and we see that the conditioned knowledge that our sample point is in B has increased the probability that it is in A also. [Is it always true that $P(A/B) > P(A)$? Suppose A and B are mutually exclusive!]

If A and B are independent then we see that $P(A/B) = P(A)$.

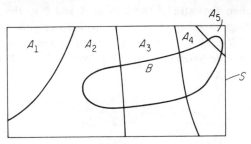

Fig. A-2.

Now suppose the events $A_1, A_2, \ldots, A_n$ form a partition of a sample space S, i.e., the events A_i are mutually exclusive and their union is S, Fig. A-2. Now let B be any other event, then

$$B = S \cap B = (A_1 \cup A_2 \cup \ldots \cup A_n) \cap B$$

$$(A_1 \cap B) \cup (A_2 \cap B) \ldots \cup (A_n \cap B)$$

where we know the $(A_i \cap B)$ are mutually exclusive. Thus

$$P(B) = P(A_1 \cap B) + P(A_2 \cap B) + \cdots + P(A_n \cap B)$$

From $P(A_i \cap B) = P(A_iB) = P(A_i/B)P(B) = P(B/A_i)P(A_i)$ we have

$$P(B) = P(A_1)P(B/A_1) + P(A_2)P(B/A_2) + \cdots + P(A_n)P(B/A_n) \quad \text{(A-2)}$$

But for any A_i we have

$$P(A_i/B) = \frac{P(A_iB)}{P(B)}$$

and hence substituting for $P(B)$ we have

$$P(A_i/B) = \frac{P(A_i)P(B/A_i)}{P(A_1)P(B/A_1) + P(A_2)P(B/A_2) + \cdots + P(A_n)P(B/A_n)} \quad \text{(A-3)}$$

Equation A-3 is called *Bayes' theorem*.

Example A-2

Three machines A, B, and C produce respectively 50, 30, and 20 percent of the total number of items of a factory. The percentages of defective output of these machines are 3, 4, and 5 percent. If an item is selected at random, find the probability that it is defective and assuming it is defective find the probability that it is from machine A.

Let X be the event that an item is defective. Then from Eq. A-2 we have

$$P(X) = P(A)P(X/A) + P(B)P(X/B) + P(C)P(X/C)$$
$$= (.5)(.03) + (.3)(.04) + (.2)(.05) = .037$$

If a piece is picked at random and is found defective, the probability that the item was produced by machine A is

$$P(A/X) = \frac{P(A)P(X/A)}{P(X)} = \frac{(.5)(.03)}{.037} = .405$$

THE GAUSSIAN DISTRIBUTION

Often one is faced with systems containing not a discrete set of points but an infinite set of possible outcomes or a continuous random variable. If we model this system by assuming that each point in an uncountable set of discrete points has probability of occurrence equal to $P(x = x_i) = p(x_i)\,\Delta x$, where Δx is the interval from halfway to the nearest point to the left to halfway to the nearest point to the right, then the probability that an outcome will lie between x_i and x_j, where $x_i < x_j$, is

$$P(x_i < x < x_j) = \sum_{k=i}^{j} p(x_k)\,\Delta x$$

If we now increase the number of points without limit such that $\Delta x \to 0$ we have in the limit

$$P(x_i < x < x_j) = \lim_{\Delta x \to 0} \sum_{k=i}^{j} p(x_k)\,\Delta x$$

or

$$P(x_i < x < x_j) = \int_{x_i}^{x_j} p(x)\,dx$$

The term $p(x)$ is referred to as the *probability density function* and must satisfy at least the following properties:

$$\int_{-\infty}^{\infty} p(x)\,dx = 1$$

$$p(x) \geqslant 0; \quad \text{all } x$$

Several quantities that describe random variables are of interest and may be defined for both the discrete random variable and the continuous random variable. These quantities are tabulated in Table T-1.

TABLE T-1. Statistical Quantities of Interest

Quantity	Discrete R.V.	Continuous R.V.
Average (mean x)	$\overline{x} = \sum_{\text{all } i} x_i\, p(x_i)$	$\overline{x} = \int_{-\infty}^{\infty} x\, p(x)\, dx$
Mean-square value	$\overline{x^2} = \sum_{\text{all } i} x_i^2\, p(x_i)$	$\overline{x^2} = \int_{-\infty}^{\infty} x^2\, p(x)\, dx$
nth moment	$\overline{x_i^n} = \sum_{\text{all } i} x_i^n\, p(x_i)$	$\overline{x^n} = \int_{-\infty}^{\infty} x^n\, p(x)\, dx$
Variance	$\sigma^2 = \sum_{\text{all } i} (x_i - \overline{x})^2\, p(x_i)$	$\sigma^2 = \int_{-\infty}^{\infty} (x - \overline{x})^2\, p(x)\, dx$
nth central moment	$\overline{(x - \overline{x})^n} = \sum_{\text{all } i} (x_i - \overline{x})^n\, p(x_i)$	$\overline{(x - \overline{x})^n} = \int_{-\infty}^{\infty} (x - \overline{x})^n\, p(x)\, dx$

In most work the gaussian distribution occurs sooner or later. This common probability density function is the well-known bell-shaped curve of grades in a classroom and is

$$p(x) = \frac{1}{\sqrt{2\pi}\,\sigma}\, e^{-(x-\overline{x})^2/2\pi\sigma^2} \qquad -\infty \leqslant x \leqslant \infty$$

The density function is plotted in Fig. A-3.

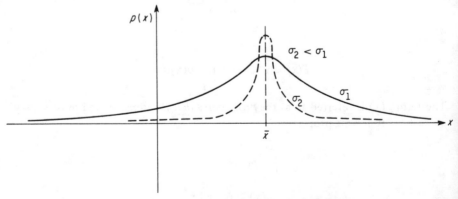

Fig. A-3. Gaussian probability density function.

The probability that an outcome will be greater than a certain value x_1 is easily found by

$$P(x \geqslant x_1) = \int_{x_1}^{\infty} p(x)\,dx$$

and is represented by the area under the probability density curve as shown in Fig. A-4.

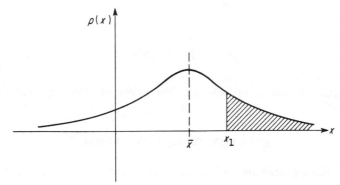

Fig. A-4. Shaded area = $P(x \geqslant x_1)$.

In the instance of two random variables (such as the reading of the output voltage out of two amplifiers simultaneously with white noise as the input or the tossing of two dice simultaneously) the joint probability density functions, if they are gaussian, may be written as

$$p(x,y) = \frac{1}{2\pi\sqrt{1 - \rho^2}}$$
$$\times e^{-1/2(1-\rho^2)\,[(x-\bar{x})^2/\sigma_x^2 - 2\rho(x-\bar{x})(y-\bar{y})/\sigma_x\sigma_y + (y-\bar{y})^2/\sigma_y^2]}$$

where

$$\rho = \text{correlation coefficient} = \frac{\overline{xy} - \bar{x}\bar{y}}{\sigma_x\,\sigma_y}$$

If the two random variables x and y are statistically independent, then $\rho = 0$ and we have

$$p(x,y) = p(x)\,p(y)$$

If the variables have zero means but finite ρ, then

$$\bar{x} = \bar{y} = 0$$

and we have

$$p(x,y) = \frac{1}{2\pi\sqrt{1 - \rho^2}}\, e^{-1/2(1-\rho^2)\,[x^2/\sigma_x^2 - 2\rho\,xy/\sigma_x\sigma_y + y^2/\sigma_y^2]}$$

and

$$\rho = \frac{\overline{xy}}{\sigma_x \, \sigma_y}$$

Notice also that

$$p(x) = \int_{-\infty}^{\infty} p(x, y) \, dy$$

and

$$p(y) = \int_{-\infty}^{\infty} p(x, y) \, dx$$

since integration over a variable has the effect of removing that variable's influence.

ECHELON CANONICAL FORM

The following example will illustrate the method of reducing a matrix to echelon canonical form. Consider the matrix,

$$\begin{bmatrix} 0 & 1 & 2 & 3 & 5 \\ 1 & 3 & 2 & 0 & 1 \\ 3 & 1 & 2 & 1 & 0 \\ 1 & 1 & 3 & 4 & 2 \end{bmatrix}$$

The first step is to locate the first column with a nonzero element, interchanging rows if the first row is all zero, and multiply that row by its first nonzero element's inverse to give a leading one. Interchanging rows 1 and 2 gives

$$\begin{bmatrix} 1 & 3 & 2 & 0 & 1 \\ 0 & 1 & 2 & 3 & 5 \\ 3 & 1 & 2 & 1 & 0 \\ 1 & 1 & 3 & 4 & 2 \end{bmatrix}$$

The next step is to subtract a multiple of the first row from all other rows to make the rest of the first column zero.

$$\begin{bmatrix} 1 & 3 & 2 & 0 & 1 \\ 0 & 1 & 2 & 3 & 5 \\ 0 & -8 & -4 & 0 & -3 \\ 0 & -2 & 1 & 4 & 1 \end{bmatrix}$$

The next step is to ignore the first row and determine where the first column with a nonzero element is located. This element is reduced to unity and the appropriate multiple is subtracted from or added to all other rows to make *all* elements in that column zero. We thus have

$$\begin{bmatrix} 1 & 0 & -4 & -9 & -14 \\ 0 & 1 & 2 & 3 & 5 \\ 0 & 0 & 12 & 24 & 37 \\ 0 & 0 & 5 & 10 & 11 \end{bmatrix}$$

Continuing, we have,

$$\begin{bmatrix} 1 & 0 & -4 & -9 & -14 \\ 0 & 1 & 2 & 3 & 5 \\ 0 & 0 & 1 & 2 & {}^{37}/_{12} \\ 0 & 0 & 5 & 10 & 11 \end{bmatrix}$$

and

$$\begin{bmatrix} 1 & 0 & 0 & -1 & -{}^{5}/_{3} \\ 0 & 1 & 0 & -1 & -{}^{7}/_{6} \\ 0 & 0 & 1 & 2 & {}^{37}/_{12} \\ 0 & 0 & 0 & 0 & -{}^{53}/_{12} \end{bmatrix}$$

$$\begin{bmatrix} 1 & 0 & 0 & -1 & 0 \\ 0 & 1 & 0 & -1 & 0 \\ 0 & 0 & 1 & 2 & 0 \\ 0 & 0 & 0 & 0 & 1 \end{bmatrix}$$

The last matrix is in echelon canonical form.

The next step is to ignore the black row and third print when the first column will again be blank (second row). The tabular is reduced to omit the first tabulate method is substituted from its start to all other rows (using to each element in the column) we may have.

TABLE T-3. Entropy of a Binary Source

p	$-p \log p$	$-(1-p)\log(1-p)$	$H(p)$
0	0	0	0
0.01	0.0664	0.0144	0.0808
0.02	0.1129	0.0285	0.1414
0.04	0.1858	0.0565	0.2423
0.06	0.2435	0.0839	0.3274
0.08	0.2915	0.1107	0.4022
0.10	0.3322	0.1368	0.4690
0.12	0.3671	0.1623	0.5294
0.14	0.3971	0.1871	0.5842
0.16	0.4230	0.2113	0.6343
0.18	0.4453	0.2348	0.6801
0.20	0.4644	0.2575	0.7219
0.22	0.4806	0.2796	0.7602
0.24	0.4941	0.3009	0.7950
0.26	0.5053	0.3214	0.8267
0.28	0.5142	0.3412	0.8554
0.30	0.5211	0.3602	0.8813
0.32	0.5260	0.3784	0.9044
0.34	0.5292	0.3956	0.9248
0.36	0.5306	0.4121	0.9427
0.38	0.5304	0.4276	0.9580
0.40	0.5288	0.4422	0.9710
0.42	0.5257	0.4558	0.9815
0.44	0.5212	0.4684	0.9896
0.46	0.5154	0.4800	0.9954
0.48	0.5083	0.4905	0.9988
0.50	0.5000	0.5000	1.0000

$$H(p) = -p \log p - (1-p) \log (1-p) \text{ bits}$$
$$H(p) = H(1-q) \quad p+q = 1$$

TABLE T-2. Logarithms to the Base 2

n	$\log n$	n	$\log n$
1	0.0000	26	4.7004
2	1.0000	27	4.7548
3	1.5849	28	4.8073
4	2.0000	29	4.8579
5	2.3219	30	4.9068
6	2.5849	31	4.9541
7	2.8073	32	5.0000
8	3.0000	33	5.0443
9	3.1699	34	5.0874
10	3.3219	35	5.1292
11	3.4594	36	5.1699
12	3.5849	37	5.2094
13	3.7004	38	5.2479
14	3.8073	39	5.2854
15	3.9068	40	5.3219
16	4.0000	41	5.3575
17	4.0874	42	5.3923
18	4.1699	43	5.4262
19	4.2479	44	5.4594
20	4.3219	45	5.4918
21	4.3923	46	5.5235
22	4.4594	47	5.5545
23	4.5235	48	5.5849
24	4.5849	49	5.6147
25	4.6438	50	5.6438

Table T-4 is for use in specifying the parity check matrix for (n, b) group codes. The quantities n and b are as defined in Chapter Six and repeated below for convenience as:

n = total number of digits per code word

b = total number of check digits per code word

In addition a third symbol k is used for tabulation purposes and is defined as:

k = total number of information digits per code word

It should be obvious that

$$k = n - b$$

In the listing of Table T-4 the group of numbers in any entry should be interpreted as follows. The first column of numbers refer to the check digit b_i. The remaining numbers refer to the position of the ones in the parity-check matrix. Thus for a $(7, 3)$ code we would have

$$n = 7, \qquad b = 3, \qquad k = 4$$

From Table T-3 we have the array of numbers

$$
\begin{array}{cccc}
5 & 1 & 3 & 4 \\
6 & 1 & 2 & 4 \\
7 & 1 & 2 & 3
\end{array}
$$

or

$$
\begin{aligned}
b_5 &= x_1 + x_3 + x_4 \\
b_6 &= x_1 + x_2 + x_4 \\
b_7 &= x_1 + x_2 + x_3
\end{aligned}
$$

and the parity-check matrix H would be

$$
[H] = \begin{bmatrix}
1 & 0 & 1 & 1 \\
1 & 1 & 0 & 1 \\
1 & 1 & 1 & 0
\end{bmatrix}
$$

TABLE T-4.   Parity Check Matrices for Various (n,b) Group Codes*

n = total number of digits per code word
k = number of information digits per code word = $n - b$
b = number of check digits per code word

	k=2	k=3	k=4	k=5	k=6	k=7	k=8	k=9	k=10
n=4	32								
	412								
n=5	312	412							
	42	513							
	51								
n=6	32	412	5123						
	412	513	6124						
	51	623							
	61								
n=7	31	413	5134	61					
	41	512	6124	71					
	51	6123	7123						
	612	7123							
	72								
n=8	31	41	5134	6134	71				
	41	512	6124	7124	81				
	52	613	7123	8123					
	62	723	81234						
	712	8123							
	812								
n=9	31	41	5134	61345	7134	81			
	41	52	6124	71245	8124	91			
	51	612	7123	81235	9123				
	62	713	8123	91234					
	72	823	9123						
	812	9123							
	912								
n=10	31	41	534	61345	71345	8134	91		
	41	52	6123	71245	81245	9124	101		
	51	63	7124	81235	912356	10123			
	62	712	8134	91234	1012346				
	72	813	9234	1012345					
	812	923	101234						
	912	10123							
	1012								
n=11	31	43	513		713456	81345	9134	101	
	41	53	624		812456	912457	10124	111	
	51	62	714		912356	1012356	11123		
	62	713	823		1012346	11123467			
	72	813	9134		1112345				
	82	912	10234						
	912	10123	111234						
	1012	11123							
	1112								
n=12	31	41				813456	91235678	10123	111
	41	52				912456	1012346	11124	121
	51	63				10123567	1112457	12134	
	61	712				11123467	1213458		
	72	812				12123457			
	82	913							
	92	1023							
	102	11123							
	1112	12123							
	1212								

*See also Ref. 5.

Table T-5 is for use in specifying the number of coset leaders of weight i for any (n, b) group code. The symbols n and b are defined as

n = total number of digits per code word

b = total number of check digits per code word

In addition a third symbol k is used for tabulation purposes and is defined as

k = total number of information digits per code word

It should be obvious that

$$k = n - b$$

In the listing of Table T-5 the listing is to be interpreted as follows. For a $(7, 3)$ group code we would have

$$n = 7 \quad b = 3 \quad k = 4$$

From Table T-5 we have the number of coset leaders of weight i for the $(7, 3)$ group code as

$$\gamma_0 = 1$$
$$\gamma_1 = 7$$

These numbers would then be useful in calculating the probability of correct decoding using a standard array table (see Eq. 6-14 and Example 6-10). If the probability of correct transmission over the channel is $p = .99$, then we have as the probability of correct decoding (from Eq. 6-10) to be

$$P(\text{correct decoding}) = \gamma_0 p^n + \gamma_1 q p^{n-1} = 1(.99)^7 + 7(.01)(.99)^6 = .9973$$

Appendix A

TABLE T-5. Number of Coset Leaders of Weight i for (n, b) Group Codes

n = total number of digits per code word

k = total number of information digits per code word = $n - b$

b = total number of check digits per code word

	i	n	$k = 2$	$k = 3$	$k = 4$	$k = 5$	$k = 6$	$k = 7$	$k = 8$	$k = 9$	$k = 10$
$n = 4$	0	1	1								
	1	4	3								
$n = 5$	0	1	1	1							
	1	5	5	3							
	2	10	2								
$n = 6$	0	1	1	1	1						
	1	6	6	6	3						
	2	15	9	1							
$n = 7$	0	1	1	1	1	1					
	1	7	7	7	7	3					
	2	21	18	8							
	3	25	6								
$n = 8$	0	1	1	1	1	1	1				
	1	8	8	8	8	7	3				
	2	28	28	20	7						
	3	56	27	3							
$n = 9$	0	1	1	1	1	1	1	1			
	1	9	9	9	9	9	7	3			
	2	36	36	33	22	6					
	3	84	64	21							
	4	126	18								
$n = 10$	0	1	1	1	1	1	1	1	1		
	1	10	10	10	10	10	10	7	3		
	2	45	45	45	39	21	5				
	3	120	110	64	14						
	4	210	90	8							
$n = 11$	0	1	1	1	1		1	1	1	1	
	1	11	11	11	11		11	11	7	3	
	2	55	55	55	55		20	4			
	3	165	165	126	61						
	4	330	226	63							
	5	462	54								
$n = 12$	0	1	1	1				1	1	1	1
	1	12	12	12				12	12	7	3
	2	66	66	66				19	3		
	3	220	220	200							
	4	495	425	233							
	5	792	300								

Appendix B

CHAPTER 2:

2-7. $H(X) = 1.5000$
$H(Y) = 1.5792$
$H(X, Y) = 3.0425$
$H(Y/X) = 1.5425$
$H(X/Y) = 1.4633$

2-8. a) $S_I(m_1) = 1.737$
$S_I(m_2) = 1.000$
$S_I(m_3) = 2.322$
b) $H(m_1, m_2, m_3) = 1.4855$

2-9. $S_I(5) = -\text{Log}_2(p_5) = -\text{Log}_2(1/9) = 3.1699$

2-10. a) $H(X) = .807$
b) $H(Y) = 1.33$
c) $H(X/Y) = .738$
d) $H(X, Y) = 2.06$

2-11. The original source is

$M = \{m_1, m_2, m_3\}$

The new source is

$M' = \{m_1 * m_1 * m_1, m_2 * m_2 * m_2, m_3 * m_3 * m_3\}$.

Then we have

$H(M) = H(M')$.

If we define the average information rate as $R(M)$ then

$R(M') = \dfrac{R(M)}{3}$.

If the channel is modeled by

$$a_i \longrightarrow \boxed{\text{Channel}} \longrightarrow b_i$$

where

$a_i \Longrightarrow m_i$ sent
$b_i \Longrightarrow m_i$ received,

then

$P(\text{correct reception}) = p(b_1/a_1)p(a_1) + p(b_2/a_2)p(a_2) + p(b_3/a_3)p(a_3).$

CHAPTER 3:

3-3. $H(A^3) = 3H(A) = 4.45643$

3-4. a)
$$\begin{bmatrix} .71 & .00 & .29 \\ .00 & .86 & .14 \\ .67 & .33 & .00 \\ .00 & .00 & 1.00 \end{bmatrix}$$

b) $P(A) = (.35, .35, .15, .15)$
d) $P(B) = (.35, .35, .30)$
e) $H(A) = 1.88129$
$H(B) = 1.58127$
$H(A/B) = .94678$
$H(B/A) = .64676$
$H(A, B) = 2.52806$

3-5. $I(A, B) = .934$

3-7. Use $\displaystyle\sum_{i=1}^{n} q_i \log \frac{q_i}{p_i} \geqslant 0,$

then $\displaystyle\sum_{j=1}^{r} p(b_j/a_i) = \sum_{j=1}^{r} P(b_j) = 1,$

and $I(A, B) = \displaystyle\sum_{i} p(a_i) X \geqslant 0$

3-8. The channel matrix is

$$P(B/A) = \begin{bmatrix} 1.0 & 0 & 0 \\ 0 & p & 1-p \\ 0 & 1-p & p \end{bmatrix},$$

and

$$C = \log(1 + 2^{1-H(p)}).$$

3-9. $x_1 = -.697$
$x_2 = -.1.15$
$x_3 = -.85$
$C = .851$

3-10. The cascaded channel matrix is

$$P \text{ cascaded} = \begin{bmatrix} p & p' \\ p' & p \end{bmatrix}^2 = \begin{bmatrix} p^2 + p'^2 & 2p' \\ 2p' & p^2 + p'^2 \end{bmatrix},$$

$$I(A; C) = H(A) - H(A/C)$$
$$= H(C) - H(C/A)$$
$$= H(C) + (p^2 + p'^2) \log (p^2 + p'^2) + 2p' \log 2p',$$

and

$$I(A, B) = H(B) + p \log p + q \log q.$$

3-14. $C = 0.80$
The mutual information = .06.

3-16. $H(A) = 1.8464$
$H(B) = 1.5006$
$H(B/A) = 1.0576$
$H(A/B) = 1.4034$
$H(A, B) = 2.904$

CHAPTER 4:

4-1. $p_{11}(3) = .250$
$p_{12}(3) = .102$
$p_{13}(3) = .648$

4-2. Transient: 1, 2, 3, 5, 6
Recurrent: 4, 7

4-3. b)

$$H(A) = \frac{q}{p+q} (1 - p) \log \left(\frac{1}{1-p}\right) + \frac{q}{p+q} (p) \log \left(\frac{1}{p}\right)$$

$$+ \frac{p}{p+q} (q) \log \left(\frac{1}{q}\right) + \frac{p}{p+q} (1 - q) \log \left(\frac{1}{1-q}\right)$$

4-5. Not regular, but ergodic.

$$S = (\tfrac{1}{2}, \tfrac{1}{2})$$

4-6. a) 3 states

b)

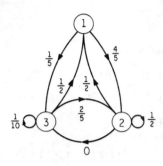

d) YES

e) YES, order 2.

f)
$$S = \begin{bmatrix} {}^{45}/_{135} & {}^{80}/_{135} & {}^{10}/_{135} \\ {}^{45}/_{135} & {}^{80}/_{135} & {}^{10}/_{135} \\ {}^{45}/_{135} & {}^{80}/_{135} & {}^{10}/_{135} \end{bmatrix}$$

4-9. We have

$$J(A/B) = \begin{bmatrix} \dfrac{1}{c_{11}} & \dfrac{1}{c_{21}} & \cdots & \dfrac{1}{c_{n1}} \\ \vdots & & & \\ \dfrac{1}{c_{1n}} & \dfrac{1}{c_{2n}} & & \dfrac{1}{c_{nn}} \end{bmatrix}$$

and

$$H(B) = H(A) + \log \| c_{ij} \| .$$

4-10. a) $p(a) = \begin{cases} \dfrac{1}{2E} & a \leqslant |E| \\ 0 & \text{elsewhere} \end{cases}$ *Note:* This is a uniform distribution

b) $p(a) = \begin{cases} \dfrac{1}{E} & 0 \leqslant a \leqslant E \\ 0 & E \leqslant a \leqslant \infty \end{cases}$ *Note:* This is a uniform distribution

c) $p(a) = \dfrac{1}{K} e^{-a/k} \; 0 \leqslant a \leqslant \infty .$ *Note:* This is an exponential distribution.

CHAPTER 5:

5-1. a) B, C, D, E
      b) B, C, E
      c) $L_B = 3$
          $L_C = {}^{31}/_{16}$
          $L_D = {}^{31}/_{16}$
          $L_E = {}^{32}/_{16}$
          $L_F = {}^{30}/_{16}$

5-2. For code D:

$$\ldots 1101001000\overbrace{1\underbrace{0000}_{a_2}}^{a_5}$$

For code F:

$$\ldots 0101101110\overbrace{1\underbrace{011}_{a_2}}^{a_5}$$

5-3. B, D.

5-4.
1   00
2   01
3 1100
4 1101
5 1001
6 1011
7 1110
8 1111

5-6. $A = \{00, 01, 101, 1110\}$.

5-7. $\overline{L} = 2.4$

5-8.

	SHANNON	SHANNON-FANO	HUFFMAN
a_1	000	00	01
a_2	001	010	101
a_3	011	011	100
a_4	100	100	111
a_5	1010	101	001
a_6	1100	110	000
a_7	1101	1110	1100
a_8	11110	1111	1101

5-9. $\overline{L}$ (Shannon) = 3.39, 86.4 percent = efficiency

$\overline{L}$ $(S - F)$ = 2.91, 99.3 percent = efficiency

$\overline{L}$ (H) = 2.91, 99.3 percent = efficiency

5-10. A = {0, 10, 11}

CHAPTER 6:

6-1. $p(b_1)$ = $^{20}/_{48}$
$p(b_2)$ = $^{17}/_{48}$
$p(b_3)$ = $^{11}/_{48}$
The decoding table is

a^*	b_j
a_1	b_1
a_2	b_2
a_3	b_3

and

$P(\epsilon)$ = $^1/_3$.

6-2. The decoding table is

a^*	b_j
a_1	b_1
a_1 or a_2 or a_3	b_2
a_2	b_3

and

$P(\epsilon)$ = .4

6-11.

ROW SPACE X	ROW SPACE Y
10011	10011
01010	11001
00101	11100
00000	00000
11001	01010
10110	01111
01111	00101
11100	10110

6-12.

	X_1	X_2	X_3	b_1	b_2	b_3
W_1	0	0	1	0	1	1
W_2	0	1	0	1	0	1
W_3	0	1	1	1	1	0
W_4	1	0	0	1	1	0
W_5	1	0	1	1	0	1
W_6	1	1	0	0	1	1
W_7	1	1	1	0	0	0
W_8	0	0	0	0	0	0

and

$P(\epsilon) = .14$ percent

b) 3 checking bits required.

$\gamma_0 = 1 \qquad \gamma_1 = 6 \qquad \gamma_2 = 1$

6-13.

	X_1	X_2	X_3	b_1	b_2	b_3	b_4
W_1	0	0	1	1	0	1	1
W_2	0	1	0	0	1	1	1
W_3	0	1	1	1	1	0	0
W_4	1	0	0	1	1	1	1
W_5	1	0	1	0	1	0	0
W_6	1	1	0	1	0	0	0
W_7	1	1	1	0	0	1	1
W_8	0	0	0	0	0	0	0

and

$P(\epsilon) = 1 - \{p^7 + 7qp^6 + 8q^2p^5\}.$

CHAPTER 7:

7-3. $F(X) = 110001010010001$

7-4.

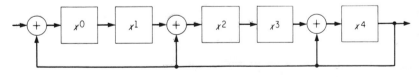

7-5. NO

References

1. *IRE Proceedings*, September 1958, p. 1647.
2. Nyquist, H. "Certain Factors Affecting Telegraph Speed," *Bell Systems Technical Journal*, 3, (1924), p. 324.
3. Hartley, R. V. L. "Transmission of Information," *Bell System Technical Journal*, 7, (1928), p. 535.
4. Shannon, C. E. "Mathematical Theory of Communication," *Bell System Technical Journal*, 27, (1948), pp. 379, 623.
5. Wiener, N. *Cybernetics*. New York: Wiley, 1948.
6. _____. "What is Information Theory?," *IRE Transactions on Information Theory*, June 1956, p. 48.
7. Feinstein, A. *Foundations of Information Theory*. New York: McGraw-Hill, 1958.
8. Bell, D. A. *Information Theory*. London. Pitman, 1953.
9. Muroga, S. "On the Capacity of a Discrete Channel," *Journal of the Physical Society of Japan*, 8, (1953), pp. 484–494.
10. Silverman, R. "On Binary Channels and Their Capacities," *IRE Transactions on Information Theory*, December 1955, p. 19.
11. Woodward, P. M. *Probability and Information Theory with Applications to Radar*. New York. Pergamon, 1955.
12. Feller, W. *Introduction to Probability Theory and Its Applications*. New York. Wiley, 1968.
13. Kemeny, J. G., and J. L. Snell *Finite Markov Chains*. Princeton, N.J. Van Nostrand, 1960.
14. Reza, F. *An Introduction to Information Theory*. New York: McGraw-Hill, 1961.
15. Khinchin, A. I. *Mathematical Foundations of Information Theory*. New York. Dover, 1957.
16. Abramson, N. *Information Theory and Coding*. New York: McGraw-Hill, 1963.

17. Kraft, L. G. "A Device for Quantizing, Grouping, and Coding Amplitude Modulated Pulses," M.S. thesis, Electrical Engineering Department, Massachusetts Institute of Technology, March 1949.

18. McMillan, B. "Two Inequalities Implied by Unique Decipherability," *IRE Transactions on Information Theory*, Vol. IT-2, December 1956.

19. Fano, R. *Transmission of Information.* New York. Wiley, 1961.

20. Hamming, R. W. "Error Detecting and Error Correcting Codes," *Bell System Technical Journal*, 29 (1950), pp 147–150.

21. Phister, M., Jr. *Logical Design of Digital Computers.* New York. Wiley, 1959, p. 329.

22. Peterson, W. W. *Error-Correcting Codes.* Cambridge, Mass.: M.I.T. Press, 1961.

23. Murdoch, D. C. *Linear Algebra for Undergraduates.* New York. Wiley, 1957.

24. McCluskey, E. J. "Error-Correcting Codes—A Linear Programming Approach," Bell System Technical Journal, 38 (November 1959), p. 1485.

25. Slepian, D. "A Class of Binary Signaling Alphabets," *Bell System Technical Journal*, 35 (January 1956), pp. 203–234.

26. Elias, P. *Handbook of Automation, Computation and Control.* New York. Wiley, 1958, Vol. 1, pp. 16-34–16-39.

27. Chung-Yen Ong. "Hybrid Tree-Block Codes," First Annual Houston Conference on Circuits, Systems, and Computers, University of Houston, May 1969.

28. Peterson, W. W., and D. T. Brown. "Cyclic Codes for Error Detection," *Proceedings of the IRE* (January 1961), pp. 228–235.

29. Prange, E. "Cyclic Error-Correcting Codes in Two Symbols," Air Force Cambridge Research Center, Bedford, Mass., Tech. Note AFCRC-TN-57-103, September 1957.

30. Forney, G. D., Jr. "Coding and its Application in Space Communications," *IEEE Spectrum* (June 1970), pp. 47–58.

31. Wozencraft, J. M., and B. Reiffen. *Sequential Decoding.* Cambridge, Mass.: M.I.T. Press, 1961.

Selected Reading List

The following references are suggested as further reading for the interested person. The reading list is organized in an order that should provide good continuity. Publications 1, 2, and 3 are interesting and informative without the burden of extensive mathematics. These references should be read before continuing a serious effort so that a broader background of more recent developments is gained. Of course each reference carries a good list of references and there is no need to repeat those here.

TEXTS

1. Shu Lin. *An Introduction to Error-Correcting Codes*. New Jersey: Prentice-Hall, 1970.
2. R. G. Gallager. *Information Theory and Reliable Communication*. New York: Wiley, 1968.
3. W. W. Peterson. *Error Correcting Codes*. Cambridge, Mass.: M.I.T. Press, Edition 2, 1970.
4. H. B. Mann (ed.). *Error Correcting Codes*. New York.: Wiley, 1968.
5. E. Berlekamp. *Algebraic Coding Theory*. McGraw-Hill, 1968.
6. D. G. Forney. *Concatenated Codes*. Cambridge, Mass.: M.I.T. Press, 1966.
7. R. Ash. Information Theory. New York. Interscience, 1965.
8. J. M. Wozencraft and I. M. Jacobs. *Principles of Communication Engineering*. New York: Wiley, 1965.

PUBLICATIONS

1. A. D. Wyner. "Another Look at the Coding Theorem of Information Theory —A Tutorial," *Proceedings of the IEEE*, June 1970.
2. G. D. Forney. "Coding and Its Application in Space Communications," *IEEE Spectrum*, June 1970.

3. I. M. Jacobs. "Convolution Coding for Channels with Memory," IT-14, No. 5 (September 1968).
4. A. Kolmogorov. "Logical Basis for Information Theory and Probability Theory," IT-14, No. 5 (September 1968).
5. G. Ott. "Compact Encoding of Stationary Markov Sources," IT-13, No. 1 (January 1967).
6. J. D. Ullman. "On the Capabilities of Codes to Correct Synchronization Errors," IT-13, No. 1 (January 1967).
7. J. L. Massey. "Uniform Codes," IT-12, No. 2 (April 1966).

The following two listings make interesting reading:

1. L. D. Smith. *Cryptography, The Science of Secret Writing*. New York. Dover, 1943, 1955.
2. D. Kahn. "Modern Cryptography," *Scientific American*, July 1966, pp. 38–46.

Index